Schoenberg and the New Music

Schoenberg and the New Music

Essays by Carl Dahlhaus

Translated by Derrick Puffett and Alfred Clayton

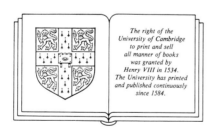

The right of the
University of Cambridge
to print and sell
all manner of books
was granted by
Henry VIII in 1534.
The University has printed
and published continuously
since 1584.

Cambridge University Press

Cambridge
New York   New Rochelle   Melbourne   Sydney

Published by the Press Syndicate of the University of Cambridge
The Pitt Building, Trumpington Street, Cambridge CB2 1RP
32 East 57th Street, New York, NY 10022, USA
10 Stamford Road, Oakleigh, Melbourne 3166, Australia

First published 1987

Printed in Great Britain at the University Press, Cambridge

British Library cataloguing in publication data

Dahlhaus, Carl
Schoenberg and the New Music.
1. Schoenberg, Arnold
I. Title
780'.92'4   ML410.S283

Library of Congress cataloguing in publication data

Dahlhaus, Carl, 1928–
Schoenberg and the New Music.
Bibliography.
Includes index.
1. Schoenberg, Arnold, 1874–1951 – Criticism and
interpretation. 2. Music – 20th century – History and
criticism. I. Title.
ML60.D158   1987   780'.92'4   87–6360

ISBN 0 521 33251 6

Contents

Translators' introduction

This book consists of essays written by Carl Dahlhaus over a period of twenty years (the earliest, 'Musical Prose', dates from 1964). The author has selected twenty-two essays from those collected in 1978 under the title *Schönberg und andere* (Mainz) and has added a further six for this new publication. Only 'Schoenberg and Schenker' has appeared in English before, in an anonymous translation published in the *Proceedings of the Royal Musical Association*. It is here reprinted with minor changes. Stephen Hinton has translated the essay on 'Form', which appears by permission of Pendragon Press.

The title, *Schoenberg and the New Music*, not only states a theme but also alludes to Adorno's *Philosophie der neuen Musik*, a central document of the New Music and one which clearly fascinates Dahlhaus. (This book is known in English as *Philosophy of Modern Music*, a title which both obscures the polemical nature of the original and fails to acknowledge the historical phenomenon of New Music as it emerged in the 1920s.) In the case of each essay the notes have been revised for the English-speaking reader, referring to standard translations where appropriate. All other translations are ours.

Writing of religious categories in 'Schoenberg's Aesthetic Theology', Dahlhaus states: 'To translate them into another language is to establish their true meaning.' Whether he would say the same of literary translation is not clear; we would hesitate to do so ourselves, if only because it is uncertain how success should be judged in relation to such a difficult original. What we can say is that our task would have been even more difficult without the help of friends. Isabella Borinski and John Halliday read the entire manuscript between them and made innumerable suggestions for improvement. Mary Whittall and Jonathan Dunsby saw large parts of it and offered valuable advice. John Deathridge, Robert Pascall and Christopher Walton helped with specific points. Thanks are due to all of them for making a difficult task a pleasant one.

'New Music' as historical category

The concept of 'New Music', which serves to pinpoint the difference between certain twentieth-century works and the mass of the remainder, seems to be one of those catchphrases which have a precise meaning as long as they are used thoughtlessly, but which turn out to be vague or self-contradictory as soon as one begins to analyse them. Is not newness, one is entitled to ask, a quality which, by its very nature, is tied to a never-recurring moment in time? And does it not seem illogical, therefore, to ascribe it to a whole epoch covering half a century? A concept which is used to characterise an unrepeatable experience is of little use as a historical label. Furthermore, one is forced to make use of the superlative, 'Newest Music', in order to distinguish between the avant garde of the past fifteen years and older New Music; and that is a rather dubious verbal construct.

The established use of the expression New Music as a name for an epoch may be paradoxical, but it has not remained without influence on historical terminology. That a term like *ars nova*, which was used in the fourteenth century to describe an *ars nova notandi*, a new notational method, albeit one which had a bearing on compositional technique, should have progressed to become a general term for French music written between 1320 and 1380 probably has less to do with the original meaning of the term than with the unconscious transfer of the later phrase New Music. Even when historians have recourse to the terminology of the past they are dependent on modern linguistic usage. At any rate, declaring newness to be the essence of a whole epoch was a notion foreign to the fourteenth century.

But what in fact is the point of referring to *ars antiqua* and *ars nova* as

1

epochs when even the most superficial consideration of the facts shows that *ars antiqua* was new music around 1250, and that *ars nova* turned into old music around 1380? How is one to explain the fact that historians tend to overemphasise unassuming work titles such as *Ars nova* and *Nuove musiche*, almost as if they had been dictated by the spirit of history wanting to place a caesura?

The concept of the 'new', which Ernst Bloch has said is in a bad way, is, taken as a historical category, as unavoidable as it is precarious. It is unavoidable in the trivial sense that the matter of history is that which changes, and not that which is static or that which repeats itself in the same form. It is precarious because the principle which states that history is to be understood as continuity urges the historian to trace the new, if at all possible, back to the old. To be precise, a historical explanation reveals the new only inasmuch as it is not new. The new is not significant in itself, but solely in relation to its antithesis, as the irreducible and unresolved remainder. Thus the new can be seen, paradoxically, as being at one and the same time the actual subject-matter and the blind spot of history.

In psychological terms newness is to be measured not only by its mere information content, but also by the expectations which it arouses. The relevance of the new is dependent upon the character of the old in question: in other words, whether the new continues a series of revolutions or whether it has to assert itself in the face of an authoritarian tradition which reaches back hundreds of years. In a sphere of music and an epoch in which little changes, such as church music at certain periods, the least alteration to the established norm seems like a revolution, whereas in the case of recent post-serial music it has become difficult to perceive changes which would perhaps turn musical thinking upside down if one were able to understand and accept them for the important events they are.

Moreover, newness is not measured by the same standards in the various strata of music. It is a question of fundamental differences, not one of degree. To be of the opinion that something is new has a different significance in popular than in esoteric music. What newness means in the case of popular music depends on how one understands its history; and it is not even certain whether one can talk about historical development in the undiluted sense of the word, or whether it would not be more appropriate to describe the changes as changes in fashion. But the kind of innovation that simply supersedes the previous year's fashion can hardly be compared to an epoch-making historical event, however much the sort of journalism that turns fashions into important events and dismisses important events as fashions might wish to attempt to obscure the difference.

The thicket of difficulties and paradoxes into which one chances even when thinking about the concept of musical innovation in the most superficial way cannot be cleared away in a few sentences. Thus I may be forgiven for attempting nothing more than a rough sketch of the features that distinguish those epochs which are felt to be times of New Music from those which are not. The suspicion that titles such as *Ars nova* or *Nuove musiche* lead to overinterpretation, the mistrust of historians who tend to exaggerate historical breaks to which scholarly labels can be attached, is understandable, but it is not justified. *Musica nova*, the title which Adrian Willaert gave to a collection of motets and madrigals in 1559, was never declared to be the classmark of an epoch of music history, though it would not be difficult to adduce arguments to support the idea that Willaert had created a New Music. It would suffice to recall the tendency to favour homophonic textures and expressive chromaticism, the Renaissance awareness of Willaert's pupils Zarlino and Vicentino, or Monteverdi's claim that Cipriano de Rore, another of Willaert's pupils, was the first composer to make use of the *seconda prattica*. Monteverdi, whom others regarded as the epitome of modernity, felt that new music around 1600 was a continuation of the Willaert tradition.

Nevertheless the question arises why a historian who is trying to decide where historical breaks occur and to assess their significance sees Caccini's monodies and not Willaert's madrigals as *nuova musica*. Broadening the question, are the events around 1320, 1430, 1600, 1740 and 1910, of which one thinks automatically when one is speaking of the 'new' in music history, more significant and momentous than what was happening around 1500, 1680, 1780, 1830 and 1950? Is Josquin's 'ars perfecta' or Haydn's 'new, special style' of lesser historical importance than Dufay's 'euphonious counterpoint' or the symphonic style of someone like Johann Stamitz? Or is it not so much the importance as the character of the changes that forces upon the historian the concept of the new? When emphatically ascribing newness to certain epochs and not to others, are we dealing with a qualitative difference, and not one of degree? Are we concerned with the profundity of the break or with its character?

I

When analysing the complex of ideas which comprise the concept of the new, we immediately come across a factor which seems trivial but which is actually rather surprising. Newness is exclusively ascribed to the beginnings of a lengthy period of evolution (a period of evolution, that is, which spans one or two centuries) and not to the middle or later stages.

Neither a classical style, be it that of the Low Countries around 1500 or of Germany around 1800, nor a mannered style, such as the *ars subtilior* of the fourteenth century or the excessive chromaticism of the sixteenth century, attracts the epithet 'new'. But it would be misguided and untenable to claim that the extent of perceivable newness, the number of unusual expressive features or, to quote Karlheinz Stockhausen, the variety of compositional 'discoveries and inventions' is as a rule greater at an early stage than at a middle or a later one. Of course, when speaking of newness in the emphatic sense, one thinks less of what has already been achieved than of what is just over the horizon, and of that contained as an unexploited possibility in what already exists. Caccini's monodies, the *Nuove musiche* of 1601, differ markedly from what immediately preceded them, such as the madrigals of Luca Marenzio, more on account of their unexpected poverty and thinness than on account of anything strikingly new. Progress, if it could be described as such, consisted in reduction. That the monodies were nevertheless and rightly felt to be the New Music of the seventeenth century was due to the consequences which followed from them. The relapse into primitivism formed the precondition for a long and far-reaching evolution. The New Music around 1600 – and similarly that around 1430 or 1740 – has the character of a programme for the future. The new style, at which the concept of New Music is directed, is to be measured not by what it is but by what it makes possible. Its apparent poverty is, as it were, a promise of future wealth.

II

The new, which asserts itself through its antithesis to the old, has a propensity to reflection and to polemics; and the more insistent the polemics are, the more unjustified they seem. Measured in abstract musical terms, the challenge to the overpowering tradition of counterpoint mounted by Vincenzo Galilei and the Florentine Camerata verged on sectarian absurdity. The fact that this challenge was nevertheless epoch-making was in no small measure a result of the literary presentation of the new by apologists and chroniclers such as Doni. Similarly, around 1740, we should not underestimate the influence of literary publications, which provided a language for the feeling of stylistic change with which that feeling could articulate and establish itself.

Furthermore, past controversies are taken remarkably seriously by historians, who like to illustrate the differences between epochs by means of symbolic events, with the result that the more emphatically the new appears in the shape of polemical documents, the greater its chances of being deemed epoch-making become. To claim that Mozart's modifications to opera buffa were not of lesser significance than Gluck's reform of opera seria and of the tragédie lyrique, and may even have been of greater significance, would be in no way absurd. Yet it is impossible to deny that the publicity which was accorded to Gluck, and which was denied to Mozart, helped the reform operas to acquire a prestige which was as important historically as the works themselves. The proclamation of an epoch sometimes resembles a self-fulfilling prophecy.

Thus literature about music, hardly different in this respect from literature about literature, forms an integral part of music as a historical event, and even as a perceived object. What one emphasises when listening to music is in part dependent on what one has read about it. Musical perception, even of the most impartial kind, which in reality does not exist, is permeated with reminiscences of what one has read, with traces of literary memory. Even the endeavour to arrive at a 'purely musical' form of listening is conveyed by literature, either as the work of aesthetic awareness or as the fulfilment of a postulate which is hardly more than 150 years old. The literary element is an aspect of music, particularly of new music, which is not directly comprehensible on its own terms.

III

That the concept of the new attaches to a whole era, instead of to an unrepeatable moment, seems to presuppose that an old style, a *prima prattica*, exists side by side with the new one, either in the shape of a peripheral tradition, as in the seventeenth century, or in that of a predominant one, as in the twentieth. A new music whose antithesis disappears within a few years, as happened around 1740, hardly needs to be declared as such.

Yet the real antithesis to the new is not music which is seen and felt to be old, but either the 'moderately modern', which Robert Schumann disparagingly referred to as the 'juste milieu', or else a dogmatism which claims that it is rooted in the nature of the thing itself, that is to say, abstracted from history, a claim which Hindemith's *Unterweisung im Tonsatz* shares with Fux's *Gradus ad Parnassum*.

Jacques de Liège's polemics against the *ars nova* of the fourteenth century were permeated with feelings of resignation. The new was bewailed as excessive, yet without calling into question its right to exist. Jacques, even if rather reluctantly, was aware that the *ars antiqua* whose passing he mourned was a thing of the past.

It was different around 1600 in the controversy between Artusi and

Monteverdi. The antithesis to the New Music of the seventeenth century, to the *seconda prattica*, the beginnings of which, according to Monteverdi, reached far back into the sixteenth century, was not an *ars antiqua*, but rather, as its apologists saw it, a timeless dogmatism which had been codified by Zarlino in 1558 as if it had been a natural law of music. It is no accident that the concept of the 'pure style', which admittedly was coined only in the eighteenth century, reminds us of the 'pure doctrine'. It seems as if Monteverdi also understood the stylistic difference between the old and the new as the contrast between a natural and a historical justification of musical techniques. Whereas the *prima prattica*, which, characteristically, was formulated as a theory, tried to give itself the appearance of having been derived from nature – Fux saw in the change of taste nothing but the ephemeral exterior of a counterpoint which remained essentially the same – the contemporaries of the *seconda prattica* already sensed, albeit in an unarticulated manner, that it was a historical phenomenon whose evolutionary stages – madrigal, monody and the concertante style – were clearly distinct. It was quite possible for Monteverdi to subsume diverging styles, the polyphony of the madrigal and the monody of early opera, under the concept of *seconda prattica* so long as they were understood historically.

In the nineteenth and twentieth centuries, aesthetics and historical theory primarily contrast the new with the 'juste milieu', the reasonable middle way, and not with the old, which is far rather understood as something that was once new, as something to which one can relate instead of having to combat it. Historical awareness, inasmuch as it is not pleasure in antiquarianism but awareness of what is perpetually new in history, becomes a vehicle of progress; and there arises the paradoxical concept of a revolutionary tradition which extends from Beethoven to Schoenberg via Berlioz, Liszt and Wagner. The opponent is moderation; the middle path is, according to Schoenberg, the only one that does not lead to Rome.

IV

Tradition is that which is self-evident, which takes itself for granted as long as it retains its predominance. It only becomes self-conscious when cracks appear in its edifice and when it begins to be assailed by doubt. A tradition that is maintained in a strenuously self-conscious manner is exposed for what it is precisely because it is on the defensive.

To its opponents, tradition seems to be the old that has been historically condemned. Conversely, the old, for those who represent it, is tradition: not something that is past and in the process of dying, but something self-evident which will survive. Thus the concept of the old, as a counter-concept to that of the new, is not at all a neutral category. Whatever is dismissed as old in the eyes of the new, be it the regulated counterpoint of around 1600, the idea of the bass as the foundation of music around 1740, or tonal harmony around 1910, seems self-evident to those who cling to it, and appears to be old only because it has always been natural and obvious. The organism model, the idea that no aspect of music is immune to becoming old and dying out, serves as a historical scheme with which to justify the new – though the concept of growth, as an antithesis to that of creation, is a conservative category.

V

It seems that both detractors and eulogists are of the opinion, though in a diametrically opposed sense, that the more abrupt the new is, the deeper the break in historical continuity it signifies. Around 1600 the contrast to received tradition was doubtless felt to be sharp. Yet nothing would be further from the truth than to exaggerate the effect that polemics against the old can have. Confronted with the tenacious power of what exists and is deeply rooted, even a successful revolution is curiously powerless. And it is precisely when the new ventures far into the unknown that it permits the old to exist alongside it unchallenged. It is no accident that in the seventeenth century, just as in the twentieth, the *seconda prattica*, new music, tolerated the existence of a *prima prattica*, old music, as a complementary contrast. And if around 1740 it seemed as though the old style was about to be eradicated, then the abrupt displacement of the 'learned' by the 'galant' (to use the language of the eighteenth century) was corrected a generation later in Haydn's quartets from Op. 20 onwards and in Mozart's return to Bach. The radical nature of the sudden change around 1740 can hardly be understood in abstract music–historical terms, in an isolated problem history [*Problemgeschichte*] of composition; it forces one to fall back on socio-historical attempts at explanation. On the other hand, the resumption of the interrupted tradition of counterpoint a few decades later represented a kind of triumph of an immanent music–historical logic independent of socio-historical factors.

VI

The new which opposes a dominant tradition not infrequently stems from an oppressed one, resembling a usurper in this respect. What had been accorded scant attention or considered to be of little value because it was regionally or socially on the fringe moves into the centre and determines the dominant style.

The New Music of around 1430, which Johannes Tinctoris acclaimed as the dawn of a new age, is based, to put it crudely, on the assimilation by French music, whose hegemony had obtained for centuries, of provincial English and Italian techniques and stylistic traits. If Heinrich Besseler is right in contending that Dufay's adaptation and artificial* redefinition of fauxbourdon was the crucial factor, then the New Music of the fifteenth century would have to be seen as the result of the ennobling of what had hitherto been peripheral and trivial.

The hypothesis which states that a hitherto secondary tradition comes to the fore whenever there is a change in style complements Hans Naumann's assertion that art on a low level is 'decayed cultural property'. It acquires added weight in that seventeenth-century *nuova musica*, Caccini's monody, is also, at least in part, the artificial formulation of a procedure which, as a peripheral musical practice – vocal improvisation over a ground bass – reaches far back into the sixteenth century. Seen in this way, monody did not arise abruptly around 1600 as a reversal of polyphony, but was merely raised from being an unpretentious occasional art form to being the dominant style.

That the New Music of the eighteenth century is characterised by traits which its adherents praised as being popular and which its opponents dismissed as being trivial is too well known for it to be necessary to cite details, such as the criticisms levelled against Haydn by the North Germans. However, it is less obvious, or at least less frequently commented upon, that in the early nineteenth century the new style also takes its starting-point from peripheral aspects of the old. Before being ennobled around 1820, the characteristic genres of Romanticism, the song, the lyric piano piece and programme music, were all of them overshadowed, secondary genres, however widely they may have been disseminated. At the same time, it is impossible to deny that the attempt to explain innovation in music as the upgrading of a peripheral or trivial tradition fails to explain the changes around 1910. The New Objectivity [*Neue Sachlichkeit*] of the 1920s would fit into this scheme much better. But however gratifying it may be that a historical–theoretical hypothesis has proved convincing, it is not sufficient compensation for abandoning the conviction that Schoenberg's transition to atonality was the decisive

---

* *Artifiziell.* Dahlhaus's many references to 'artificial' music should be taken in the literal sense: music made up of artifices, or 'art music' as opposed to popular music. See J. B. Robinson's preface to Dahlhaus's *Foundations of Music History* (Cambridge, 1983), p. x. [Trans.]

event in the music of the first half of this century – and probably of the second half as well.

VII

The observation that a new musical style not infrequently takes its cue from peripheral traditions suggests making use of the idea advanced by the sociologist of literature Levin Schücking, that stylistic change in general terms is bound up with a change in the 'type of the upholder of taste'. According to this theory a change in taste is the taste of a different social stratum or of a new public. But the attempt to transfer Schücking's interpretative scheme to music history, which seems plausible at first sight, proves unsuccessful; the caesuras in the history of music do not coincide with those of social history.

The *ars nova* of the fourteenth century was doubtless destined for the same 'literati' who, according to Johannes de Grocheo, formed the audience for the motet around 1300, inasmuch as one may term retiring scholarly circles an audience. However great the musical differences between them may seem, *ars antiqua* and *ars nova* are impossible to tell apart in sociological terms. And again, a century later, at the historical break around 1430, nothing points to a change in the 'type of the upholder of taste'. The social structure of the Burgundian court at Dijon was in essence the same as that of the Papal court at Avignon, the centre of the *ars subtilior*, the musical mannerism of around 1400.

Early seventeenth-century monody was esoteric music, an art for aristocratic humanistic circles. Yet these had already sustained and encouraged the *musica reservata* of the sixteenth century, the expressive polyphonic art of the madrigal. What was new in terms of the history of music was based sociologically on tradition.

That stylistic change around 1740 is linked to the rise of bourgeois musical culture, as described by Eberhard Preussner, has become a scholarly commonplace. But although the hypothesis seems plausible because of its simplicity, it is questionable. In the first place, sixteenth-century bourgeois musical culture was hardly inferior to that of the eighteenth century. Secondly, England, the bourgeois nation par excellence, did not play an important role in the history of music after the death of Handel. Thirdly, the eighteenth century saw the parallel rise of Metastasian opera seria and of its bourgeois counterpart, opera buffa. That the Enlightenment was a bourgeois epoch in literature does not mean that it was also one in music. Finally, it seems as if the proposed connection between stylistic change and a change in the 'type of the upholder of taste' is of no avail even in the twentieth century. For it would be rather difficult, using tangible sociological criteria, to prove the truth of the assertion that the New Music audience, though it is doubtless a special one, differs from that of older music. But then the attempt has not as yet been made.

On the other hand, a distinction has to be made within the category 'type of the upholder of taste', inasmuch as the group that is crucial in music–historical terms does not have to coincide with the representative audience in music–sociological terms. Yet the concept of what is representative in terms of music sociology is ambiguous. It does not signify the mass of listeners, which tends to prefer the trivial and make no bones about it, but the group whose taste ranks highest in public opinion. An empirical study, which remains to be carried out (though it would not be difficult), would probably show that the listeners at chamber music and symphony concerts represent the ruling 'type of the upholder of taste', both in their own estimation and in that of most other people. In contrast New Music is tolerated without being socially accepted. In everyday parlance 'modern music' is considered to be jazz. Yet a single group, which according to the criteria of music sociology would be considered a sect, such as the audience of the 'Society for Private Performances of Music', which its detractors referred to as the 'Schoenberg clique', can in retrospect turn out to be of crucial importance in music history. There is a discrepancy between historical and sociological relevance. But if the group that supports a new music lacks social prestige, then the concept of the 'type of the upholder of taste' becomes vague and difficult to pin down.

VIII

The epoch-making new music of around 1600 or around the middle of the eighteenth century was poorer than the old which it replaced. Compared with the tradition which it destroyed it seems a relapse into poverty, which should not however be misunderstood as naivety. A penchant for the calculated, even for the aggressively constructive, is unmistakably present in both Caccini's and Monteverdi's monodies and, a century and a half later, in the symphonies of Stamitz and the sonatas and fantasias of C. P. E. Bach. The new – though based on reduction and on the polemical reaction against the move towards increasingly complex polyphony which preceded it – was more mannered than innocently primitive, a fact which went unnoticed as long as there was a tendency to regard beginnings as simple and to seek in the simple the popular, which, with dubious logic, was considered to be the antithesis of mannerism.

Scholars no longer dispute that mannerism is a style in its own right and not merely a decadent form. Despite this, however, the prejudice that it always represents a late stage, the end of a development, has proved particularly tenacious – even though the concept of experiment, with which one tries to overcome one's perplexity in the face of certain manneristic conceits, in itself implies that we are dealing with beginnings which provoke consequences.

The *musica reservata* of around 1600, which Helmut Hucke has described as mannerism, comprised – and this has hardly ever been realised – not only the madrigal but also the monody, and not only the late, excessively chromatic style of Saracini and Belli but also the early one, the simplicity of which is a stylistic mask. In spite of Caccini's polemics against counterpoint, madrigal and monody were not felt to be expressions of antithetical 'cultures of music', that is, to quote August Halm, of the polyphonic and the homophonic, but as extreme, mutually interacting forms within a single style, the *seconda prattica*, which, according to Monteverdi, reached back to the middle of the sixteenth century and included madrigalists such as Cipriano de Rore and Marenzio. But if the *seconda prattica*, of which it cannot be said that it was of no historical importance, was a kind of mannerism, then the idea that mannerism is always a late stage which is followed by nothing but stylistic decay must be abandoned, as must the complementary prejudice that beginnings are always popular and simple. The organism model is a questionable historical–theoretical paradigm.

There is seldom talk of eighteenth-century mannerism. Admittedly the fact has never been overlooked that the mangled syntax of the Mannheim symphonists and their use of surprise dynamics, which are not so much evolved out of the composition as thrust upon it, are manneristic traits. Yet scholars have fought shy of proclaiming a mannerism in music history to which analogies in literature and art history are lacking. Instead of this they have spoken of musical *Sturm und Drang*, which preceded that in literature by decades.

The label would be of little importance if there were not a characteristic common to all mannerists, Marenzio and Gesualdo as well as Stamitz and C. P. E. Bach, and, later, Berlioz: the combination of technical ostentation and an extreme degree of expressiveness. The means are not fully subsumed in the result. They are not concealed but presented for all to see. On the other hand calculation and effect are closely connected and dialectically related, instead of, as prejudice would have it, being mutually exclusive or cancelling each other out. To believe in the naivety of the expressive element in the sonatas and fantasias of C. P. E. Bach is itself naive.

Those who tend to equate rationality and emotional expression must be prepared to counter the argument that they are defending something which is not genuine but artificial. The answer to this would be that it is illogical to upbraid an enacted emotion – and a musical affect is not unlike a theatrical one – for not being 'genuine'. 'Genuineness' is a dubious category, not only in aesthetics, and it would be one of the tasks of a theory of mannerism to demolish it.

IX

Epoch-making new music represents a beginning whose rudimentary and meagre nature one is prepared to overlook on account of its far-reaching consequences. The decisive factor is not so much what the new directly signifies in the isolated work as what it brings about indirectly as a historical event. Peri's and Caccini's Florentine opera is undoubtedly a model instance of New Music; but without the historical influence that emanated from it, it would be nothing but one experiment among countless others that were all inspired by antiquity, an experiment which historians would dismiss just as lightly as the humanist's composing of odes or Nicola Vicentino's enharmonics.

The concept of historical influence, which is inextricably bound up with that of the new, seems however to be more a category of political than of art history. A political event which leads to nothing is historically of no importance whatsoever; indeed, to call it a political event at all is in itself already an exaggeration. A work of art, however, remains what it is even if it has no historical influence. If Albert Schweitzer was right in claiming that Bach's historical impact was negligible it would still do nothing to alter Bach's significance. What belongs to the history of music – a history which consists of works handed down and not of a mere chain of interacting events – is decided not only by historical but also by aesthetic judgment. To put it bluntly, it is the dilemma of writing music history that one is forced to alternate between the criteria of historical influence and aesthetic quality, between two poles, that is, which often complement but which not infrequently contradict each other. Even if they conceal the fact, historians of music work on the principle of double standards, a state of affairs which becomes clearly apparent when one compares the concepts of newness and classicality.

At first it seems as if the one merely designates the beginning of a development and the other its culmination. Yet even thinking about it in passing is enough to make one aware that newness is primarily a historical category, classicality an aesthetic one. New Music such as Caccini's monodies or the symphonies of Stamitz, which represent a preliminary stage, is completely absorbed in history, the further progress of which it thereby ensures. It is so to speak swallowed up, whereas the classical seems to jut up out of history. It survives in the shape of an isolated, self-contained work. The new, on the other hand, does not continue to exist in itself, but is subsumed in the events which it brought about. Compared to the classical, the new has more the character of an event than of a work.

Yet at the same time one should not deny that newness is also an aesthetic factor, which for example is inextricably bound up with the earliest atonal works, Schoenberg's Op. 11 Piano Pieces and the final movement of the Second String Quartet. What is seemingly most transient – the quality of incipient beginning, of 'for the first time' – acquires a paradoxical permanence. Even half a century later it can be felt in almost undiminished form, and as an immediate aesthetic quality at that, not as a purely historical one which can be perceived only by bringing into play one's historical awareness.

This attempt to provide a rough sketch of how the habit of speaking of New Music came about, perhaps justifiably, not only in the twentieth but also in the fourteenth and seventeenth centuries – the attempt, in other words, to analyse the concept of New Music as a historical category – would be wholly misunderstood if one were to regard the tangible result as the establishment of an eternally recurring historical type, that of 'New Music'. Much less was intended: to suggest an analogy. And an analogy is not a result, but an attempt to clarify concepts in order to show areas of agreement and of disagreement, or to enable them to appear with greater clarity than would be possible from other perspectives. It would not be surprising if the impression has been conveyed that the features common to the epochs compared are less relevant than the features that set them apart. It is normal for hypotheses to fall apart in the course of his-torical investigation. Historians are used to the fact that the concepts which they employ have to be refined until they finally dissolve. Yet if they were to deny themselves the use of such hypotheses, the facts would remain mute instead of being compelled to speak.

Progress and the avant garde

I

'Ce qu'on appelle en général progrès n'est que transformation' (Fétis). The idea of progress, except in a scientific or technological sense, is regarded with so much mistrust that one almost has to force oneself to think about the problem involved. Yet it is not one of those problems which can be solved by not talking about them. 'The idolisation of progress', wrote Paul Valéry, 'was countered by the idolisation of the rejection of progress. That was all; and it led to two clichés.'[1] Yet belief in progress is not quite as deluded as its detractors would have us believe. It is more a matter of hope than of arrogant presumption, and its modern version is Ernst Bloch's idea of utopia, which was developed in the context of a philosophy of music.[2]

Yet the notion of progress[3] has less to motivate it in the theory of art than in sociology or anthropology. The idea that social history is nothing but a sequence of self-contained events and states of being is unbearable in the face of the 'mass of real evil', as Hegel put it.[4] The philosophy of history is thus to be understood as an attempt at a theodicy, a justification of the ways of God to man;[5] and indeed the idea of progress seems to be a secular formulation of a concept which was originally a theological one.[6] 'It may well happen', Hegel tells us, 'that the individual will suffer an injustice, but that is of no interest to World History, which individuals serve as a means to further its progress.'[7] The future is conjured up because the existing state of affairs or an isolated event fails to be meaningful in itself. The word 'meaning' acquires the significance of 'goal'; and, in a progression which passes over and beyond it, the present is thus supposed to acquire that meaning which it does not in itself possess.

14

In the case of art, by contrast, the here and now is never a preliminary stage. No art worthy of the name requires justification by a future which will make good, in the case of subsequent works, the misfortune that has befallen present-day ones. But if the need for a theodicy is absent, then the idea of progress has lost one of its motives.

II

Originally a military term, 'avant garde' is a questionable figure of speech when it comes to art criticism. It would be erroneous to imagine that the word is the slogan of composers of serial and post-serial music. Pierre Boulez uses it, not exactly as a term of abuse,[8] but certainly with irony.[9] That it is nonsensical to speak of an avant garde when judging something written today should have become generally clear, at least since the appearance of Hans Magnus Enzensberger's essay 'Die Aporien der Avantgarde' ('The Aporias of the Avant Garde'). 'For who', he states, 'apart from it [the avant garde] is to decide what is "in front" at any given time remains wide open. . . . One can only be sure about what *was* "in front", not about what *is* "in front". . . . The "avant" in avant garde contains its own self-contradiction, for it can only be described as such *a posteriori*.'[10]

To claim that one is anticipating the future, or that one is taking possession of something which no one as yet knows, cannot be justified in any way whatsoever. But it is also quite foreign to the composers who are referred to by the expression 'avant garde'. Karlheinz Stockhausen declared that he was composing for the present. The future he left to those born after him. 'If we of today expect that much more music of our time will be performed . . . then we must also expect of future generations that they will produce *their* new music. . . .'[11] Stockhausen conceives of history in terms of a 'fury of disappearing', as of a process which threatens works of art with loss of substance, however much they may be handed down ostensibly unquestioned. 'There is', wrote Eduard Hanslick in 1854, 'no art which, like music, uses up so quickly such a variety of forms. . . . Of a great number of compositions which rose above the trivialities of their day, it would be quite correct to say that there *was* a time when they were beautiful.'[12]

Thus 'avant garde' is hardly an appropriate title with which to talk about the new music of the past few decades. Yet the catchwords on which the debate among the composers themselves was based are probably too familiar to require repetition. What people thought around 1950 about integration and determination, and a few years later about chance, indeterminacy and ambiguity, suffered the fate of being talked to death, a fate which was to some extent implicit in the object itself. From the time when the aesthetics of emotion and inspiration fell into disrepute and the imagination of composers was stimulated rather by intellectual operations, practice and theory – composition and reflection – have become closely interlinked. It is a state of affairs for which there is no lack of historical precedent,[13] and which it would be sentimental to regret. The creation of works and the development of musical poetics complement one another, and not infrequently the one merges into the other.

III

Insofar as they are motivated by social criticism of an Eastern European variety, the polemics against serial and post-serial compositional techniques are based on the idea that musical progress is dependent on that of society as a whole. As a mediator between social facts or postulates on the one hand and musical phenomena on the other there is the content of the music, the affect or the subject-matter. Whereas the exponents of new music believe that it is the latter's autonomy, its independence of external ends, which represents as it were its self-evident aesthetic morality, their opponents rely on the principle of heteronomy as propagated by the nineteenth-century 'progressive party', whose most important theorist was Franz Brendel. In dialectical opposition to Eduard Hanslick's aesthetic of the specifically musical, Zofia Lissa maintains that it is indeed part of the specific quality of music not to be specifically musical, but 'to pass beyond itself and conjoin with literary elements'.[14] To quote Walter Benjamin: 'It is only . . . the cooperation of the word, as Eisler puts it, that can transform a concert into a political meeting.'[15]

An unfortunate and exaggerated remark by Stravinsky concerning the impossibility of musical expression has meant that the aesthetics of the specific, to which both music theory and poetic theory[16] have assigned the label 'formalism', are sometimes presented by their opponents in terms which make them seem easy to refute. Yet in fact it is not a matter of denying that music is capable of conveying emotions and associations, but of formulating an idea which can do justice to a work of art. It is of decisive importance to establish whether aesthetic perception, as the literary critic Northrop Frye puts it, is 'centrifugal' or 'centripetal':[17] whether it aims beyond a musical structure at its meaning, or whether it turns back from the meaning, albeit without neglecting or underestimating it, to the contemplation of the structure itself. The aesthetics of the specific emphasise the object character, and not the sign character, of musical phenomena. To put it in the language of Romanticism: the aesthetics of content, which assign to music a representational function, are, according to Ludwig Tieck, 'prosaic'; viewed 'poetically', a musical work of art is a 'separate world of its own'.[18]

IV

That a composer continues to believe in artistic autonomy does not mean that he refuses to think about the function that he consciously or unwillingly performs.[19] What the principle of 'l'art pour l'art', which Jean Paul called 'poetic nihilism',[20] means in a social sense is not clear; rather, it forms the subject of a controversy. It is a matter of debate whether the hermetic nature of modern art, its abstraction from familiar emotional content and retreat to problems of form and material, is to be construed as constituting disagreement with or adaptation to the existing state of affairs. 'Abstraction', Alfred Andersch wrote in an essay based on some of Theodor W. Adorno's ideas, 'is the instinctive or conscious reaction of art to ideas which have sunk to the level of ideology. . . . Abstract art is not art without content, but art which protests, by withdrawing itself, against content which has sunk to the level of ideology. It performs its socio-critical function, whether or not the individual artist creating abstract works of art is aware of this, or whether he feels himself to be solely an artist.'[21] While Andersch conceives of the 'withdrawal of self' as criticism, Arnold Gehlen explains it in an opposite sense, as 'successful irresponsibility', which is removed from social reality and therefore does not impinge upon it.[22] In considering hermetic art to be 'irresponsible', Gehlen, who can be reckoned to belong to the conservative camp, is of the same opinion as Eastern European socialists, whereas Adorno and Andersch, who represent an unorthodox Marxism, feel that the 'withdrawal of self' constitutes opposition to existing reality.

At the same time it is a dilemma for the proponents of the opposite aesthetic position, the eulogists of socially committed art, that the kind of society they are aiming at does not as yet exist. It is difficult to decide whether works of art should be judged with regard to the future, the social utopia come true, or with regard to their direct utility value at the revolutionary intermediate stage. The number of those able to follow music on a high formal level has always been small, in all past forms of society. But what Marx had in mind was not the suppression of the complex for the sake of a mass audience which had not as yet had the chance to cultivate aesthetic sensibilities, but the exact opposite, the attempt to make universally available those accomplishments which had been developed by a privileged few. When Anton Webern, not without naivety, said that he was convinced that his music would, a few decades later, be as popular as

Puccini's, he was nearer to the intentions of Marx than is an art censor who dismisses dodecaphonic and serial techniques as decadent because they are of no use at the revolutionary intermediate stage.

The charge of arrogant elitism, which turns an idea of Ortega y Gasset[23] on its head, is beside the point. Anyone who raises it should become aware of the conditions under which the concept of elitism is suspect. An élite in the disreputable sense is a group which, in the first place, exercises power without rational legitimacy and, secondly, shuts itself off against outsiders. Yet it would be absurd to accuse the composers and audiences of new music of one or the other of these traits. Equally without foundation is the continually repeated and rather servile attempt to denounce sympathy for serial or post-serial music as snobbism. A snob – Stravinsky called him the 'pompier of the avant garde' – tries to acquire prestige by aping the views of a ruling class and by adopting opinions that are not rooted in his own personal experience. But a ruling class whose conspicuous consumption includes serial music does not exist.

V

The constitutive category of autonomous aesthetic awareness is the concept of the self-contained work of art. 'The highest reality in art', as Walter Benjamin put it, 'is an isolated, complete work.'[24] In contrast to this the proponents of social commitment, who see in art a tool of social change, are concerned less with the individual works than with their 'cultural function'.[25] The ethically defined criteria of evaluation derive from the sentimental belief in progress and education of the eighteenth century, a time when Kant's statement that music was 'more pleasure than culture'[26] was the most damning verdict imaginable.

But 'progress', the dogma of the eighteenth century, is more a category of the philosophy of history than of scientific history, with the result that the dispute about the concept of the progressive threatens to become a quarrel between disciplines. Whereas Hegel regarded common sense with the undisguised contempt of the philosopher who considers himself to be above the nether regions of empirical knowledge, empiricists such as Karl Popper[27] view the philosophy of history as being merely a tissue of superfluous or even pernicious speculation, to put it mildly. The method of argument is simple, consisting in the claim that the problem of whether an epoch as a whole signifies progress or regression is not capable of being solved, and is thus irrelevant in a scholarly sense. One can speak of progress only within clearly defined limits and not without making certain assumptions about value. When these are disregarded, the claim that

progress has been made evaporates. It is however evident that the extent
of what can be regarded as belonging to music is not clearly defined, and
that there are several competing views and criteria. Compositional–
technical progress can be coupled with regression in musical hearing; and
it is not *a priori* clear whether composition or reception* is the crucial
factor. The tendency to encompass the whole, which is a characteristic of
the philosophy of history, thus encounters difficulties which are hardly
capable of being solved. If a philosopher of history speaks of progress,
then he can always be accused of being arbitrary in that he makes a part
the measure of the whole. At the same time, a historian who does not
move beyond a restricted area, such as that of compositional technique,
must put up with the reproach that his thinking is one-sided – Hegel
would say, 'abstract'. It seems as if the dilemma of having to choose
between speculation and abstraction is inescapable.

VI

In stating that works of art cannot be compared, Benedetto Croce[28]
expressed a widely-held view. Yet much of a music historian's time is
devoted to comparison, and he must, if he is not to lose his self-respect,
attempt to interpret the idea that works cannot be compared in a way
which will not hinder his endeavours. For what Croce is in fact saying is
that it is impossible to compare works of art taken as a whole. The process
of observing differences or similarities in order to formulate stylistic concepts involves placing certain aspects and individual traits side by side.
But by extrapolating them the work as a whole and as an individual entity
is abrogated, for it changes from being an object of aesthetic contemplation to being a document for a style or a technique.

In undissected form works of art stand next to each other without
transitional links. For that reason Kant[29] made a sharp distinction
between the continuity of progress in a scholarly discipline and the discontinuity which is characteristic of changes in the sphere of art. Adorno's
idea[30] that there is a standard of musical awareness or of progress below
which a composer must not fall if he does not wish to produce irrel-
evancies thus seems without foundation inasmuch as it is aimed directly
at the works as aesthetic forms. In order to make sense it presupposes
that, despite the discontinuity of the works, it is possible to decide a level
on which musical 'discoveries and inventions' (to quote Karlheinz

---

* *Rezeption*, referring to the way in which a work is understood, both at the time of its composition and subsequently. The related term *Rezeptionsgeschichte* ('reception history') conveys the entire subsequent history of a work and its critical reception. [Trans.]

Stockhausen)[31] come together to form a unity or a continuum. Only then is it possible to speak of a musical development which admittedly is at times interrupted and externally determined but which obeys an immanent logic. Thus Fétis, although he insisted 'que la musique se transforme, et qu'elle ne progresse que dans ses éléments matériels', admitted that progress was nevertheless possible in the 'éléments matériels'.

Yet the level at which attempts were made to determine musical progress has changed. From the late eighteenth to the early twentieth century it was, next to the development of harmony and instrumentation, above all the growing richness of expression and characterisation that was considered progressive.[32] In the past few decades, however, the emphasis has tended to be placed on compositional–technical discoveries and hypotheses, on methods of musical thinking. (Acoustical–technical innovations such as the synthetic production of tones and noises or the employment of changing sound directions are of lesser importance.)[33]

The transitions from atonal to dodecaphonic and from serial to postserial music have been described by Theodor W. Adorno[34] and György Ligeti[35] on the lines of problem history. Karlheinz Stockhausen's development from pointillist technique via group form [*Gruppenform*] and the statistical method to moment form[36] can serve as an example, showing clearly that difficulties which at first seemed insoluble provided the stimulus for works at a second level on which earlier problems were solved. Admittedly, others arose in their stead, but these in turn urged musical thinking onwards. This seems to suggest that musical development in a restricted sphere, that of compositional technique, shares certain traits with the progress of a scholarly discipline. Yet one should not overlook the differences. The problems of a first level of musical technique can indeed be solved on a second level, but earlier results have to be discarded in the majority of cases. It is impossible to foresee how one might weigh up profit against loss in this context. So one can hardly speak of progress in the exact sense of the word. Modern physics includes classical physics; yet it would be a gross overstatement to say the same about modern compositional technique.

VII

'Like all of nature's creatures the arts and sciences only grow to perfection gradually. The space between first beginnings and utmost perfection is filled with such a multitude of intermediate creatures that one becomes conscious everywhere not only of the stepwise progression from the simple to the complex, and from the small to the large, but also that one can examine every single link in this series of steps alone and as a complete entity. In this respect the sciences and the arts resemble an octopus, the hundred different arms of which all live independently, yet which all seem to be complete, even if smaller, octopuses.'[37] Johann Nikolaus Forkel's bizarre octopus metaphor expresses in a drastic manner the paradox of the idea of progress. It would, it is true, be blindly presumptuous to ascribe a higher rank to the musical present than to the past; yet Forkel believed that the language of music – Adorno would say: the 'material' – was engaged in 'stepwise progression'. According to Adorno, 'one cannot speak' of progress and regression 'with respect to the qualities of individual works written at different times. . . . Progress means nothing other than now and then to grasp the material at the most advanced stage of its historical dialectic.'[38]

Forkel's historical paradigm, the idea of a development 'from the simple to the complex', still dominates discussion about progress nowadays. August Halm saw the goal of music history as a synthesis of fugue and sonata, the 'two cultures of music'[39] – an idea which was not foreign to Anton Webern. And Arnold Schoenberg did indeed recognise that profit had up to now been paid for by loss.[40] But nevertheless he was convinced that there was a developmental tendency towards a work structured in all directions. 'This is why, when composers have acquired the technique of filling one direction with content to the utmost capacity, they must do the same in the next direction, and finally in all the directions in which music expands.'[41]

Yet it seems as if, contrary to Forkel's scheme, the move from the old to the new in earlier centuries was sometimes bound up more with simplification and retrenchment than with complication and emancipation.[42] Johannes Tinctoris in the fifteenth century and the *Summa Musicae* in the fourteenth characterise the respective modern styles as restrictive: 'Sciendum tamen est modernis, quod eis non licet, quidquid antiquis licebat.'[43]

But it was precisely a restricted and regulated style that constituted progress, both indirectly and directly. Directly with regard to the remnants of chance dissonance in the fourteenth and fifteenth centuries, indirectly as a precondition of musical rhetoric. The classification of dissonances into regular and irregular in the sixteenth and seventeenth centuries did not mean that the irregular ones were strictly excluded; they could be and were employed, but in full knowledge of their special character – as 'figures' similar to those used in rhetoric, which, on occasion and for artistic reasons, disregarded the prescriptions of grammar. Thus progress consisted in a growing complexity of musical thinking, of the categories and criteria which were at one's disposal.

VIII

Progress in music is not like that in science, but can be compared to that in philosophy, which is similarly debatable and which seems to consist, inasmuch as it exists at all, less in the solution of problems than in their discovery. It cannot be denied that composers such as Boulez, Stockhausen, Nono, Kagel and Ligeti, composers who can reasonably be described as the avant garde, have enlarged musical thought; and that the questions to which their works represent an answer cannot be dismissed as being insubstantial. Enzensberger's assertion that no one is capable of deciding who is 'in front' retains its validity. But the arrière garde, the camp followers of naive or obdurate epigones, can be quite clearly discerned. Progress, it is true, is uncertain and endangered; but regression is clearly evident and an everyday occurrence.

Avant garde and popularity

The subject 'Avant Garde and Popularity' (historical implications prevent me from using the word 'Volkstümlichkeit') seems to be ill-conceived, inasmuch as it links a term signifying a group with an expression which is aimed at a certain socio-psychological phenomenon. One could, if one were trying to justify the use of this phrase, fall back on the contention that one was really trying to talk about 'Popularity as a Problem of the Avant Garde', of an avant garde that felt itself hemmed in by an esotericism from which it was trying to escape. Yet it is equally clear that 'avant garde' and 'popularity' – 'Volkstümlichkeit' – are the slogans of diametrically opposed musical or musico-political parties. And that the contrast in the formulation of the subject is grammatically distorted, even though it is itself essentially a matter that is clearly defined, gives an idea of the sort of difficulties that stand in the way of a sensible dialogue between the warring factions. Almost all the key categories appear with two meanings; and clarity can therefore not be obtained without making things more complicated.

The pleasure derived from destroying the expression avant garde philosophically and historically, in order to harm the object it signifies – in other words, to say that we know little about the future of music and therefore cannot state with certainty which of today's composers and groups of composers will in retrospect turn out to have been the avant garde – has become rather jaded. This is not to say that a well-worn argument loses its validity. It is irrefutable that we do not know who in fact represents the avant garde. Yet the kind of pedantic philosophy of history that makes the term avant garde seen untenable can be qualified by taking into account considerations based on historical experience.

In the first place, there can in general be little doubt about who does *not* belong to the avant garde. Positive claims are as dubious in theory as negative claims are difficult to refute in practice. Schoenberg's statement that the golden middle way – the path, that is, where avant garde and popularity seek a hollow truce – is the only one that does not lead to Rome has lost none of its topicality. Secondly, the judgment of the present is not without influence on the future. It is more than likely that a composer who is assigned to the avant garde by his own time will exert a historical influence precisely for that reason. This justifies *a posteriori* the view which initially anticipated it.

The real subject of the musico-political debate, then, is not *who* is to be regarded as avant-garde and who is not, but *whether* the concept of the avant garde still represents a central category at all – a category on which a proper understanding of music-historical development can be based – or whether we are dealing with an outmoded stereotype which the onward-moving spirit of the age has left behind as an empty conceptual shell.

The concept of the avant garde is a historical category which arose in the eighteenth century together with the notion of originality and the idea of the autonomous work. One may therefore assume in theory that it will change and finally wither away and die. But for the time being it is hardly possible to say that it has paled into insignificance. It seems rather as if the uncompromising delight in the new, the characteristic feature of the avant garde, is incapable of being suppressed as long as social alienation persists. This has become such a commonplace that it is tedious to call it by name. 'There is only one way', wrote Roland Barthes, 'to escape the alienation of present-day society: *to retreat ahead of it*: every old language is immediately compromised, and every language becomes old once it is repeated.'[1] But an end to alienation is not in sight, even in countries whose rulers claim to have established socialism.

II

If, then, the concept of the avant garde is a category which arose historically and which is subject to change, and which one can in theory imagine as deprived of all meaning, even though at present this hardly seems likely (the political irritation caused by the musical avant garde is a sign of its right to exist), then by analogy the idea of popularity or 'Volkstümlichkeit' (it is not difficult to demonstrate that we are dealing with an idea) must also be understood historically. Like the concept of avant garde, it stems from the eighteenth century; and the two contrasting categories are related in such a way as to complement each other.

Anyone who regards popularity as signifying nothing more than mass consumption falls short of the mark and stifles the problem we hope to discuss, instead of solving it or bringing us – at least theoretically – nearer a solution. To speak in the same breath of avant garde and mass consumption would be absurd. No one – except certain demagogues with whom it is not worth arguing – would claim that a mass audience which is accustomed to popular hits and marches is an authority in whose name one can sit in judgment over the avant garde, whatever its outward appearance. Vis-à-vis the public as it is, the avant garde has not only the objective right, but also the moral and social right, to be unpopular. It would doubtless be malicious to insinuate that the proponents of popularity were basing their case on nothing more than the reluctance or hostile reactions of the existing public when accusing the avant garde of a lack of popularity. Anyone who argues against the avant garde – and not merely inveighs against it – always bases his argument, tacitly or explicitly, on an idea of popularity which has not as yet materialised. It is an idea that he must define more precisely if the discourse is not to become vague and rhetorical; and if he wishes it to be better understood, he must indicate with what means – educational, revolutionary or authoritarian – it could be put into practice.

The usual and indeed popular debates about the merits and shortcomings of the musical avant garde are thus almost always pointless. On the one hand, protests against the real avant garde are made in the name of an ideal popularity without mentioning the difference in conceptual levels. On the other hand, in response to this, supporters of the avant garde insinuate unknowingly or intentionally that the champions of popularity base their arguments on the actual, musically corrupted mass audience in order to demonstrate to the avant garde with spiteful intent that it is a peripheral phenomenon bordering on the superfluous. Yet the misunderstandings are so crude that even the most superficial analysis of the basic concepts should suffice to invalidate them – provided that emotion does not impede rational analysis.

Ever since the eighteenth century, the idea of popularity has been aimed at 'the people'. This never meant an existing audience, whether 'educated' or 'humble', but rather the common human substance which transcended the social divides. From the eighteenth to the twentieth century 'true popularity', existing primarily in the mind and only in rudimentary form in reality, has repeatedly been distinguished from the 'false' kind which retains its grip on the greater part of everyday life. The history of the idea of popularity consists of the changing content of the formal concept of 'true popularity'.

However undisputed it may have been that existing society, formed by 'convention' instead of by 'nature', did not represent the people for whom art was 'really' intended, vast disparities became apparent as soon as the attempt was made to attach the idea of 'true popularity' to part of the real world, that is to say, to single out a fragment of reality which could be used to bring the idea down to earth from the realms of the abstract. Rudiments of the 'real' people – seen as a universal human substance – were sought in the relics of a past peasant culture which had survived into the present; in a feeling of humanity transcending class boundaries evoked by works such as *Die Zauberflöte* or *Die Schöpfung*, which were at one and the same time classical and popular; and in the beginnings of a proletarian culture which was believed to contain the promise or anticipation of future classless art.

Thus, inasmuch as 'the people' was understood as a universal human substance which was, to be sure, latent and prefigured in existing society but which still needed to be realised and urged to manifest itself – in other words, a substance which was a piece of the future – the idea of 'true popularity' did not necessarily have to clash with the music of the avant garde, which in the nineteenth century was at first mocked and then praised as 'music of the future'. 'The people' – in this context, a figment of the imagination – was far more like the authority to which Wagner clung when he felt himself rejected by the prejudices of the 'educated' on the one hand and by the rough treatment of the 'mob' (it would be right to include the 'aristocratic mob' of the Paris *Tannhäuser* scandal) on the other. The ideas of the 'music of the future' and of 'true popularity' assume complementary roles in Wagner's aesthetic and political programmes. 'The art-work of the future' was intended to be the form of expression of an audience which had been emancipated in the direction of the universal–human – in other words, of the people.

On the other hand the aesthetic of the avant garde, whose central tenet seems to be the maxim that art has to be new in order to be authentic, has been combined, since the late eighteenth century, with the idea of the autonomous work, a work which, as Tieck put it, forms 'a separate world of its own'. For the postulated novelty was understood primarily, even if not exclusively, as the newness of artistic means and expressive features, and only secondarily as the newness of the subject-matter on which a work was based, or of the function it performed. (In the case of Wagner, however, artistic means, expressive character, subject-matter and function are inseparably interlinked, and it would be ahistorical to project onto the nineteenth century without further ado the one-sided emphasis placed on artistic means by the Russian formalists – whose ideas in turn influenced Adorno when he forged his concept of material, which profoundly altered musical thinking. The autonomy concept is a category which is subject to historically changeable and changing interpretations.)

The view has almost become a commonplace that the autonomy of art is a slogan used by those who look upon human emancipation with indifference, suspicion or hostility, and that only politically committed art can have a liberating effect. This is a mistaken and sometimes perfidious prejudice. According to concepts current in the nineteenth century – and the extent to which these are outmoded is not at all clear – art represented an element of freedom precisely because it was autonomous, that is, because it was abstracted from the 'realm of necessity', as Fichte called the socio-economic sphere. It was the concept of freedom, of the abolition of social and economic constraints, that proved to be the focal point for those ideas which aimed at a concrete designation of the universal human substance.

The conceptual conglomeration characteristic of the nineteenth century, the attempt to unite and correlate the concepts of universal human substance, of the realm of freedom, of true popularity, of the autonomy of art and of the newness of artistic means and expressive character can be described as being one of the 'heroic illusions' of the bourgeois age. But one can also interpret it as a promise which, because it was never fulfilled, has lost none of its right to be realised. (The practice of denunciation which is spreading like an intellectual epidemic – the method, that is, of dismissing and suspecting the mental anticipation and elaboration of the aspired moral–social condition as being an evasive move on the part of those who do not really wish to change anything – is based on a crude theory of milieu, on the conviction that people do not need to change inwardly but that it is sufficient to change the circumstances under which they exist.)

III

In his manifesto 'Einiges über das Verhalten der Arbeitersänger und -musiker in Deutschland' ('Some Observations on the Behaviour of Worker Singers and Musicians in Germany', 1935), Hanns Eisler wrote:

In the bourgeois world the modern musical style has led to a serious conflict of opinion, for it does little to pander to the comfort and pleasure of the bourgeois listener. The modern musical style has never been able to conquer a large audience. Only small circles of specialists and intellectuals find it interesting. From a revolutionary point of view this modern style can be described as one which is progressive within capitalism. It does not simulate connections between people which no longer exist in bourgeois society; it does not awaken cosy 'feelings'; it does not deliver harmonious connections; and it demands an ever-increasing level of education from the listener, that is, it posits ever-larger material preconditions if he is to understand it. Thus it is truly capitalist; and thereby it is very timely indeed, for it mirrors the confusion of capitalist conditions without glossing over them, though also without criticising them.[2]

This is an ambiguous passage. Eisler's objections to the esoteric nature of New Music and the unpopularity into which it has fallen do not descend to the level of simplistic polemic, and he interprets it as an expression of the state of bourgeois society, which is supposedly so depraved that it cannot bear to contemplate its own likeness. The same coldness and the same fear that exist between people in everyday life also emanate from the music – music which, just because it is abstract, is 'its age rendered in sound' (to parody Hegel). That it expresses an inhuman state of affairs is its merit, because it conceals nothing; and at the same time this is its misfortune, for by being a mirror of inhumanity it becomes inhuman itself.

Eisler's thesis was challenged by Adorno's counter-thesis which proposed that music is human precisely because it speaks of inhumanity and resists it. And it performs – contrary to Eisler's verdict – a critical function in that it does not transfigure or obscure what exists but calls it by name. In rejecting a false positivism, which manifests itself aesthetically as kitsch, Eisler and Adorno were of one opinion.

The difference between Eisler's and Adorno's interpretations of esotericism can be decoded politically. It means that for Adorno, who did not believe in a mitigation of alienation in socialist states, in other words, in their basic socialism, resistance against the existing state of affairs came together in the form of internal criticism, which found a refuge in art. Eisler, however, saw himself on the right path to socialism, to an active criticism of alienation. Therefore he only allowed music which formed a tool of active, and not merely of contemplative, criticism, to pass as 'critical music'.

The autonomy of music to which Adorno adhered is open to the accusation of being ideological, of deceiving us about social reality. The contrast between autonomous and functional music is an illusory one in the opinion of those who are in favour of politically committed art; for them even music which considers itself to be autonomous in fact performs a function. They believe it is not a question of distinguishing between functional and autonomous music, but between music that admits its function – and that means its partiality – and music that conceals it.

The argument may seem logically compelling, yet it is empirically flawed. First of all it denies or misunderstands the difference between essential and accidental features of a thing. No one denies that the reception of a Beethoven symphony can be corrupted to a greater or lesser extent to become conspicuous consumption. Yet the functional element, even if it should happen to predominate in socio-psychological terms, remains extraneous to the object – the Beethoven symphony – in aesthetic terms; whereas in the case of music conceived with a function in mind, such as that accompanying a liturgical or ceremonial act or a dance, the intended function belongs to the object itself, being an essential element and not merely an accidental one.

Secondly, the argument that autonomous music cannot escape the clutches of functionality suffers from the flaw that a difference of degree, which is what really matters, is suppressed or treated as irrelevant. (The logical pattern – the procedure whereby a crucial difference of degree is allowed to seem unimportant by stating that it is not a basic contrast – reminds one of the intellectual practices of moral zealots.) Without bothering about the difference between essential and accidental features, one demonstrates that the asserted autonomy of music is not universally valid and then arrives at the horrendous conclusion that there is therefore no significant difference between musical propaganda and esoteric art, except perhaps the difference between honesty and hypocrisy.

Thirdly, the attempt to demonstrate the functional character of autonomous music remains deliberately abstract. Those who despise the aesthetics of autonomy make light of the far-reaching differences between the functions that can be discerned in autonomous music, as if it were of no importance whether a piece of music serves conspicuous consumption or is felt to be the expression of inner resistance. The difference is played down to make bourgeois society seem like the night in which all cats are grey. (That Adorno heard an element of inner resistance in esoteric music shows quite clearly, incidentally, that, without actually sacrificing the idea involved, he did not deny the functional character of autonomous music and even emphasised it.)

Fourthly, one must distinguish between functional character in the narrow and in the wider sense, between liturgical or political music tied to a specific purpose and the educative function which autonomous music is able to perform precisely because of its autonomy and abstraction from the 'realm of necessity'. The reference to the fact that autonomous music is or can be functional in the wider sense is not sufficient to justify the polemical claim that there is no difference between it and functional music in the strict sense of the word.

Fifthly, the urge to deny or even to slander artistic autonomy is, strictly speaking, incomprehensible in the case of socialists whose avowed aim or utopian vision is the overcoming of alienation. One can indeed question the extent to which the compositional activity of the avant garde is truly autonomous, but it can hardly be denied that where it attains autonomy it represents one of the few paradigms of non-alienated work in the existing forms of society – and that means all forms now in existence. It is nonsensical and depressing when declared socialists suspect autonomy, to the idea of which the avant garde rightly clings (even if in reality it is restricted), of being merely arrogant and escapist, and deliberately misunderstand the fragment of aesthetic–moral utopia which it contains.

IV

One can, if one is sufficiently interested in rational discourse, differentiate between the elements of the dispute between the supporters of the avant garde and the proponents of popularity without thereby obscuring the differences which are of crucial importance.

1. There are those who accept the current conflict between the esoteric and the popular – in other words, who either, while enjoying *Gebrauchsmusik*, speak scornfully of 'opus music', which they would prefer to ignore, or, as initiates of New Music, consider the distance separating it from trivial music to be the essential feature of the avant garde – and the number of these conservatives is not small. Yet a debate which is based on reasons rather than on interjections can hardly be envisaged, on account of the hardening of attitudes between the musically 'highbrow' and the musically 'lowbrow'.

2. But it is almost impossible to expect the sort of zealots who demand either a different avant garde for the existing mass audience or a different mass audience for the existing avant garde to indulge in ideas that are more than just masks for their emotions. On the one hand, the slogans which baldly declare the working class as it is, or as it has been fashioned by the system, to be the authority to which music has to justify itself are evidently dictated solely by political tactics, and are not founded on objective considerations which would be of interest to a political outsider. On the other hand, the attempts to popularise the music of the avant

garde as it is by direct educational measures have for the moment failed, either externally or internally: externally on account of failures, and internally because of distortions of the very object that was supposed to be understood. More precisely, they have failed by turning music, part of whose significance consists in its relationship to a complex musical past, into ahistorical objects of sound which are to be made acceptable to inexperienced listeners by means of the technique of calculated mis-understanding.

3. If the argument concerning avant garde and popularity is not to remain pointless – that is, a mere exchange of misunderstandings – one would have to be able to assume that the basic characteristics of both the present audience and the avant garde can be regarded as being open to change. (The fact that a decidedly sudden alternation of compositional methods belongs to the concept of the avant garde does not preclude the possibility of speaking of a phenomenon with persistent basic traits or of a sustained structure.) Of course, the musico-political programmes, which were designed in the belief that nothing is constant, are very different in character. Either a false avant garde and an equally false popularity appear as two aspects of the same impasse which can only be overcome by over-throwing existing society (whose antagonisms lead to the collapse of musical culture) by means of a revolution based on the proletariat. Its musical consequences must therefore preserve the tradition of the popular, however questionable it may be, rather than that of the avant garde. Or, vice versa, one is convinced that the music of a more humane future is prefigured, not in the popular or semi-popular, but in the advanced, even if not in a distinct form. It is a future which one believes can be reached by reforms without resorting to revolution. A third musico-political concept based on the idea that a cultural revolution, though proletarian in nature, could and should in fact be orientated towards advanced and not popular art was stifled in Russia after 1930. Yet the feeling that it should actually be possible to let the music of the revolution and the revolution in music converge instead of diverge is not dead by any means – even if it is difficult to translate this feeling into practicable concepts and thoughts.

New Music and the problem of musical genre

The fact that in the last decade and a half the works of the musical avant garde have no longer presented themselves as sonatas or symphonies but as 'Constellations', 'Figures' or 'Prisms', even though composers showed no inclination towards programme music, provoked the critics to express disagreement and derision. They sensed the unnatural character of the titles without noticing the technical motives which fashion concealed. There is hardly a discipline, be it physics, astronomy or linguistics, the vocabulary of which composers have not ransacked. Taken out of their original context, the borrowed words acquire a picturesque quality, yet without completely losing their sober technical or scientific resonance.

There is a clear affinity with the modish titles in painting. Yet the similarity in the linguistic exterior should not blind us to the difference in the underlying motives. In painting, the title of a picture has become a problem because of the abstraction from the object; in music it is the disintegration of genres that forces composers to look incessantly for new titles – titles which are supposed to designate a work as a special, individual shape not tied to a genre, and which are nonetheless abstract enough not to contradict the essence of instrumental music. The task is a paradoxical one and almost incapable of being solved; hence the mannerism of the titles, which is more an expression of the predicament than of snobbish one-up-manship.

Arnold Schoenberg, who detested being called a revolutionary, remained faithful to the traditional genre names, however much he may have revolutionised compositional technique. Even in the late dodecaphonic works, they are not simply empty verbal shells but express an inner affinity with the past. This becomes apparent as soon as the tonal surface ceases to strike one as surprising. The Op. 33 A Piano Piece draws on the tradition of the character piece; the Third and Fourth String Quartets refer back to Brahms; *Moses und Aron* is a music drama.

This submission to the norms of genre, which he must have considered to have become devoid of meaning, contains an element of inflexibility, almost as if Schoenberg had resisted the consequences of his own compositional technique. That the New Music has a tendency to abolish genres and make works wholly individual first becomes clearly apparent in the case of Anton Webern, who dissolved the genre-determining connections between formal models, movement structure and types of scoring – though he too, and in this there was no difference between him and Schoenberg, did not wish to deny himself the use of the genre names symphony, concerto and string quartet. Nevertheless, it would be an exaggeration to speak of an abrupt break with tradition in the case of Webern. The reasons for the disintegration of genres, the final consequences of which are the individualising yet abstract titles of the last decade and a half, reach far back into the nineteenth century.

I

There are only tentative beginnings when it comes to a theory of musical genres. Characteristic of the difficulties involved is the fact that it is impossible to decide in a reasoned and unambiguous manner whether a fugue is a genre, a form or a technique. Anyone who embarks upon an attempt to design a system of genres which does not violate their historical nature comes up against a logical difficulty at a very early stage, namely that at different times in history genres are determined by changing points of view, with the result that the order of main and subsidiary concepts becomes confused. It is unclear whether it is function, scoring, form, texture or text that constitutes the decisive feature. Older music history differs from newer music history not only in its repertoire of genres but also in that the concept of genre itself is differently defined. Using a rough formula which merely indicates the evolutionary tendency, one could say that prior to the seventeenth century function, text and texture are the primary factors that determine a genre, whereas later on these are scoring and form.

Organum and discant, which were types of polyphony current in the late twelfth century, differ neither on account of the texts on which they were based nor on account of their liturgical function, but merely on account of the nature of the counterpoint – the rhythmic shape of the cantus firmus and the relationship of the principal voice to the counter-melody. However, a sixteenth-century motet differs from a madrigal less on account of compositional features than on account of the liturgical or ceremonial function that it performs and the prose form and Latin text on which it is based.

It was only in the eighteenth century that formal types such as the sonata and the concerto began to determine the genre. The concept of form in the theory of form, which must be distinguished from the concept of form in aesthetics, is a historically recent category. It is not at all self-evident that large-scale movements which reach out beyond the confines of a song are determined by a form laid down by theory, which states that they should represent a clear, plastic whole divided into sections which are palpably related by means of repetition and contrast as well as by thematic–motivic connections. It would be wrong or at least misleading to speak of the form of a sixteenth-century motet, inasmuch as the mere concatenation of wholly new sections which stand side by side without motivic connection cannot be reconciled with a formal concept which is based on repetition and thematic relationships. On the other hand, in the eighteenth- and nineteenth-century symphony, string quartet and sonata, the formal type which they constitute determines the genre. And even in the twentieth century, in the works of Schoenberg and Bartók, the expectation that the first movement of a string quartet should be based on the sonata-form model is seldom frustrated.

Scoring began to determine genre together with form: a symphony is nothing but an orchestral sonata. Yet if the scoring and sometimes the number of voices was variable or not stipulated in earlier epochs, in the seventeenth and eighteenth centuries it gradually became an established and even primary feature of musical genres.

In the seventeenth century, the transitional period between older and newer music history, it is sometimes almost impossible to decide whether it was the function of the works, the use of a sonata in the liturgy or in the princely chamber, or whether it was the scoring, the difference between three-part and four-part writing or between solo and orchestral performance, which constituted the decisive mark of a genre; that is to say, whether sonata da chiesa was the concept under which sonata a tre and sonata a quattro were subsumed, or whether sonata a tre was the concept under which sonata da chiesa and sonata da camera were subsumed. On the one hand Corelli makes a distinction between the sonata da chiesa a tre (Opp. 1 and 3) and the sonata da camera a tre (Opp. 2 and 4), with the result that it seems as if he were grouping his works primarily according to their function. But on the other hand the Op. 5 violin sonatas and the Op. 6 concerti grossi contain both sacred and secular works. The inclusion of pieces with the same scoring but with a different function in one printed work does not necessarily mean that the scoring was felt to be the primary feature of a genre, with the function taking second place. It cannot be ruled out that the grouping into solo, trio and orchestral sonatas was less dependent on ideas of musical genre than on seventeenth-century publishing practice. Printed copies of works with the same scoring, even if with a different function, were presumably easier to sell than those with the same function and different scoring, given that the very same musicians played both in the church and in the chamber. But if it had not coincided with internal compositional factors, the external motive would hardly have made itself felt. The decisive factor was that the scoring in the seventeenth and eighteenth centuries changed from being a matter of performance practice to being an aspect of composition. The idiomatic character of the vocal and instrumental parts, which had in the past been left to improvisation, was now written down. The social and technical aspects – the growth of the publishing business in musical culture and the increasing importance of scoring in the history of composition and musical genres – interlock with and support each other.

II

In the early history of music, as we have seen, a genre was determined primarily by the function it performed and by the texts on which it was based. This indicates that musical genres developed less as a result of compositional assumptions than as a result of external circumstances, which were however assimilated as internal determining factors. Functional music is part of a process which reaches beyond itself, a liturgical act or a celebration, a procession or a dance. And as an art of courtly or bourgeois entertainment even a genre which was compositionally as subtle as the madrigal was functional music without, to put it in crude and anachronistic terms, the utility value endangering the art character [*Kunstcharakter*]. The liturgical, ceremonial or social function and the aesthetic, compositional claim supported each other rather than cancelling each other out. The mass composed in a more complex manner was at the same time the more dignified one.

It has become a scholarly commonplace to contrast the functional music of earlier epochs with the autonomous music of the eighteenth to twentieth centuries. Yet the contrast is too crude and direct for the purpose of conceptualising the changes in eighteenth-century musical thinking. One of the predominant ideas in the Classical and even in the Romantic era was the notion of an aesthetic education which did not remain encapsulated in the realm of aesthetics in which it was rooted, but which reached beyond it with the result that the distinction between autonomous and functional art became blurred. Haydn's *Die Schöpfung*, Beethoven's Ninth Symphony, Mendelssohn's oratorios and Wagner's music dramas – those works, that is, in which bourgeois musical culture recognised the idea of itself in music – can be classified neither as functional nor as autonomous music. They stand apart from the two alternatives to the same extent as the religion of emotion on which they were based sought to escape the distinction between sacred and secular. The nineteenth century was an era which sought to overcome growing contradictions with attempts at reconciliation which may be regarded as successful mediation but also as murky compromise.

While the idea of aesthetic education was bound up with a concept of music which mediated between the idea of the functional work and that of the self-contained, autonomous one, it was characteristic of the musical thinking of the 'artistic era' that in aesthetic theory it adhered unswervingly to the primacy of vocal music at a time when in musical practice, at least in Germany, instrumental music had long since attained the same significance. It is no accident that Beethoven was not mentioned once in the lectures on aesthetics given by Hegel in Berlin in the 1820s. In the aesthetics of the eighteenth and early nineteenth centuries, which were later called 'aesthetics of content' after their predominance had been broken or at least weakened by 'formalism', the procedure of developing concepts and views one-sidedly on the basis of sacred music and opera was considered natural and apposite – just as in the second half of the century it was self-evident to a 'formalist' like Eduard Hanslick that the real music which had attained its true essence, and which aesthetics needed to take as their starting-point if they did not wish to miss the object of enquiry, was instrumental music.

In the age of aesthetic education, to put it bluntly, instrumental music was listened to as if it were vocal music whose text the composer had either suppressed or concealed. Music was meant to speak even if there were no words. And instead of understanding them as formal processes, people sought to understand the symphonies and sonatas of Haydn and Beethoven by attributing content to them in the form of esoteric, unavowed programmes. But the tendency to translate music into poetry, almost invariably of a mediocre kind – the programme Wagner drafted for Beethoven's C sharp minor Quartet is a good example – provided the impetus for Liszt's programme music, which on the one hand put the aesthetic theory into compositional practice, as it were, and on the other sought to counter the spreading dilettantism of musical poeticising by making use of world literature – Dante, Shakespeare and Goethe.

The relationship of the aesthetics of content or emotion to the traditional musical forms and genres is ambivalent. The emphasis on the affect, on the subject-matter or on the 'poetic idea' can have a constructive and stabilising effect, but it can also have a destructive one. Heinrich Christoph Koch, whose *Versuch einer Anleitung zur Composition* (three volumes, 1782–93) is representative of early Classicism, conceives of the aesthetics of emotion as being correlative to formal schematicism. 'I come now', he writes in Volume 2 (p. 117),

to the form of the movements of a piece of music. One cannot deny that on the one hand the form of the same is an accidental feature which in actual fact has little or no influence on the inner character of the piece; and on the other hand one has little reason to complain much about the form of our movements, both in the larger and in the smaller pieces. And this is presumably the reason why many great masters have worked virtually all of their arias, for example, according to one and the same form.

Since form, understood as an outer accoutrement, was of no concern or at least of secondary importance, it could be conventional and was even supposed to be. Thus it is no accident that the sonatas of the Romantics Weber and Chopin, in which the 'poetic idea' is the decisive factor, are formally more schematic and self-conscious than those of the Classicist Beethoven, for whom form, precisely because it was of greater importance, became a problem which posed challenges continually requiring new solutions.

Yet, as the example of Liszt shows, the primacy of content can also lead to fundamental and historically significant changes in musical form. That form is of secondary importance means that it is dependent on content instead of creating an established and never-changing framework to which it adapts itself. The conviction that content is of primary importance justifies unwonted formal designs. These, however, emancipate themselves from the conditions which gave rise to them, and become independent as absolute musical forms. If it is primarily through a tendency to more precise determination of the content that the symphonic poem reaches out beyond the symphony, then at the same time it also turns out to be a more modern genre in formal terms – a genre which provides a spur for further development.

While the idea of aesthetic education, on which the musical culture of the 'artistic era' considered itself to be based, was closely bound up with the convictions and prejudices of the aesthetics of content and with the idea of the primary and model character of vocal music, it also encompassed the idea that in music, just as in poetry, classicality or the classical was possible. Admittedly the concept first gained currency in musical aesthetics after 1780, together with the rise of modern historical awareness. In the nineteenth century aesthetic and historical education were closely linked. But a classic, a *classicus auctor*, was, before the concept of the classic dwindled to become the name of an epoch, thought to be the model author of a genre. According to Thibaut, whose book *Über Reinheit der Tonkunst* (1825) was of crucial importance for the idea of the classical, Palestrina was held to be the classic author of church music, including that of the Protestants; Handel of the oratorio; and Gluck of musical drama. The appeal to the classical could thus, depending on the age of the model, which one copied as an *exemplum classicum* or which one attempted to emulate, justify both a restoration, such as the return to the style of Palestrina, and a mere link with the past, as in the case of Mendelssohn's attitude to Handel, or even an unbroken stylistic evolution, such as the continuation of the Gluck tradition in French opera. But in each case the idea of the classical, as long as it was attached to the concept of the *classicus auctor*, was one of the conservative factors in musical thinking that strengthened the genre traditions which revolved round the idea of aesthetic education.

III

The disintegration of musical genres in the twentieth century is the result of a development determined by the idea of an individual, self-contained work, in the course of which the constituent features of a genre – text, function, scoring and formal model – gradually lost their importance. The text was felt to be of secondary importance or even regarded with indifference; music tied to functions degenerated into triviality; and the increasing complexity and individualisation of scoring and form led to a dissolution of the stereotypes on which traditional genres had been based.

In the eighteenth century an older way of hearing, which took its bearings primarily from the text and how this was rendered in musical terms, was superseded by a new one, which sought to understand music by concentrating on form and on thematic–motivic connections. Typical genres clearly marking the two extremes are the sixteenth-century motet and the nineteenth-century sonata. In order to understand a motet, whose aim is the musical rendering of language as meaning and structure, in the manner in which it was intended, one must listen to the text as a kind of string along which the sections of the composition corresponding to the individual movements or parts of movements are arranged in order. As opposed to this it is the aim of structural hearing that the parts of a work, though they are perceived one after another, should come together at the end in imaginary synchronicity to create an image of the form. Succession turns into simultaneity. And Hans von Bülow's claim that form is large-scale rhythm says nothing more than that large extended sections, for example the thematic groups of a sonata exposition, are linked on the basis of the same principle of correspondence which joins beats so that they become bars, bars so that they become phrases, and phrases so that they become periods.

Yet even the help provided by texts and literary subjects and by real or imputed programmes was abandoned by listeners who could not cope with the difficulties associated with perceiving form. The older manner of hearing vanished without the new one having become sufficiently well established. Whereas it was characteristic of the aesthetics of the eighteenth and early nineteenth centuries, both in theory and in practice, to look for concealed texts or contents in instrumental music, in recent decades the opposing tendency, which is to disregard the texts and to hear vocal music as quasi-instrumental music, has gained the upper hand. And if in serial and post-serial works linguistic fragments are treated as mere noise complexes, then it seems that compositional conclusions have been drawn from an evolutionary tendency of hearing.

This indifference to the text has resulted in a loss of its significance as a feature determining the genre. Developing musical genres on the basis of literary or dramatic ones, which was the rule in earlier epochs, has become a rare exception in New Music; and where it has happened, as in the case of Brecht's and Weill's kind of opera, it remains doubtful whether or not the musical part should be classified as *Gebrauchsmusik*.

The functions of music have become similarly irrelevant. In the nineteenth century, the epoch of 'art religion', art became an object of selfless and immaterial contemplation in the manner described by Schopenhauer. And the idea of a work of art in the emphatic sense, in whose name music, raised to the status of tonal art, was lifted to infinite heights, seemed incompatible with the idea that music could also preserve its aesthetic dignity when it was subsumed in the performance of a function and, as one of several factors, joined in a process which reached out beyond it. It is not that the amount of functional music that was produced and consumed declined in the nineteenth century; and there was also no dearth of new functions which led to the creation of musical genres. Yet functional music remained excluded from the concept of art. There was a yawning gap between utility value and art character, both in liturgical music, which degenerated to the level of an archaising craft, and in light music. But if functional music is regarded with contempt, it runs the danger of becoming as banal as one expects it to be. Reality corresponds to one's prejudices about it. Wagner's *Zurich Waltz* and Bruckner's *Apollo March* are unbelievably bad pieces, almost as if it had been their purpose to demonstrate the inner compulsion to divide music into advanced and trivial categories.

In the twentieth century the gap between utility value and art character has not narrowed; indeed it has probably increased. It almost seems as if New Music were continually trying to escape banality. That it might be possible to discover additional functions for music, even in industrial society, which would enable one to develop new musical genres without falling behind state-of-the-art compositional technique is the hope of composers who feel unhappy about the present isolation of the avant garde. But attempts to close the gap between utility value and art character in the name of New Objectivity forced even composers of the calibre of Hindemith and Krenek to turn away from New Music. And proclamations which dismissed atonal and dodecaphonic music as being the decline and fall of Romanticism, and which extolled efforts to create a kind of *Gebrauchsmusik* on an artistic level as representing what was really modern, could conceal only for a short time the fact that the compromise had been a failure.

The symphony, the string quartet and the lyric piano piece form genres in that there is an established connection between a formal model and a type of scoring. And the genre norms correspond to listener expectations, the frustration of which proves disconcerting. In the nineteenth century the idea of assigning a short lyric piece to a string quartet would have offended against the aesthetic code of manners, the sense of what was musically appropriate. The extreme brevity of Webern's bagatelles was all the more confusing around 1910 in that they were pieces for orchestra and for string quartet. They contradicted all too brusquely established ideas about the meaningful relationship between form and scoring which had become genre norms.

Webern's procedure, seemingly a peripheral experiment, had a historical significance which no one was able to perceive in 1910. It meant nothing less than that the aesthetic, compositional and technical basis of musical genres, and not of individual genres but of the concept of genres taken as a whole, had begun to crumble. In Webern's music there is no typical connection between form and scoring which corresponds to a genre norm, but a special, individual nexus rooted in the unrepeatable character of the single piece. Both the forms and the scoring pursue a path towards individualisation, the extreme consequence of which is the abolition of musical genres.

The displacement of stereotype by variable scoring is the reverse of a process which one might call the emancipation of tone colour. Of the various sound qualities, colour was the last to become a constitutive factor in composition, after pitch, duration and dynamics. Instrumentation first acquired an essential significance in the music of Berlioz, where the writing is often incomprehensible when abstracted from the tone colour. And Wagner emphasised that it was pointless to evaluate the harmony of *Tristan* or of *Parsifal* independently of the instrumentation. In certain works written in the last few years, which have taken the *klangfarben* technique of Schoenberg's Op. 16 as their starting-point, tone colour has even become the central sound quality.

But *klangfarben* technique presupposes a variability of instrumental resources which runs counter to the establishment of certain patterns of scoring as genre-determining types. The tendency to replace the orchestra by varying ensembles became apparent at the beginning of the century in Schoenberg's Chamber Symphony for Fifteen Solo Instruments, and in the growth of the orchestra since Berlioz one may even discern a trend to greater variety – and not merely to monumentality. The enlargement of orchestral resources makes possible a richer variation of scoring within a single work.

As was the case in scoring, musical form emancipated itself from the types and models on which it had been based and which had hemmed it in. The individual shape, without the support of a model, is supposed to stand on its own feet as an unrepeatable entity and not as an example of a genre. It is the work, and not only the genre, that is supposed to survive in history. The consolidation of the repertoire is one of the reasons why the emphasis changed from the genre tradition to the individual work.

If the Classical concept of form was characterised by the fact that, to quote Jacques Handschin, the 'plastic' and 'logical' factors – clear structure and thematic–motivic work – were held in a precarious balance, then music in the nineteenth and twentieth centuries tends to split up into opposite extremes. To put it bluntly, the plastic structure falls victim to triviality, and the development of compositional technique leading to New Music is primarily determined by the 'logical' factor, through the spread and growing complexity of thematic–motivic work, the logical consequence of which is dodecaphony, 'composition with twelve notes related only to one another'.

In the eighteenth and nineteenth centuries formal clarity was ensured by the interaction of tonal harmony, based on the cadential model, and regular syntax. But according to August Halm harmony and syntax represent the general element of musical form, whereas the thematic and melodic aspects represent the special, individual element. (Complex harmony which dissolves or disguises the cadential scheme cannot structure large forms, and stereotype thematicism does not permit the kind of further elaboration that gives a whole movement inner coherence.) Thus the growing significance of thematic–motivic work is the compositional aspect of a process which appears in aesthetic terms to be the individualisation of form. The forms of New Music tend to be unrepeatable. They detach themselves from the traditions of genre, the substance of which has been whittled away.

IV

The abrogation of musical genres, whose importance had already declined in the course of the nineteenth century, is the result of the reverse of an emancipation of the individual work which is directed not only against functional constraints but also against dependence on types and models. The autonomous work is at the same time the individual work which carries within it its own formal law. It is however not enough to describe the tendency towards the individualisation of musical form. One should attempt a sociological explanation, even though there is considerable danger of failure or of digressing into speculative regions.

One of the reasons for the disintegration of genres is, paradoxical as it may seem, the consolidation and historicising of the concert and opera repertoire since the middle of the nineteenth century. The fact that symphony concerts consisting of an introductory piece, a solo concerto and a symphony emerged and firmly established themselves means of course that certain groups were privileged and, so to speak, institutionally supported. The idea that the genre traditions of the symphony and of the solo concerto would for this reason be guaranteed unbroken continuity is an illusion. It was not genres but single works, the mainstay of the repertoire, that were canonised in the nineteenth century. What Heinrich Rickert said of the historical method is true of historicising musical practice: it proceeds by individualisation.

The genre ensured historical continuity as long as the music that was performed was contemporary music, with the result that it was not the individual work but only the genre, whose evolution transcended the individual entity, that survived. At the same time, the historicising of the repertoire meant that individual works, extrapolated from the genre tradition from which they stemmed, were passed down and preserved.

Historicism, one of the pillars of the tendency to individualisation, ends up by becoming the antithesis to tradition.

The consolidation of the repertoire is connected with the fact that the mediocre, which in the eighteenth century was not looked down upon and was even considered indispensable, became superfluous in the nineteenth and twentieth centuries, however much it might pullulate and spread. Anything that does not rise above the level of the 'juste milieu', as Schumann called it, has no aesthetic right to exist as far as New Music is concerned. It was, however, one of the conditions of an unbroken genre tradition that it should be allowed to exist without being ashamed of itself. The history of genre disintegrates when the mediocre degenerates to the level of aesthetic vacuity. For instance, anyone who attempts to describe the evolution of the mass in the nineteenth century feels prompted to speak only of important, exceptional works, of Beethoven's *Missa Solemnis*, Liszt's *Graner Festmesse* and Bruckner's F minor Mass, of works, that is, which stand unrelated side by side without being linked by a genre tradition elaborated in lesser works. But a history of exceptions is no longer a history of a genre.

The craving for what is new and for the infringement and abolition of norms stands in a curiously ambivalent relationship to the consolidation and historicising of the repertoire. The fact that works continue to be performed, instead of being rapidly used up, means on the one hand that old music which reaches into the present from the past prevents what is new at any given time from entering the repertoire. But on the other hand the possibility that pieces may be repeated years and decades later supports the decision to venture forward into the unknown. As long as music was subject to the constraint of having to be understood and accepted immediately, uncompromising newness was hardly possible; or at least it was possible to a lesser extent than in an age in which a composer can hope for repeat performances which can gradually impress a work upon an initially reluctant audience and make it comprehensible.

The extreme form of the individualisation which led to the dissolution of genre norms is a tendency to favour the exceptional. This is not something that first appeared in New Music; it was in fact already present in the music of Berlioz, Wagner, Mahler and Strauss. Although in the first instance it brought the composers into conflict with the audience, it can doubtless be explained in socio-psychological terms, for it seems to be the result of having to maintain one's position in the market place without the backing of a patron. The inner compulsion which led to what had never been heard before was thus at the same time an external pressure. And the postulate of originality, coupled with the idea that one should not offend against good taste and aesthetic manners, is not all that different from the rule obtaining in the case of trivial music, which says that a piece will succeed if it manages to combine the charm of what is unusual or even disconcerting with what is seemingly familiar.

Problems of rhythm in the New Music

Whenever it has tried to express itself, the resistance to the New Music has always brought the concept of atonality into the centre of the argument. It is a concept better suited than any other to fruitless squabbles because it describes a fact, namely, the dissolution of major-minor tonality, and because it can be used for angry outbursts if one thinks the word implies the absurd idea of music without tones. But it is not by chance that both the polemical and the apologetical literature latched on with dogged one-sidedness to problems that deal directly or indirectly with tonality, with the result that even twelve-note technique was regarded primarily as a substitute for it. For the absence of traditional harmonies and progressions is the most trivial, and therefore the most obvious, negative characteristic of modern music.

The neglect of other elements of composition, especially rhythm, could therefore be understood as long as the New Music still lived up to its name. But after half a century there is no excuse for the fact that hardly anything relevant to the problems of rhythm has been said in detail other than in Alban Berg's essay 'Why is Schoenberg's Music So Difficult to Understand?'. Rhythm in Stravinsky is unremittingly cited, extolled and adorned with a critical vocabulary whose vagueness stands out strangely from the precision of the object described; analysis, however, has hardly been attempted. So I may be forgiven for discussing Stravinsky before I sketch out some principles of rhythm in serial music and deal with the problems which arise with regard to Webern's Orchestral Variations, Op. 30.

45

I

The following attempt to describe types or principles of rhythm in Stravinsky is not meant to be a watertight classification or even a system, but merely a list of observations. A discussion of their relationship to each other that tried to deal with Stravinsky's rhythm in its entirety would have to be carried out with greater precision than is possible in a sketch, which is more concerned with demonstrating phenomena clearly than with laying down a theory. I shall also avoid the temptation to move from descriptions to suppositions regarding their historical ancestry, because the method of ascribing to folklore all the phenomena that cannot be explained on the basis of the tradition of European art music – a folklore which cannot be properly understood by someone who has not grown up in it – is probably of questionable methodological legitimacy, to say the very least.

A rhythmic technique the principles of which are new instead of merely enriching older forms leads to problems of notation. The composer has the problem either of changing the notational system or of the reverse, namely, expressing rhythmic phenomena in a notation which, by virtue of the historical meaning it has acquired, contradicts that which is to be conveyed. One would have to be blind to history to see in our notation, which even Stravinsky uses, because it is the only universally readable one, a neutral supply of signs, independent of any style and capable of doing justice to any style. It is the expression and equivalent of the metrical rhythm that evolved in the seventeenth century, and it implies assumptions which Stravinsky does not share. The attempt to understand Stravinsky's rhythm, and to understand it in such a way that the immediate, non-conceptual musical view becomes a categorically precise one, embroils us in the problem of an inappropriate, even an unavoidably inappropriate notation; unavoidably so because the alternative – of inventing other signs – would have been suspect to Stravinsky, on account of its sectarian overtones.

But if one is searching for a method to show how Stravinsky's novel use of rhythm deviates from tradition, it would not be the worst course of action to start out from the contradictions between rhythm and the notational system Stravinsky was compelled to use, from the gulf between the object itself and its external representation. This 'detour', in the course of which the import of Stravinsky's rhythm will be examined, consists in the observing of inaccuracies in the notation.

1. The bassoon solo at the start of *Le sacre du printemps* is rhythmically imprecise. One hardly needs the indication *Tempo rubato* for it to be clear that the notation should not be taken too literally (Ex. 1). The presentation of the E minor broken chord in semiquavers, quaver triplets and

Ex. 1

semiquaver quintuplets is not meant as rational augmentation and diminution – the proportion 1/4: 1/3: 1/5 – but as an uncertain, vague broadening out and acceleration. And the apparent shift of accent in the first bar, the displacement of the stress from the first to the second note of the E minor broken chord, is nothing other than a deception inherent in the notation. In the irrational, melismatic rhythm that Stravinsky has in mind, only the turn before the figure's first note acts as an accentuating factor. But in rational metrical rhythm, whose notation Stravinsky uses, the stress moves from the first to the second note when four semiquavers are exchanged for four quaver triplets (Ex. 2).

Ex. 2

2. The second section of the 'Danse sacrale', the final movement of *Le sacre*, begins with chords at intervals of quavers and crotchets (Ex. 3). The

Ex. 3

time signature changes between 3/8 and 2/8. But after twenty-one bars the opening rhythm is repeated in a different metrical scheme, without the change in notation being comprehensible as rhythmic variation (Ex. 4).

Ex. 4

One cannot hear how the 3/8 and 2/8 bars change position so that the third chord stands in the middle instead of at the beginning of the second bar. The musical insignificance of this difference suggests that the time signatures, being interchangeable, mean nothing; they are in fact irrelevant. The barlines are not markings of stress, but merely a method of ordering the notes.

Apart from this operational aspect, their only meaning is a negative one: a short note surrounded by two long notes stands at the beginning of each bar and thus apparently draws the accent onto itself. This is no more than a means of preventing us from giving in to custom and associating 'long' with 'accented' and 'short' with 'up-beat'. In order to present rhythm which is not subjugated to the metrical scheme, Stravinsky permits the separate elements of notation tied to the metrical rhythm (long notes and accents) to cancel each other out.

The only principle adhered to by the arrangement of 'longs' and 'shorts' is an irregularity in which neither repetition nor rhythmic motifs and their variants can be distinguished without the interpretation being forced or arbitrary. One could speak here of a technique of 'intervallic rhythm', in analogy to 'intervallic melody'. 'Intervallic melody' means that only the distance between the notes is or should be deemed relevant, not the degree of consonance between the intervals. 'Intervallic rhythm' means, then, that mere time intervals and not the degree of stress accorded to them determine the rhythm.

The need to hear 'intervallic rhythm' as such and not to reinterpret it as irregular barring is greater than it at first seems. Our perception of the relative durations of notes is imprecise and rudimentary. We can still grasp the relationship $2:1$ as a proportion, the reduction of a 3/4 bar into $2/4 + 1/4$. But a quaver at the end of a 3/4 bar is no more than a short upbeat to the next 3/4 bar; the quaver's relative duration is not precisely defined, since the relationship $5:1$ is not a musical phenomenon as far as we are concerned. Even the relationship $2:3$ touches the limits of what we can perceive accurately when the tempo is fast and the beats are not subdivided. The *Aksak* rhythm which Bartók termed 'Bulgarian rhythm' comprises $2/8 + 2/8 + 2/8 + 3/8$. Yet one does not hear the proportion $2:2:2:3$, but a 4/4 bar with a slightly lengthened final beat.

The prerequisite for this phenomenon of the 'lengthened beat', however, is that the rhythmic grouping is repeated regularly, thereby constituting a bar. The phenomenon that I have tried to describe as 'intervallic rhythm' occurs when the impression of a bar dominated by 2/8 and 3/8 values is contradicted – on the one hand by an irregular chain of 2/8 and 3/8 values and on the other by indiscriminate accentuation.

3. If the first type, the melismatic rhythm, is founded on irrational extension and contraction, and the second, intervallic rhythm, on the distance
between notes – a distance that is measured, but not subject to a metrical
scheme except in a superficial, operational sense – then there is also a
third type, which should be described as 'counting' rhythm and which is
confined to a single time value. Basic values form irregular groups which
should not be understood as bars, and whose differences should not be
interpreted as bar changes, even though the notation may suggest such a
misunderstanding (Ex. 5).

Ex. 5

The first choral section in *Les noces* begins with an eleven-syllable line
and a twelve-syllable line. Stravinsky divides the 11 + 12 = 23 syllables
into three 6/8 bars and one 5/8 bar. But the metrical scheme is fictitious.
Real accents fall on the first syllable of each line in order to identify it as
a beginning and as a new entry, and also fall on the natural accents of the
names that are emphasised more than the rest of the lines (in the manner
of a litany). If we were to notate each real accent as the first beat of a bar,
the result would be the metrical scheme 6/8 + 5/8 + 7/8 + 5/8. Instead of
5/8 + 7/8, Stravinsky writes 6/8 + 6/8 in order not to confuse the conductor. The result is that the first syllable of the second line appears as a
sforzato accent and not as the first beat of a bar. But both the first five
syllables (in the Russian version) and the music correspond in each of the
two lines, and it would be absurd to take the notational difference literally
as a change of bar and as a displacement of the musical accents by a
quaver. The metrical scheme does not have the essential meaning of determining the main stresses, but is a purely functional means of clearly
distributing the conductor's beats.

The caesural accents by which the lines are divided in this 'counting'
rhythm do not always fall on the opening notes as in the choral section
from *Les noces*, but sometimes stand as isolated beats between the lines,

thereby confusing the notation of the bars. Any attempt to hear the single beat that divides two identical lines as part of a bar would have the absurd consequence that, when the line following this single beat is repeated, the stress would be displaced by one beat. And to do justice to Stravinsky's rhythmic technique, this single beat that divides the lines must be understood as a phenomenon unknown to metrical rhythm. It is a beat that stands alone, linked rhythmically neither to what has gone before nor to what follows. One must suspend the habit of hearing a beat as an antecedent that requires a consequent, or a consequent that presupposes an antecedent.

4. The concept of metrical rhythm that emerged in the seventeenth and eighteenth centuries implies a hierarchy of stresses; metrical rhythm has a subordinating effect. In a 4/4 bar, it is not merely the case that the first and third crotchets are stressed, the second and fourth unstressed; in addition the first crotchet has the primary stress as opposed to the secondary stress of the third crotchet. And the principle of subordination goes still further, for whole bars can be stressed or unstressed in relation to each other. But whereas a multilayered hierarchy is the distinctive feature of metrical rhythm, a rhythm in which the individual beats can be divided into stressed and unstressed parts, but where there is no question of an overall antithesis of accented and unaccented beats and groups of beats, cannot be subsumed under the concept of metrical rhythm. To define the difference terminologically, one could speak of 'beat rhythm'.

In the 'Danses des adolescentes' from *Le sacre*, Stravinsky notates in 2/4 motifs that span two, three or four crotchets, with the result that a

Ex. 6

contradiction emerges between the regularity of the barring and the irregularity of the length of the motifs (Ex. 6). If one takes the barlines literally, one is compelled to shift the accents of the motifs. The stress in *a2* falls on the first and third crotchets (bars 7–8) or on the second crotchet (bars 10–11). In *b* the accent falls on the first (bar 3) or the second crotchet (bars 8–10). In order to avoid the apparent absurdity of this shift of accent, one would have to alter the notation and turn bars 6 and 9 into 3/4 bars (dotted lines). But neither the change of accent nor the change of time signature would do justice to the rhythmic effect that Stravinsky had in mind. The crotchets are to be understood as equal beats, not divided into ups and downs, but juxtaposed in a non-hierarchical manner. The barlines are mere indications of division and orientation without a rhythmically qualitative meaning, with the result that it is of no consequence where in fact they divide the motifs. Thus the barlines are neither musically absurd nor notationally incorrect; but they are rhythmically irrelevant.

That the subordinating principle of metrical rhythm does not apply to these beats does not preclude them from forming groups. But the grouping in beat rhythm is no universal, predetermined scheme governing the rhythmic details, but the result and manifestation of the particular rhythmic and melodic impulse. In metrical rhythm, a change of time signature is a departure from the norm of regularity, a norm that is founded in the very nature of metrical rhythm. But in beat rhythm what was the exception in metrical rhythm becomes the rule. It is in the nature of a rhythmic technique that consigns itself to the momentum of its smallest parts without the support of an overall scheme that the groupings should change. Yet in modern notation the groupings in beat rhythm appear as bars, and their regroupings as changes of time signature (Ex. 7).

Ex. 7

The trumpet melody of the 'Action rituelle' in *Le sacre* reveals unmistakably the beat principle, none of the beats being more or less stressed than the others. The groups are written as bars, the first as a 3/4 bar, the second as a 2/4 bar. They are repeated, but altered through slight elongation; the variant causes the notation to become confused. The figure b^1–c^2 sharp–b^1, the second beat of the example, is supposed to be understood as a unit even in its augmentation, as an elongation or doubling of the duration of the beat. But when the beat is thus augmented, its subdivision into a stressed and an unstressed half corresponds to an alternation of stressed and unstressed groups through which beat rhythm approximates to metrical rhythm. Therefore, in this augmentation, the notation of the bars is real, not fictitious, for the first crotchet has more weight than the second. But at the same time the notation of the bars acts as a distorting factor, for the first note of the melody (given in the example as the first beat of the bar) appears in the variant as a weak beat. It is really neither a strong nor a weak beat, but a beat that has as much weight as any other. It would be musically absurd to interpret this as a metrical change in the meaning of the note, and this in itself confirms the hypothesis that the melody makes manifest a beat rhythm which is more likely to be hidden by the notation of the bars than revealed by it.

5. That Stravinsky recognises types of rhythm that undermine or evade the metrical scheme does not mean that metrical rhythm is foreign to him. Some of his rhythmic points presuppose the awareness of a metrical rhythm in order to be understood in the way they were intended. They are deviations from the accepted norm, not the expression of an unusual one (Ex. 8). In this quotation from *Le sacre*, the principle of metrical rhythm is unmistakably revealed. Both the crotchets and the minims are complicated metrically: the first has more weight than the second. But the row of 4/4 bars is interrupted by single 6/4 bars; or, more precisely, the row of 2/2 bars by single 3/2 bars. The surplus beat – the final minim of the 3/2 bar – is an anticipation of the opening of the following bar. It is heard first as if it were the beginning of a bar, that is, as a stressed beat, then recognised as the anticipation of one and consequently reinterpreted as an unstressed upbeat.

Ex. 8

In Hugo Riemann's system, the most sophisticated theory of metrical rhythm, the metrical reinterpretation of whole bars is described, but not that of beats. And without doubt the reinterpretation of beats is a more substantial deviation than that of whole bars. Yet the principle of metrical rhythm is not negated by this reinterpretation of beats, for the disruption may be perceived as an accidental deviation and related back to the norm. In the example given, the time change is a musical reality, and not a mere pretence conjured up by the notation, behind which another kind of rhythm may be hiding.

Addition by means of repetition of a beat is the primary form – but not the only form – of true metrical change in Stravinsky's *Le sacre*. A secondary form was also described by Hugo Riemann with respect to whole bars, and we have only to apply it to the relations between beats. It is the extension that occurs when a metrically stressed phrase-ending is followed immediately by a metrically stressed phrase-opening (Ex. 9). In this quotation from *Le sacre*, the doubling of the stressed beat is notated as the extension of a 4/4 bar into a 5/4 bar instead of isolating it as a single crotchet in a 1/4 bar. It does not need to be demonstrated that it would be nonsensical to interpret the opening of the second phrase as an unstressed beat. Stravinsky counteracts this possible misunderstanding by means of an abrupt change in dynamics and orchestration.

Ex. 9

6. To bring time to a standstill in and through music is something on which Stravinsky's musical thinking has always focused, independent of any stylistic changes. But even if the idea of a 'cessation' of time passing is circumscribed in ever different ways in Stravinsky's oeuvre, one can still name one type of texture which comes closest to it and reveals it most emphatically.

Its hallmark is a 'floating' rhythm, the idea for which Stravinsky may have found in works of the fourteenth and fifteenth centuries, but which he pursues with musical means that are very far removed from those of the late Middle Ages. The proximity to early settings of the Ordinary, which Stravinsky evokes in his Mass, should not obscure the fact that a difference in techniques stands behind the stylistic affinities, a difference in which the historical distance separating us from the fourteenth century is expressed.

The decisive element in the second section of the *Gloria*, the *Laudamus te*, is rhythm; harmony and melody are rudimentary. The impression of 'floating' that comes from the rhythm, of internally active immobility, is based on a method that could be termed 'neutralisation'. In order to understand this better, we must distinguish between four types of stress: first, the accent on a word; second, the stress on the bar; third, duration; and fourth, the emphasis created by the entry of a chord in the instrumental accompaniment. If one analyses the *Laudamus te*, it becomes clear that Stravinsky places at least one of the possible means of emphasis on every syllable, and not more than two on each one. Duration, the accents on the bar, the accents in the declamation and the entries of a chord all neutralise each other. There is an undeniable danger that the effect will be feeble and monotonous; and to combat this, one must retrace the process of neutralisation through active listening, instead of accepting a state of vague uncertainty through passive listening. Only then is this resultant immobility in time – which differs from monotony only in the smallest details – an active one of the kind Stravinsky had in mind.

II

Some of Webern's late works, such as the Concerto, Op. 24, and the Orchestral Variations, Op. 30, might not be models of serial composition, but they certainly contain a number of hidden prerequisites for it. But attempts to use the problems to understand the methods that are supposed to solve them, instead of merely describing historical relationships between the results, will produce differences and even contrasts as well as similarities. It is difficult to decide without being arbitrary which elements are to be regarded as fundamental and which as accidental.

The aesthetic value of serial composition is not decided by the theory on which it is based, but by the quality of the works it produces. Just as it would be inappropriate to use shortcomings in the theory to conclude that the works were aesthetically insubstantial, so it would hardly suffice to base a defence of the theory on the works. It may be disconcerting, but it cannot be denied that important works may be produced on the basis of questionable theories.

Serial rhythm, the construction of rhythmic rows, is not based on a single unchanging method but on several different methods, of which one can say without exaggerating that the theoretical legitimacy of one can be called into question by another. One basic way of organising rhythm in analogy to a twelve-note row is to establish a correlation between pitch intervals and differences in durational value. This procedure is open to the misunderstanding that it does no more than relate pitch and duration. It appears at first sight to be based on the principle that the twelve degrees of the chromatic scale correspond to twelve durational values which themselves result from the multiplication of a unit, a *chronos protos*, ranging, for example, from semiquaver = 1×1 to dotted minim = 12×1. If one imagines a descending scale in which $b^1 = 1$ and $c^1 = 12$, then the notes b^1–f^1 sharp–a^1 correspond to the rhythmic figure semiquaver:dotted crotchet:dotted quaver (Ex. 10).

Ex. 10

But, as a more exact analysis shows, it is not pitch and duration that are correlated but the distances between pitches and the differences in durational value. The use of the semitone as the unit of measurement for the interval between pitches corresponds to the use of the semiquaver as the unit of measurement for differences in duration. The element of the method that decides its legitimacy is therefore not that the note e^1 is assigned a minim and c^1 a dotted minim according to the ordering of the scale, but that the crotchet difference between e^1 = minim and c^1 = dotted minim coincides with the difference between b^1 = semiquaver and g^1 = crotchet plus semiquaver. The difference between durations (in this case a crotchet) always corresponds to the interval between pitches (in this case a major third).

However, it cannot be denied that the scheme is hampered by a number of difficulties, which are partly avoidable and partly unavoidable.

1. A basic rhythmic pattern corresponds to a melodic one, the rhythmic retrograde to the melodic retrograde. The rhythmic analogy to inversion is the reversal of addition and subtraction in durational values. If, for example, an ascending whole tone is inverted to form a descending whole tone, then the rhythmic correlative of the whole tone – the difference of a quaver – occurs not between the crotchet and the quaver but between the

crotchet and the dotted crotchet. And if one takes the durations themselves as the substance of the rhythmic row and not their differences, then the rhythmic changes that correspond to the inversion of intervals bear no logical relation to the basic rhythmic pattern. A true relationship between the figures crotchet plus dotted crotchet and crotchet plus quaver – one which would make it possible to talk of a rhythmic analogy to intervallic inversion – only becomes evident when one realises that what matters is the differences in durational value. Yet it is questionable whether the differences in durational value are a rhythmic phenomenon at all, or merely a figment of the imagination. In metrical rhythm they are irrelevant; in a 6/4 bar the rhythmic figure dotted minim:minim:crotchet is heard not as a progressive crotchet reduction of the durational values, but as a dotted minim followed by another dotted minim divided into a minim and a crotchet. But just because this concept of difference in durational value is unusual does not mean it is fictitious.

2. According to the 'Two-Component Theory' of music psychology, which is of fundamental importance for serial music, a pitch comprises two elements: its 'tone quality' [*Tonqualität*] and its 'brightness' [*Helligkeit*]. The tone quality of d^1 is its 'D-quality', which remains constant at every octave: some musical psychologists talk of a 'D-ness'. Its 'brightness' is its octave register, the localisation of the 'D-quality' in the octave above middle c^1. In serial technique as applied to rhythm, relative duration corresponds to tone quality: for example, the dotted crotchet corresponds to the specific note f^1 sharp when referring to a semiquaver on the note b^1. Corresponding to the 'brightness' or octave register is the unit of rhythmic relation, that is, the semiquaver value of b^1. Any change in the unit of rhythmic relation, however, negates the correlation between the pitch intervals and the differences in durational value. In contradiction to the principle of the system, the durational value of b must be less than that of c^1 if the durational value of c is not to increase immeasurably by being multiplied by twelve. At the octave limits, the rule that the difference recurring between durational values corresponds to the interval recurring in another octave becomes invalid.

3. Relative duration in the rhythmic row is, as we have seen, the correlative of tone quality. In every octave, then, when a descending scale is constructed, the note B has the shortest value, C the longest. And inasmuch as duration signifies emphasis, serial rhythm contradicts the principle of atonality, the dogma that no note is to be accorded lasting priority. (At the local level, primacy of certain notes is unavoidable and does the principle

no harm.) It seems, therefore, that the hierarchy of notes dissolved by the twelve-note technique has been brought back by the use of serial rhythm.

In order to resolve the contradiction between the assumptions and consequences of the method, one must abandon the notion that longer values always and necessarily imply emphasis. One does not need to deny that a natural affinity exists between duration and emphasis, just as it does between ascent and crescendo, to be able to say that it is not musically absurd to have a crescendo on a descending sequence of notes, and that the connection between duration and degree of emphasis can be inverted as well as completely suspended. Set among a lot of long notes, a single short note acts as an accent. But if a reversal of the natural affinity is possible, then so is its negation – a rhythm, that is, in which neither the long notes nor the short notes stand out in relation to each other, but where the differences are neutral and perceived as mere differences in duration. This is not as absurd as it might seem at first sight.

A second method of creating rhythmic analogies to twelve-note rows is based on the idea of correlating not the pitch intervals and durational differences, but the proportions of the intervals and of the durational values. The chromatic scale contains eleven intervals, from the semitone to the major seventh. The simplest, the fifth, represents the proportion 2:3 when comparing frequencies, and 3:2 when measuring string lengths. The most complicated, the tritone, has the proportion 32:45, or, in another tuning, 5:7. In the corresponding rhythmic scale, the rhythmic proportion 1:2 (= crotchet:minim) becomes the equivalent of the octave proportion 1:2, filled out with intermediate values. The fifth (= 2:3) corresponds to the relation between crotchet and dotted crotchet, the fourth (= 3:4) to the relation between dotted crotchet and minim (Ex. 11).

Ex. 11

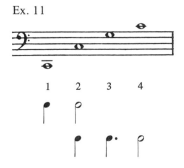

One problem that was insurmountable in the first method of rhythmic row construction is avoided in the second. It consisted in the dilemma that a break in the rhythmic scale resulted from a change in octave – if the durational values were not to increase beyond measure. But if the rhythmic octave-scale extends not from the semiquaver to the dotted minim but only from the crotchet to the minim, then the difficulty is removed, for the transition to a lower octave can correspond to a doubling of the unit of rhythmic relation, without the augmentation of the durational values becoming incomprehensible.

But the dubiousness that is avoided at one point appears at another. The concept of intervallic proportion has a double meaning, and false conclusions thrive under the protection of ambiguity. It can mean either the proportion that forms an interval, such as the proportion 2:3 for a fifth, or the proportion that one interval forms with another, such as the proportion 2:3 with respect to the interval of the whole tone (equal to two semitones) and a minor third (equal to three semitones). The proportion that forms an interval is not perceived as such. The idea of a fifth does not suggest any proportion. That a fifth represents the relationship 2:3 is not shown directly by the phenomenon itself, but only indirectly – by measuring strings which produce the notes a fifth apart. In contrast to the proportions of a single interval that can only be imagined and not heard – the proportion 2:3 in a fifth – the relationship between two intervals, the relationship 2:3 between the whole tone and the minor third, is a matter of musical perception – or of possible musical perception – and not of mathematical or acoustical knowledge. But the method of relating the proportions between pitch and the proportions between durational values is based on the abstract, rather than the concrete, concept of intervallic proportions, that is, on the imaginary instead of the audible. It creates an analogy between the rhythmic relation 2:3 = crotchet:dotted crotchet, which can be perceived as a proportion, and the interval of a fifth, which represents the relationship 2:3, without making it manifest. So the theoretical assumptions which lie behind the correlation between rhythm and intervallic structure are not secure. As we have seen, this does not say anything against the works themselves.

III

Webern's Variations for Orchestra, Op. 30, is one of those works that are always cited whenever a serial use of rhythm has to be justified by referring back to historical models. It is undeniable that rhythm in the Variations is related to twelve-note technique instead of independently

forming its own motifs in the traditional sense. Yet the differences
between Webern's method and serial technique are no less striking than
the similarities, and it would be inappropriate to dismiss them as secondary, or to interpret them on the basis of a pattern of historical development leading from exploratory experiments to a perfect system – as if
Webern's rhythmic technique were a rudimentary precursor of that of the
serialists.

Ex. 12

The row on which the Variations are based is confined to three intervals: the semitone, minor third and major seventh (Ex. 12). The poverty
of material is matched by a richness of relations: the retrograde of the row
is a semitone transposition of the inversion; the retrograde inversion
therefore a semitone transposition of the basic set. Essential for the
rhythm is the fact that notes 7–12, transposed by a semitone, form the
retrograde inversion of notes 1–6. A rhythmic retrograde corresponds to
the melodic retrograde, and a change in the unit of rhythmic relation
corresponds to the melodic inversion: notes 1–4 are diminuted to form
notes 12–9, notes 5–6 augmented to form notes 8–7. One could argue
that the change in the unit of rhythmic relation can be understood as the
correlative of the semitone transposition instead of the inversion, but the
later transformations show that the inversion is what is intended.

    There is an element of arbitrariness associated with the method of treat-
ing the change in the unit of rhythmic relation as a function, as a variable
dependent on melodic inversion; the serial scheme that makes the change
in unit of rhythmic relation analogous to the change in octave is logically
more rigorous than this. Webern's method results from the compulsion
either to forgo a rhythmic correlative to inversion or to change the unit of
rhythmic relation. For this is apparently the only rhythmic variation that,
apart from the retrograde, can fulfil the condition of leaving the relative
durational values unaltered. That a third possibility exists will be shown
below.

    It would be wrong to speak of a rhythmic row. An analogy between
melody and rhythm does exist in Op. 30 in the techniques of altering the

set, but not in the structure of the material. The rhythmic material does not consist of the six durational values from crotchet to demisemiquaver that occur in the formulation of the basic set, but of three rhythmic figures or relationships: $1:1$ = crotchet:crotchet; $1:2$ = quaver:crotchet; and $1:3$ = semiquaver:dotted quaver (together with their retrogrades). That Webern uses three melodic intervals on the one hand, and three rhythmic figures on the other, is a coincidence which may or may not be the result of pure chance; but no consequences are drawn from it. There is no definite connection between the intervals and the rhythmic figures.

The row is divided in two ways: abstractly, as mentioned above, into $6 + 6$ notes, the second half being the retrograde inversion of the first; and concretely, into $4 + 4 + 4$ notes, the three groups being divided from each other by pauses and changes in instrumentation. The concrete, not the abstract division is the basis for the rhythmic changes that correspond to the inverted and retrograde forms of the whole row. The correlative to the retrograde of the whole row is not a retrograde of the individual durations but a retrograde of the rhythmic groups. Group 1 (the crotchet-crotchet-quaver-crotchet rhythm) appears unaltered as group 3.

Thus the basic rhythmic shape for Webern is the four-note group as a closed form, not the series. And the apparent irregularity in the motivic character of the rhythmic groups is due to the fact that in the basic set the third rhythmic relation, $1:3$, is first heard in its inversion. The 'irregular' form, $3:1/1:3$, is clearly defined as a motif; the 'regular' $1:3/3:1$ would be vague.

The motivic character of the rhythmic groups provides Webern with the possibility of varying the motifs by shifting the stress in such a way as is denied to serial rhythm. It should be obvious that the stresses of metrical rhythm, to which Webern adheres in essence rather than for merely notational purposes, are not subsumed in the dynamics, the latter being one of the parameters of serial music. For in the first place, dynamic emphasis is a superficial way of marking the stress of a bar, and in complex music it is superfluous. Secondly, if a group of notes sounded as if it were focused around the loudest one, this would invalidate the whole point of serial dynamics, which regard each note as a step on a dynamic scale. The emancipation of dynamics, which is the goal of serialism, would be negated and cancelled out by the habit of regarding dynamic levels merely as a means of grouping notes together and not as independent elements with a scale of their own.

But the price that has to be paid for this emancipation is the renunciation of the technique of shifting stresses, which Webern applies in the Op. 30 Variations with a truly systematic consistency. One should not expect mechanical permutation, for the system is subject to limitations inherent in the nature of the rhythmic motif. First, two stresses must be separated by at least one unstressed note, for even though stresses that are directly juxtaposed are to be found in Stravinsky (as we have seen), they are foreign to and incomprehensible within the traditional metrical rhythms that Webern preserves (albeit in a most sophisticated way). Secondly, in contrast to upbeats, motif-endings can hardly be elongated. There is virtually no limit to the number of unstressed notes that an upbeat can encompass, but not more than one unstressed note may follow the stress at an ending if it is to remain unambiguously an ending.

So if one considers the limitations inherent in the nature of the motif instead of expecting a perfect permutation, it emerges that the five placings of the accent that are really possible have already all been employed by Webern in the exposition of the four forms of the row, the 'theme' of the Variations (Ex. 13). The notes that can be employed as accents in a four-note phrase (and are so employed in Webern's Op. 30) are 1 and 3, 2 and 4, 1 and 4, 4 on its own and 3 on its own.

Ex. 13

Besides the retrograde and the alteration of the unit of rhythmic relation, the shifting of stresses is a third method of rhythmic variation that leaves the relative durations unaltered. And thus a modification of the Webernian method seems to emerge: the compositional possibility of using a shift of stresses instead of a change in the unit of rhythmic relation as a correlative to the inversion, and of recognising the analogy between the unit of rhythmic relation and the octave position of notes. But in observations such as the ones sketched out above, there is a tendency towards consolidating the relationship between melody and rhythm – something that was foreign to Webern. Despite certain analogies to twelve-note technique, his rhythmic technique is still the traditional one of motivic composition. And the seemingly precarious state in which elements of the past are still present and elements of the future are already present is perhaps aesthetically the richest.

Tonality: structure or process?

I

When we seek – in the first instance, without any scholarly ambition – to come to grips with the problems of musical practice, the terms we use are of little significance provided that their shortcomings do not unduly inhibit an understanding of the object in hand – especially when it is by no means clear what that object actually is. In any case it would be sheer illusion to expect anything objectively illuminating to emerge from an etymological and conceptual discussion of the expression 'tonality', which simply denotes either centralised tonal relations or tonal relations as such. The debate that was conducted about tonality and atonality in connection with the emancipation of the dissonance and with dodecaphony – a debate clouded over by polemics and apologetics – finally led to nothing but the trivial insight that regulated tonal relationships, which could be made to form the basis of a composition as a system of reference, need not always be centred on a tonic or principal note. To call systems without a centre tonal is possible and admissible on both etymological and conceptual grounds.

If there is a problem with tonality at the present time, when it would be absurd to revive the controversy that surrounded atonality and its historical and aesthetic legitimacy, it cannot consist merely in the fact that composers who feel they belong to the post-modernist movement are not afraid of interpolating harmonic–tonal relics of nineteenth-century music into their stylistic montages. Rather, a fundamental, more profound difficulty which has worried composers lies in the experience that the less the tonal relationships – or relationships of tone quality* – are emphasised aesthetically, the more urgent becomes the need for a regulating element which reduces the composer's responsibility. Or to put it the other way round: to the extent that tonal relationships, instead of generally being preformed, must be justified specifically and individually, in other words from the context of the unique, particular work, the composer's compulsion to draw attention to them aesthetically increases.

The fact that the establishment and justification of regulated tonal relations attracts an intense interest is thus perfectly understandable in the light of the disintegration of general structural models. At the same time, however, it is problematical inasmuch as the idea that the parameters of pitch, duration, dynamics and tone colour should be equal in principle is a legacy of the 1950s which cannot simply be discarded. A development aimed at restoring to compositional thinking the traditional hierarchy of sound qualities, that is to say, the primacy of pitch or tone quality, and to a lesser extent duration, would represent a profound change, all the more so because the hierarchy of sound qualities, even though it may appear to be a self-evident fact, has really always been problematical. The idea that dynamics and tone colour are only peripheral parameters – not constitutive but merely supportive ones – was a premiss of compositional technique for hundreds of years, a premiss which was reflected strikingly in notation but which scarcely had anything to do with the way music was perceived. The aesthetics of production and of reception, to use the currently fashionable vocabulary, not infrequently went different ways. And in a certain sense the abolition of the difference between central and peripheral sound qualities has meant that a psychological state of affairs which had always existed has been translated into a compositional procedure, a change which initially made it seem as though everything had been turned upside down.

If the restoration of a hierarchy is therefore a rather risky undertaking from the psychological point of view, it nonetheless seems that even a cursory (albeit unavoidable) reflection about tonal relations will show that the most difficult problems, which seem almost insoluble, lie in the fundamentals: that is, in the area that conventional music theory labels as general musical knowledge, as if we were dealing with a number of facts to be learnt parrot-fashion. It is easy to understand that in dodecaphony the connection between basic set, inversion, retrograde and retrograde inversion constitutes a system of relations, and a closed system at that. Strictly speaking, however, it is by no means clear why the interval

---

* This term is explained above, p. 56. [Trans.]

between D and F, or between F sharp and G sharp, constitutes a relationship at all, if all we can do after the principle of consonance has been abolished is to define the intervals according to the principle of distance as sums of semitones. The relationship between part and whole that exists in the case of individual intervals and the twelve-note row can be interpreted as just as much of a relationship as the quantitative differences between the parts of a row, the larger or smaller intervals. The interval itself, however, as an element of the system, remains a theoretical blind spot, or so it seems. And what is actually being sought after under the name of 'tonality' in the present context – no matter whether the name is well chosen or not – is plainly a viable way out of an awkward dilemma: the dilemma of either restoring the principle of consonance, the victim of atonality, or having to concede that intervals are tonal distances and nothing more.

II

Faced with problems of tonality such as those we have just outlined – problems which can hardly be solved by merely plundering the store of historical and ethnological knowledge – one tends to seek support in natural phenomena (or phenomena which one believes are natural). This tendency is the reverse of a growing distrust of the maxim that has been dominant for decades, namely that if a composer does not wish to produce superfluous work he must entrust himself to the course of history, which in the last resort is held to decide what is musically significant and what is not. In the 1950s, under the influence of Adorno and in accordance with the habit of interpreting serial music as a historical consequence and as a compensation for a deficiency in dodecaphony, the idea of musical 'nature', which Paul Hindemith still clung to, was largely displaced in the aesthetic thinking of composers by the principle of historicism. By the 1970s, however, the concept of history had lost its hold on the general consciousness, because the idea that there is 'history' in the singular – a history whose stage of development determines what is timely and what is not, and therefore what can succeed and what is doomed to failure – came to be seen as a myth. Real history consists of histories in the plural: of events and chains of events which, at times autonomous and at times interwoven, emanate from a whole range of heterogeneous origins and lead to diverging results.

Of course, the fact that a myth which had upheld the general consciousness was shattered is no reason to revive an older one, which for decades everyone had thought was long dead. To put it bluntly, to invoke the concept of nature as a sort of court of appeal for a music theory that is related to present-day compositional practice is to attempt to bring the dead back to life. And the restorational tendencies which are more and more in evidence are bound to provoke dissent, even if the objections that must be raised are in part as outmoded as what they are objecting to.

First, the fact that a phenomenon of sound is, or seems to be, 'natural' is no guarantee that it has any musical meaning. A composer who, because a complex of tones can be deduced from the overtone series, believes himself relieved of the necessity of making the notes 'speak' through his own subjective effort, sacrifices musical reason to a chimera about whose true character one should not let oneself be deluded by the physical nomenclature with which this fiction can be decked out in a pseudo-scientific way.

Secondly, natural phenomena, in the form in which they appear in music theory, are almost always phenomena that have been placed into and interpreted in terms of a category: in other words, they represent nature as it has been appropriated or manipulated, and not nature in its original raw state. The classifying of sonorities according to their degree of consonance – from the octave through the fifth and fourth to the third and sixth and ultimately to the seventh and second – may, as far as the psychology of perception is concerned, be a fact of nature, or, more precisely, an anthropological structure going back to time immemorial. But to claim that the octave is a more perfect interval than the sixth and thus, as a sonority, its natural goal is an interpretation whose philosophical implications are, on the one hand, the Pythagorean premiss that the more simple thing is the more perfect and, on the other, the Aristotelian idea that the imperfect strives towards the perfect as to its *telos* – implications which should by no means be regarded as self-evident but which should be recognised as specifically European (and indeed as fundamental to European polyphony). Moreover, the sense of direction in the relationship between simple and more complex is subject to variation; and in view of the fact that in individual cases we regard a reduction in complexity (the resolution of a dissonance onto a consonance) but in general an increase in complexity (a gradual increase in the wealth of harmonic relations) as a 'natural' principle of musical structure, it is indeed possible to reflect on the illusory nature of the obvious.

Thirdly, the 'freedom to posit axioms'* which Ernst Krenek, influenced by David Hilbert's philosophy of mathematics, appropriated on behalf of composers has unquestionably been effective in all periods of European

---

* See below, p. 276. [Trans.]

music history together with the orientation towards natural data and towards historical preconditions. When Alexander Scriabin or his commentators tried to show how the *Prometheus* chord could be derived from the overtone series, they provoked the objection that it was in actual fact a dominant-ninth chord with flattened fifth and with a 'Chopin sixth' as added note. Beyond the controversy about nature and history, however, which proved so confusing, one less obtrusive but more essential fact remained clear: namely, that the decision systematically to compose out the relationship between part and whole, between the individual chord and the chord centre, in order to establish a rigorous musical coherence, was founded in the composer's freedom to posit axioms and nothing else.

III

Those who are of the opinion that, in the connection and interaction between natural data, historical preconditions and compositional positing of axioms, the decisions of composers or groups of composers represent the final, decisive authority must find the attempt to influence them through theory arrogant and misguided. Nonetheless, the fact that abstract reflection cannot be used to influence compositional practice from the outside does not mean that it should not be used to sketch out and discuss the various possibilities that remain open in principle. And an up-to-date discussion of regulated tonal relations becomes firmly established (or so it seems) only when we reconsider the difference between tonality as structure and tonality as process with all its implications and consequences – a trivial difference, but one that is not always sufficiently borne in mind.

The idea that harmony is a goal-directed process can by no means be taken for granted. Without indulging in a long-winded historical digression, we can make it clear in broad terms that the idea which originated in the twelfth century, that a tendency or affinity whereby a first sonority led inexorably to a second constituted musical connection or progression, became the absolutely fundamental idea determining the development of European polyphony for hundreds of years. That sonorities do not simply exist side by side, linked by melody or voice-leading, but have their own inherent momentum is a principle whose historical significance was underestimated by the older school of music historians only because they took it for granted instead of regarding it as surprising.

Once the basic idea is clear, the distinction as to whether a fourth resolves onto a unison, a major third onto a fifth, a dominant-seventh chord onto a tonic triad, or a chromatic collection onto a fourth-chord – in other words, the distinction which enables us to distinguish between the musical techniques of the twelfth, fourteenth, seventeenth and twentieth centuries – becomes secondary, though not inessential. For the fundamental idea which allows us to interpret the relationship between a lower and a higher degree of consonance as a bias or gravitation, and thus as a harmonic basis for musical progression, did not change at all between the twelfth and the early twentieth centuries.

The union of opposing forces which we call harmony has been understood since as far back as the twelfth century as a process, therefore, and more particularly as an affinity of opposing tone qualities for one another. In earlier epochs and in non-European cultures, by contrast, as well as in large areas of the New Music of the twentieth century, harmony appears primarily as a system. (We can pass over the trivial point that processes presuppose systems of reference and that, conversely, systems that are realised in sound always contain processive elements: what we are discussing are shifts of emphasis, not principles that are contrary and mutually exclusive.)

In order to attain an initial overview, we can make a distinction between closed and open systems, as well as between centred and non-centred ones, and so isolate the basic patterns from the historically variable redefinitions through which they were first made accessible to the composer.

The chromatic scale, if understood according to the principle of distance, as in dodecaphony, that is, without distinguishing between diatonic and chromatic semitones, is a closed complex – as is the pentatonic scale, which has no semitones at all. On the other hand the overtone series, which can in theory be extended into infinity, is an example of an open system – as is major-minor tonality, whose ability to accommodate remote harmonies is unlimited.

Open systems are and must be centred, since, in a situation where there are no limits, the grouping around a central point seems to be the only way of ensuring systematic coherence. Similarly, closed systems may indeed also contain a tonic or principal note, yet having a centre is not necessary, as dodecaphony shows; and where a centre is prominent in a closed system – as in a mode in non-semitonal pentatonic music – it has the appearance of being a secondary structure or something that has been superimposed. A centre is not essential in closed systems, though it is in open systems. A tonic in pentatonic music, where it exists, is, so to speak, an additional determining factor; in the overtone series and the tonal complexes derived from it, by contrast, it constitutes the basis of tonal coherence.

When we come to the redefinitions of systems the composer's freedom to posit axioms, which was mentioned by Ernst Krenek, comes manifestly into its own, as can be seen in the following seemingly banal, but actually rather confused, matter: the contrast between consonance and dissonance. The habit of treating consonance and dissonance as opposites, as if they represented a dichotomy like plus and minus, is misleading and obscures the fact that the series of degrees of consonance in theory does not just permit the inclusion of caesuras in different places, but in addition to these, apart from the division into two classes of intervals, also permits divisions into three or four, as long as they can be justified by the compositional ideas. (Fourteenth-century music was composed using three classes of interval, in that on the one hand the tendency of the so-called imperfect consonances to resolve onto the perfect was used as a means of constituting a musical progression, whereas on the other hand dissonances were treated as added notes and colouristic stimuli whose resolution did not so much represent an element that propelled and motivated the harmonic development as a simple means of cancelling out a deviation from the norm.)

The concept of redefinition, though it cannot be avoided, contains the possibility of misunderstanding inasmuch as it gives a clear impression that there are basic elements underneath. One must bear in mind, however, with the older polyphony as well as with that of the twentieth century, not only that the higher levels are supported by the lower, but, conversely, that the deep structures are influenced and modified by the surface structures, with the result that the nomenclature is actually inappropriate. The fact that in the fourteenth century the fourth, contrary to the ordering of the degrees of consonance, was explained as a dissonance on the basis of the internal logic of the compositional-technical system – a system in which the fourth was supposed to have the same relation to the third as the seventh had to the sixth – shows how the positing of axioms could predominate over a fact of nature. And the initially irritating circumstance that, in twelve-note works, intervals which are not even present in the row can acquire not only melodic identity but even motivic significance through the transposition of intervening notes into the vertical plane or into other voices – this becomes truly comprehensible only when we realise that the dodecaphonic reason and the motivic reason for the tonal relationships, though they frequently coincide, are in principle two separate things. The motivic connections are by no means based throughout on the dodecaphonic ones, but only in part, and to some extent take the place of the twelve-note system as an authority for creating relationships. That the motivic construction tears holes, so to speak, in the dodecaphonic substructure is compensated for by the fact that it in its turn, and in like manner, is performing the function of establishing connections.

IV

In the New Music of the twentieth century the idea of a harmonic process has been universally demoted in favour of that of a harmonic system, but without the dialectical relation that exists between system and process being abolished. The shift of emphasis is as clearly apparent in the dodecaphony of Schoenberg and (most especially) Webern as it is in the methods of layering or stratification developed by Stravinsky.

Certainly, if we wish to do aesthetic justice to the complex techniques of superimposition in *Le sacre du printemps* or to the ironically ingenuous ones in *The Rake's Progress*, we must not fail to appreciate that Stravinsky's neutralisation of tonal functional chords should not be understood as a given, so to speak self-contained fact which we have to accept for what it is, but as a procedure which can be comprehended – though not always without some effort. When a tonic is, so to speak, crippled functionally by having a dominant placed on top of it, the listener should become aware that this is the result of a conflict and not just a mute fact.

While the inner tension of what we call Stravinsky's static harmony is due to its suppressed dynamic element, Schoenberg's harmony – as the systematisation of which the dodecaphonic technique may be interpreted – is a consequence, taken to an extreme and ultimately inverted, of the chromaticism of *Tristan*, and one which similarly represents a phenomenon of neutralisation. The connection between chords, the second of which uses those notes of the chromatic scale which are absent from the first, is based on the principle of complementarity, the adding of parts to make a whole, but also – and primarily, in the first instance – on leading-note movement in the voices, and thus on an expressive and dynamic element which Ernst Kurth described as 'energetic'. And it is difficult to define the historical limits at which this leading-note character, which initially dominates in complementary harmony, recedes in comparison to the abstract complementary relationship between the chords to the extent that one can say that dynamic–processive chromaticism is replaced by a static–structural complementarity such as exists between the notes or note-complexes of a twelve-note row: a complementarity one of whose essential aesthetic features is that – unlike chromatic harmony – it can in principle be reversed in time.

At this point, against the background of several decades of New Music in which compositional thinking generally, while not free of contradictions and dialectical struggles, has tended to move from the processive to the systematic, we shall try to discern a line of development in the present situation – a line of development which is not only based on the technical details of a few works but which is linked in a comprehensible way with the aesthetic decisions of the so-called post-modernist movement. The fact that the undisputed hallmark of the 1980s is an emphasis on the subjectively expressive suggests the idea that efforts to create a dynamic and processive type of harmony would not come amiss, though of course not in the sense of restoring past practices but in the sense of reconstituting them under different conditions. Certainly, the association of the subjectively expressive with the dynamic and processive, which derives from the legacy of the nineteenth century and can therefore scarcely be deemed to belong to basic anthropological data, cannot be taken for granted. And the contrasting idea of a kind of hovering music that girates around itself and is nonetheless not cosmic rapture, but unmistakably subjective and expressive, is by no means fiction, strange as it may seem.

A further objection to any attempt to revive a dynamic form of harmony is the simple fact that the atmosphere of ahistoricity which is one aspect of the vague philosophical assumptions held by the otherwise generally unphilosophically-minded post-modernists is bound up with the tendency to regard everything as usable and blithely to heap layer upon layer of a whole heterogeneous host of different stylistic fragments and quotations. The virtually inevitable result of all this is an effect which, in Stravinsky, was a precisely calculated technique with clearly established aesthetic assumptions designed to neutralise the processive element, but which at present often seems to be no more than a blind grab into the biscuit tin of the past. In other words: as compositional techniques and ways of thinking, the processive and the static layering methods have become diametrically opposed in the confused situation of the 1980s, and a resolution of this antithesis remains in abeyance for the time being. It is not even clear whether this antithesis is an example of a living dialectic or whether it is no more than a dead, unproductive contradiction.

V

If we attempt to unravel, though not to simplify, this situation, and even if we do so in abstract form and with the sole intention of embarking on an intellectual experiment, then we must first remember the freedom to posit axioms brought to our attention by Ernst Krenek which allows a composer to regulate the features of chords that were either natural or determined historically by various postulates that permit the creation of a dynamic and processive form of harmony – despite the fact that several aesthetic tendencies of post-modernism are moving in a different direction. And an age that regards itself as a kind of post-history really ought to be attracted by the idea, inherent in Krenek's thesis, that an autonomous subject should not allow itself to be tyrannised by history.

At the same time, however, a composer – if one accepts that music is generally created in relation to earlier music rather than being derived from everyday life – is never entirely independent of the historical events which form the background to the present. And for this reason it is sensible to keep the consequences that stem from the thought-patterns of the immediate past in mind – a past that can be counteracted, but which cannot simply be eradicated by ignoring it.

But, if we assume that the continuing and intensifying reflection, which serial and post-serial music have forced us to regard as a necessity, concerning the analogies, the differences and the mutual interaction that exist between the parameters of pitch, duration, dynamics and tone colour cannot be reversed by an intellectual coup d'état, then we are almost forced – in our intellectual experiment, at least – to confront the goals and intentions of the 1980s with the achievements of the 1950s and 1960s. Of course, these achievements cannot be simply swept aside and forgotten, and they consisted in a high level of reflection which cannot be relinquished without disadvantage rather than in compositional techniques. Thinking in parameters was also a way of thinking about possible relations, whether they had been realised or not. In rough terms, Giacinto Scelsi's highly sophisticated way of linking harmony and tone colour led to a pronounced neutralisation of rhythm and, conversely, Edgard Varèse's indissoluble blend of tone colour and rhythm to the exclusion of harmony, at least in the usual sense of the word. And while we should not permit ourselves to indulge in the type of generalisation that is embarrassingly reminiscent of a profit-and-loss scenario, we can nonetheless clearly see from the models, whose topicality can scarcely be denied, that there are some contradictions between the legacy of the immediate past and the tendency towards a subjective and expressive dynamicism. These need not stand in our way, but they do nevertheless represent a challenge. To link harmony and tone colour in a way which reduces the role of rhythm is in fact problematical – if we are trying to restore a dynamic and processive form of harmony – insofar as harmonic processiveness appears to be difficult to create without including the dynamic elements of rhythm – at least going by the history of music up to the present time. The fact that even the broadest kind of historical experience has never been able to demonstrate convincingly that something is impossible hardly needs reiteration. But it nonetheless gives an indication that obstacles do exist that must be overcome.

The kind of abstract reflection directed at composers by someone who is not himself one is almost always rather disquieting, if not worse. And even if one is not deceiving oneself, one must still admit to oneself that in the final analysis these intellectual experiments are nourished by nothing more than the dubious conviction that, to cite Walter Benjamin, we have to pile up the difficulties in order to be able to solve them: a conviction that makes the principle of progressive and irrevocable reflection seem absolutely inescapable at least as theory, even if it is not useful in practice.

Schoenberg's poetics of music

I

The difference between aesthetics and learning a craft, which Schoenberg emphasised, not without a touch of irony, in the first chapter of his *Harmonielehre* (1911), is, strictly speaking, of quite secondary importance. For the aesthetics, the claims of which Schoenberg was attempting to ward off, were classical and constricted; and though the *Harmonielehre* was praised, largely in order to discomfit the aestheticians, this was not so much because it was a decisive authority as because of the sincerity with which it remained within its bounds. (It was not Schoenberg's intention to provide an apologia for craft in the way Stravinsky and Hindemith were later to do.)

When he talks of composing in the emphatic sense, Schoenberg refers to his feeling of form; explaining what the feeling of form has produced by means of theory is held to be possible in principle, but for the time being of no pressing concern. Schoenberg conceives of music history as a process which brings forth and makes manifest what is contained and prefigured in the nature of music as a possibility longing to be realised, as a process sustained by the composing genius, who is infallible. As decisions are a matter for the genius, theory is a *cura posterior*. Yet, inasmuch as we are dealing with the unfolding of factors that lie embedded within nature itself, and not with phenomena that are historical through and through, we can conceive of a theory which formulates comprehensive principles instead of restricting itself to the mere codification or rationalisation of epoch or personal styles. Nature as the origin of music, history as unfolding, the genius as the executor of what nature has prefigured, and the masterpiece as the end result: in Schoenberg's thinking these form a complex, the individual components of which seem to be inextricably intertwined.

But if we abandon Schoenberg's metaphysical idea of nature – and in a description which considers itself to be empirical nothing else is justified – then theory no longer appears as the reconstruction of the musical fundamentals of nature, which sustain the composing genius, more intuitively than consciously, but as the essence of historically determined principles and categories, which are at the root of a composer's musical thinking. And the theory of an individual oeuvre we can call poetics, to use a word from the realm of literary scholarship.

Thus the concept of musical poetics, a concept which preserves the memory of its Greek origins, signifies an idea, permeated by reflection, concerning the making and production of musical compositions. The thought structure to be uncovered is contained on the one hand in compositional procedures and on the other in theories of explanation or vindication. But this does not mean that a composer's theoretical statements may be accepted at face value as the final word on the meaning of his musical works. Rather, they are the objects of the enquiry, and not its precondition. They belong to the material from which – in reciprocal interaction with the interpretation of the works themselves – the musical poetics are to be reconstructed.

Compared with the older tradition of poetics, attempts to develop systems of musical poetics for the works of the nineteenth and twentieth centuries are forced to limit themselves to operating in a descriptive and individualising, and not in a normative and generalising, manner. They differ from the systems of rules that were called poetics until the eighteenth century in that they do not formulate norms which a work is required to fulfil if it is to satisfy the demands of a genre tradition and a stylistic standard, but merely demonstrate connections and fundamental conditions within a group of principles and categories on which an individual oeuvre is based.

To outline a system of musical poetics in which the technical factors merge into aesthetic ones, and vice versa, would be impossible if Schoenberg's sharp distinction between what a work 'is' and the manner in which it 'is made' had to be taken literally. One should not, however, as in the case of the inversely emphasised contrast of aesthetics and theory of craft, disregard the apologetic function which Schoenberg's theories were supposed to perform. If in 1911, after the transition to atonality, Schoenberg felt pressed by critics who accused him of having violated aesthetic norms, then later, in the dodecaphonic period, he acquired the notorious reputation of being a musical mathematician or engineer. In the first instance he played off the theory of craft against the aesthetics invoked by his opponents; in the second he played off the fact that his works are music in the same sense as those of Beethoven or Brahms, against the tendency of the critics, both well-meaning and hostile, to cling to the manner in which they were made.

That the theories are thus dependent on or partly determined by practical considerations does not mean that they are without foundation, for something that is true does not stop being true by serving an interest. Yet the fact that the relationship between the technical and the aesthetic aspects of music could be emphasised by Schoenberg in very different ways permits us to conclude that the frequently cited aphorisms are one-sided squibs which do indeed to some extent cover up, but do not wholly obscure, Schoenberg's real conviction that the way something is made and what it means are two sides of the same thing – a conviction, the theoretical elaboration of which is to be understood as a system of musical poetics.

II

The categories that combine to make up Schoenberg's musical poetics, categories such as idea [*Gedanke*], development, consequence and logic, are an expression of the tendency to conceive of a musical work in an almost unmetaphorical sense as discourse, as a tonal thought process. Not that the concept of musical thinking was new around 1910, at the time when Schoenberg's poetics assumed coherent form. But the emphasis with which Schoenberg took at its word a terminology which Forkel, Hanslick and Riemann had employed more by analogy than with theoretical intent was quite unusual. At the same time, Schoenberg's manner of thinking has proved to be epoch-making and in subsequent decades has significantly changed the way in which people – even Schoenberg's opponents – understand and talk about music.

But however much the tendencies on which Schoenberg's musical poetics are based become apparent, it is difficult to say precisely what he considered a musical idea to be. The aesthetic aspect is closest within reach, the distinction between musical ideas that are worthy of the name and mere *topoi*, flourishes or formulas. Schoenberg's concept of the musical idea is replete with a kind of pathos which reminds us of the ardour with which Adolf Loos battled against the ornament and Karl Kraus against the empty phrase.

To describe the concept of the musical idea in technical or formal terms hardly seems possible. Putting it on a par with the categories motif and theme would narrow it down in a way which would bar us access to Schoenberg's poetics. Inasmuch as they were products of inspiration and not mere *topoi*, Schoenberg also conceived of chords as ideas, and it would doubtless not infringe upon his manner of thinking if one were even to reckon abstract interval structures such as those discovered by Jan Maegaard, which form a common denominator for whole groups of motifs and chords, as being musical ideas. Furthermore, in certain contexts it is not a definite intervallic structure, but rather an expressive gesture, that forms the substance of a musical idea – a gesture whose intervals can change as long as the outline remains distinct.

If a motif, a theme, a gesture whose intervals can change, and even an abstract interval structure which appears in changing rhythmic guises and either in melodic or in harmonic form can pass as a musical idea, then the category would seem to melt into thin air. There is no hard and fast, recurring feature which is common to all the manifestations of that which can signify a musical idea in Schoenberg's thinking. And yet the term is not devoid of meaning.

Schoenberg's musical poetics can be understood as the attempt to mediate between postulates which the unfortunate party strife in music aesthetics between formalism and the theory of the affects projects as opposites, that is, between the demand for convincing expressivity at every moment on the one hand and for total interrelatedness of the musical events on the other. In Schoenberg's scheme of things the essence of a musical idea is that it both emanates from a need for expression, which can virtually assume the character of an imperative, and also has formal consequences and establishes far-reaching connections instead of exhausting itself in a momentary effect. In other words, a musical idea constitutes itself as what it is on account of what it is related to. Contrary to popular belief, expressiveness is also to no small degree a function of context.

The unity of the expressive and the structural, as guaranteed in traditional music by themes and motifs which determined the 'tone' and character of a movement as well as being the starting-point and the material of developing variation, was however endangered in Schoenberg's case in particular by the divisibility of the gestural factor from the intervallic one. That a gesture makes its mark and develops in changing intervallic forms is a different musical process from the deduction of different melodic phrases and chords from an interval structure. And the procedures can be distinguished not only in analytical thinking but also in compositional practice, whereas in traditional thematic–motivic work they were more closely interwoven. Gesture and interval structure seem like antithetical abstractions from the traditional concept of the motif, and indeed like abstractions which have acquired a life of their own.

At the same time Schoenberg sought to retain the aesthetic function of the Classical motif, the connection of the aesthetic and the structural, even when he had greatly changed the compositional–technical preconditions. One could even claim that the concept of the musical idea represents the belief that it should be possible in problematical circumstances to restore a unity of the factors which in the case of the traditional motif and its development were present in unproblematical form. To put it paradoxically: Schoenberg *thought* 'motivically', even when he did not *compose* 'motivically'.

Only detailed analyses would demonstrate how in a single work or movement the process of spinning out formal connections from interval structures relates to the events that are described by the gestural patterns. But whether the mediation turns out to be comprehensible or not, it is always Schoenberg's fundamental intention to make structural features felt as expressive ones and vice versa.

III

The conviction that a musical idea only becomes an idea at all on account of the context in which it exists meant that Schoenberg, hardly different in this respect from Wagner, considered what was isolated and unrelated to be incomprehensible and insupportable. The intelligibility of the individual feature depends on the logic of the whole.

The belief that the isolated event was incomprehensible did however pose problems for Schoenberg when he attempted to justify the emancipation of the dissonance. The compositional decision that a dissonance could stand on its own, instead of having to be resolved, was based on the theoretical assumption that it is musically comprehensible independently of the consonance on which it leans, without it being absolutely clear what the expression comprehensibility really means in the case of an emancipated dissonance, for it can hardly mean the mere intelligibility of the interval structure.

Emancipation meant that the forward-moving tendency of the dissonance, which made for coherence, was abolished together with the obligation to resolve. Instead of producing musical motion the dissonance remains, seemingly at least, as an emancipated form of its own without consequences. Isolation proves to be the reverse of emancipation.

The first way out of the dilemma was the principle of complementary harmony – which was, however, practicable only to a limited extent. A second one was to treat a chord as if it were a motif. The increase in the notes available, and equally the transformation of a harmonic interval structure into a melodic one, could be understood as musical consequence, as logic.

But Schoenberg's attempted solutions to the challenge posed by the conflict between the emancipation of the dissonance and the conviction that isolated musical events were essentially incomprehensible are in their turn closely linked to other aspects of the system which the observer perceives as Schoenberg's musical poetics. Complementary harmony tends towards twelve-note writing, towards total chromaticism. And thinking of a chord as a motif is the expression of a 'structural' manner of thinking which finally resulted in the serial principle – a manner of thinking which conceives of connections between notes as abstract interval structures, the vertical presentation of which is a variant of the horizontal and not a different phenomenon in principle. The problems that grew out of the emancipation of the dissonance under the preconditions of Schoenberg's musical poetics – under the domination of the idea that the isolated event was incomprehensible – thus belong as generative factors to the prehistory of dodecaphony. And conversely, the genesis of twelve-note technique remains to some extent unfathomable if one does not relate the compositional–technical facts, as revealed by an analysis of the notes on the page, to the musical poetics, in the category system of which the individual phenomena and procedural methods first acquired the significance from which the consequences they had in Schoenberg's career derived.

IV

Schoenberg referred to the process of spinning out a network of relationships from the musical idea as developing variation. Yet Schoenberg's category differs from the traditional account of thematic–motivic work in that the interaction of the diastematic and the rhythmic components, such as was characteristic of the traditional idea of a theme or a motif, can be dispensed with. Schoenberg also subsumes under the concept of developing variation diastematic connections not linked to rhythm and rhythmic ones not linked to pitch.

Descriptions of methods of developing variation or of thematic–motivic work almost always suffer from a kind of one-sidedness which is all the more disturbing because one hardly seems to notice it. Anyone who analyses a piece of music emphasises involuntarily the recurring, structuring aspects – in order to demonstrate the inner coherence of the movement – and neglects the no less important task of investigating the various kinds of deviation from the model, and the reasons for them. However, the point of a variant is decided not only by its dependence on a model but also by the reason why just this variant and no other appears at a certain juncture in the course of a piece.

In traditional music – the substance of which Schoenberg did not wish to abandon, but whose basic tenets he sought to preserve, to restore under changed circumstances or to replace by equivalents – the impression of coherence emanating from a series of variants was based, first, on the harmonic logic of the chord progressions which carried the variant-forming process; secondly, on a certain consistency of the rhythmic or diastematic expansions or contractions to which the model was subjected; and, thirdly, on the relationship of the syntactical and formal functions that the various variants performed.

Of these means for achieving consistency Schoenberg dispensed merely with the tonal foundation of the succession of variants – the constitution of musical logic in a series of variants by means of harmonic functionality. At the same time, it was precisely the relationship between harmony and motif in thematic–motivic work that formed a perceptual model from which Schoenberg took his bearings in order to pursue reflections which led ultimately to atonality.

One thing fails to fit in with the usual belief that harmony – the harmonic logic of a tonal structure – belongs to the essence of a musical idea or is indeed its central characteristic. It may be trivial, but it seems that the consequences attendant upon it have never been fully investigated; and that is the fact that in thematic–motivic elaborations a melodic shape is repeatedly harmonised in different ways without thereby becoming unrecognisable. In situations of this kind the identity of a motif rests more on the rough melodic outline and its gestural–expressive character than on exact diastematic formulation and the harmonic meaning thereof. Or to put it the other way round: it is not so much that the tonal functional context forms the musical idea itself, but rather that it represents one of the means of linking up variants of the idea in such a way that it creates an impression of consistency.

But the thematic–motivic work – and not the usual concept of melody, whose hallmark is diastematic and harmonic straightforwardness – forms the precondition or background for Schoenberg's concept of what a musical idea is. For the Schoenbergian category has the following implications, which it shares with the melodic substratum of motivic–thematic elaborations: first, that it is the vague melodic outline – as expressive gesture – that constitutes the essence of a musical idea; secondly, that an idea only turns out to be an idea in the course of a development which proceeds from it; and thirdly, that harmonic tonality appears not as the substance of a musical idea, but as a means with which to render it comprehensible – and by this Schoenberg understands the elaboration into a self-contained musical discourse.

The abandonment of tonality resulted, as we have seen, in the loss of one of the means which gave a series of variants a directional tendency. Not a diastematic or rhythmic link as such, but only a functionally based link can pass as musical logic, as developing variation in the full sense of the phrase. The abolition of tonality was therefore an emancipation which at the same time represented a loss. And it seems as if the invention of dodecaphony – which he construed as a discovery – was felt by Schoenberg to be a way out of an impasse which had come about due to the renunciation of the backing provided by tonality.

Not that dodecaphony is an equivalent of tonality in any palpable sense. The idea that a configuration of twelve notes related only to one another is to be explained as 'pantonality', that is, as a kind of expansion and differentiation of traditional tonality, in which the notes gathered around a single centre, is abstract in the negative sense of the word. Dodecaphony is not to be compared with tonality as regards its substance, but rather, if at all, as regards its function. It does not take the principle of tonality as its starting-point, but performs in part an analogous function in the elaboration or developing variation of motifs. If in tonal works the harmonic logic – next to the formal functions and the directional tendencies of the melodic and rhythmic process – formed one of the means of determining the reason why at a certain point of a development a certain variant and no other is appropriate, then under the conditions of atonality dodecaphony serves a similar end. For the diastematic formulations in which an expressive gesture – which represents the substance of a musical idea – is expounded and developed are to a certain extent (but only to a certain extent, seeing that it can be manipulated) dependent on the twelve-note structure. Dodecaphony, like the tonality which it supersedes, is a vehicle of consistency in the representation of a musical idea.

Thus historians investigating the prehistory of dodecaphony should not only search for substantial preconditions – for twelve-note complexes or permutations of interval structures – but should also reconstruct the problems as the solution to which, within the system of reference of Schoenberg's musical poetics, dodecaphony acquired a significance that would hardly have been accorded to it if it had been merely a technique, a procedure capable of being described in a few sentences.

Schoenberg's aesthetic theology

I

In 'My Evolution' (1949), his draft of an inner biography, Schoenberg wrote: 'This is also the place to speak of the miraculous contributions of the subconscious. I am convinced that in the works of the great masters many miracles can be discovered, the extreme profundity and prophetic foresight of which seem superhuman.' Then, using a music example, Schoenberg demonstrates a latent connection between contrasting themes in the Op. 9 Chamber Symphony 'solely in order to illustrate the power behind the human mind, which produces miracles for which we do not deserve credit.'[1]

Dubious though the thematic connection which Schoenberg thought he had discovered in his work decades later may seem, it is unusual and characteristic that the inspiration that he felt had been conferred on him did not consist of a theme, but rather of a connection between themes. The inspired idea, in the face of which Schoenberg felt moved to make use of the language of art religion, occurred unconsciously, remained initially latent and manifested itself in a relationship and not a substance. The idea which assumes concrete form in a work such as the Chamber Symphony is thus realised less in the musical shapes that make up the surface than in the tissue of relationships which, hidden beneath, connect the ideas with one another.

The principle on which the interconnection of themes in the Chamber Symphony is based is that of 'contrasting derivation'. It was formulated by Arnold Schmitz in 1923 with regard to Beethoven sonata movements. And the very fact that both Schmitz's analyses and those of Schoenberg contain certain questionable features, and yet were produced independently of each other, enables us to see them all the more clearly as the expression of a tendency characteristic of the time, which transcends their inherent differences: the tendency to regard hidden connections as being the most important and convincing ones.

Yet the most striking thing about the quotation from Schoenberg's 'My Evolution' is the seemingly self-evident manner with which, in one and the same sentence, there is talk of the workings of the 'subconscious' and of a 'miracle', with the result that categories taken from religion and from psychology or depth psychology intermingle as if they were interchangeable.

It would be completely unjustified to dismiss the word 'miracle' as being a mere metaphor lacking religious substance. In the essay 'Composition with Twelve Notes' from the year 1935 Schoenberg makes use of the language of aesthetic theology in a way which requires us to take him at his word, and with a seriousness and an insistence which prevent us from suspecting his manner of expressing himself of being pardonable pseudo-religious rhetoric:

To understand the very nature of creation one must acknowledge that there was no light before the Lord said: 'Let there be Light'. And since there was not yet light, the Lord's omniscience embraced a vision of it which only His omnipotence could call forth. We poor human beings, when we refer to one of the better minds among us as a creator, should never forget what a creator is in reality. A creator has a vision of something which has not existed before this vision. And a creator has the power to bring his vision to life, the power to realise it.[2]

This mingling of religious and psychological categories, which irritates in the 1949 'My Evolution', reaches back in Schoenberg's thinking at least to the year 1911. In the essay 'Franz Liszt's Work and Being', 'faith', which Schoenberg contrasts sharply with mere 'conviction', moves close to 'instinctive life':

Liszt's importance lies in the one place where great men's importance can lie: in faith. Fanatical faith, of the kind that creates a radical distinction between normal men and those it impels. Normal men *possess* a conviction; great men are *possessed* by a faith. . . . But the work, the perfected work of the great artist, is produced, above all, by his instincts; and the sharper ear he has for what they say, the more immediate the expression he can give them, the greater his work is. That is exactly the relationship, or perhaps it is even more direct, between faith – faith independent of reason – and instinctive life.[3]

The Romantic religion of art to which Schoenberg subscribed wholeheartedly – a religion of art which his opposite Stravinsky felt to be inadmissible and dishonest, as regards both religion and aesthetics – was rooted in an assumption which seemed as natural to nineteenth-century Protestant theology as it seems suspect to that of the twentieth century: the assumption that the substance of religion consisted in subjective emotion, which one could then interpret as the guarantee of religious truth, as in the case of Schleiermacher, or as the source of religious illusions, as in the case of Feuerbach, but which in any case formed the starting-point of both apologetics and polemics. Theology was – contrary to the name, which it continued to bear – anthropocentric.

However, it is not the business of a historian to subject the roots of religion in subjective emotion to theological criticism for which he is not qualified. What matters is to recognise that the art religion which spread in the aesthetics, and particularly in the popular aesthetics, of the nineteenth century was a variant of the religion of emotion which was considered to be legitimate theology by Protestantism of the time. Dogmatism, the decline of which seemed inexorable, was replaced by philosophy of religion, and this finally turned into psychology of religion. Thus it is not surprising that the basis of art religion changed progressively from Wackenroder's emotional devotion via Schopenhauer's metaphysics of the will to Sigmund Freud's psychology of the instincts, which was adopted by Schoenberg.

If as a result of this the proximity of 'faith' and 'instinctive life' in Schoenberg's thinking is capable of being interpreted in the context of the history of ideas, then the aesthetically decisive factor lies in the conviction that the idea of a musical work, in which a composer's 'instinctive life' manifests itself, consists primarily of relationships, and indeed of relationships which in essence remain latent. In Schoenberg's thinking there is a configuration of three factors: faith, to which reason cannot attain; the urge which emanates from the expressive need of the subconscious; and the expression of a musical work idea less in terms of themes than in terms of thematic relationships which are not capable of being perceived directly and which, precisely for that reason, seem all the more convincing. The configuration proves difficult to explicate inasmuch as to concentrate on one of the factors to the detriment of the others – be it the theological, the psychological or the aesthetic, compositional–technical component – would be one-sided, inadequate or heavy-handed.

The extent to which the aesthetic categories of the eighteenth, nineteenth and twentieth centuries are secularised theological concepts has never been underestimated. As a result, the fact that the reverse of the consecration of the profane, which one calls art religion, is a deconsecration of the sacred, led to a situation where the various interpretations of the phenomenon veered from one extreme to the other. Because of its legal origins, the term 'secularisation' was associated with the idea of taking other people's property; but this did not stop the view that the acquisition was illegitimate from being countered by the opposing view that the transformation was legitimate because it was a historically necessary formal change. While on the one hand the art religion of the nineteenth century could be suspected of investing the musical expression of earthly and sometimes all-too-human emotions with a metaphysical dignity which was a mere aesthetic illusion, on the other hand Richard Wagner claimed, in commenting on *Parsifal*, nothing less than that the substance of religion, which had petrified in the form of ecclesiastical Christianity, should be saved and incorporated by art as the living manifestation of the spirit of the age.

A belief in origins which considers the primary ownership of a thing to be the only legitimate one is the antithesis of a philosophy of history aimed at the future which adheres to the possibility that the real substance, or at least the part relevant to the present, which lies concealed in theological ideas and concepts, can be brought out into the open by translation into the realms of aesthetics, psychology or politics; and that this secularisation does not represent an illegitimate appropriation, but the fulfilment of a promise contained in the religious categories. To translate them into another language is to establish their true meaning.

Yet Schoenberg's texts cannot be interpreted unequivocally in either way, and, in any case, it is probable that similar formulations from the turn of the century have to be assessed differently from those of the last few decades. Whether Schoenberg, like Freud, conceived of psychological categories as being the roots of religious ones, or whether he simply regarded the subconscious as a place where religion manifests itself without being psychologically reducible must remain in the balance, at least for the time being.

In general one can interpret the process that one calls secularisation in at least four ways: first, as the questionable appropriation and transformation of theological substance; secondly, as historical evolution, to which as a historian one already accords a claim to validity, without openly coming to a conclusion, in that one concedes continuity to the process – and in the language of historians that virtually amounts to historical legitimacy; thirdly, as a structural analogy in which the direction of the transfer – for example, between depth psychology and theology – remains just as open to question as does its legality; and fourthly, as a metaphorical interpretation, the substantiality of which depends on how close to the truth one considers an 'unreal', poetic language to be.

To apply the various schemes of interpretation available in hermeneutics to Schoenberg's art-religious confessions would not be impossible, though it would be like going for a walk in a labyrinth, the exit of which is very difficult to find indeed.

II

Schoenberg's output consists to roughly equal extents of vocal and of instrumental works. Yet his aesthetic theory – sometimes at odds with his compositional practice – is one-sidedly determined by instrumental music. Schoenberg's claim, in his essay on 'The Relationship to the Text', that, when composing a song, he permitted himself to be led solely by the initial sound of the poem, turns out to be all the more revealing in the context of the history of ideas on account of the fact that an analysis of the George songs proves it to be blatantly untrue. However implausible the idea may seem, faced with a work like *Erwartung*, that in the period of early atonality the text was merely a means of building large-scale forms without the support of tonality, it does tally with the fact that dodecaphony, the primary function of which Schoenberg considered to be the purely musical foundation of larger forms, at first formed the basis, on the whole, of instrumental works.

Thus the fact that instrumental music, particularly in the form of a discourse based on musical logic, represented what Schoenberg considered to be 'real' music is doubtless connected with the influence of Schopenhauer's metaphysics of absolute music, a metaphysics which, transmitted by Wagner and Nietzsche, had around 1900 become the aesthetics of all German composers from Strauss and Mahler to Schoenberg and Pfitzner. Yet if one is not afraid of a hypothesis for which there is no tangible documentary evidence, one can also reconstruct a link back to the time around 1800, which, even though Schoenberg may not have been aware of it, makes his aesthetics appear more comprehensible.

The 'vision' which, in Schoenberg's words, characterises a musical 'creation' that may be referred to as such without arrogance or blasphemy is the outline of a distinct world of one's own. Mahler, for example, spoke of a 'world' constructed by a symphony 'with all the technical means at one's disposal'. That music is 'a world of its own' was however the fundamental idea with which, in 1799, Ludwig Tieck, in his *Phantasien über die Kunst*, founded the Romantic metaphysics of music, which was in essence an aesthetic of instrumental music, or, to be more precise, an aesthetic of the symphony as the paradigm of large-scale instrumental music. That aesthetic theology, which was centred on the concept of musical creativity, believed it had found its proper subject in instrumental and not in vocal music was by no means an accident, as can be shown by a short digression into the history of ideas.

The claim that man, God's likeness, is an 'alter deus' as a poet and only as a poet, who does not imitate but creates, had been advanced as early as 1561 by Julius Caesar Scaliger, the compiler of Renaissance poetics. But the idea, as Hans Blumenberg pointed out, first acquired philosophical substance and historical importance in the eighteenth century, when it combined with Leibniz's idea of the possible worlds to form a configuration from which emanated the idea, crucial to modern poetics, that a poet is the creator of another, that is, of a possible world. Johann Jakob Breitinger's *Critische Dichtkunst* of 1740, as Oskar Walzel realised, puts 'Leibniz's idea of the possible worlds to aesthetic use'.

But the concept of the creative formed an exclusive antithesis to the traditional imitative principle moulded by Aristotelian philosophy. Planning a world of one's own could not be reconciled with imitating nature as it is – be it the empirical appearance or the metaphysical essence of nature.

Yet vocal music – to return to the starting-point of the argument – had since the sixteenth century been declared to be the imitation of that which was expressed by the text. Instrumental music without a text, the content of which remained imprecise as long as it did not regress to primitive tone painting, seemed both to the sixteenth-century humanist and to the eighteenth-century encyclopaedist to be an inferior kind of vocal music, to say nothing of more negative ways of describing it.

But from 1800 onwards there is a gradual change in the order of precedence of the genres. If for thousands of years the lack of a text had been regarded as a deficiency in music defined in principle by harmony, rhythm and language, then this was reversed in the writings of E. T. A. Hoffmann and Eduard Hanslick, where the text appears as an 'extra-musical' addition to a tonal art whose 'real' being manifested itself in 'pure' instrumental music. Yet there is, it seems, a close and direct connection between the change of paradigms in music aesthetics from vocal to instrumental music, and the transition from the imitative principle to the idea of the creative. If vocal music in general remains an imitation formally dependent on a text or on the contents of a text, then instrumental music, inasmuch as it aspires to the heights of the symphonic style, can be understood as the construction of a world of its own. In the symphony the composer adopts a claim which had previously been made for the poet: the claim that a poet, as opposed to a painter or a sculptor, does not imitate the real world but founds a possible one. (Scaliger spoke of 'condere' as opposed to 'narrare'.)

But if one acknowledges the connection which existed between the emancipation of instrumental music and the use in music aesthetics of the poetological idea of the creative, then it becomes clear why it was instrumental music, which had liberated itself from poetry, that Tieck called 'poetic'. Poetry, understood in the sense in which Breitinger had formulated it, was the paradigm of the generation of a personal, possible world; and music became 'poetic' in advancing a similar claim and substantiating it convincingly in works such as Beethoven's symphonies and Bach's fugues – which Goethe felt to be a musical symbol of a possible world prior to the creation of the real world.*

Tieck's metaphysics of instrumental music were adapted by Schopenhauer, and Schopenhauer's philosophy was in turn adapted by Schoenberg. It is hardly possible to deny that the aesthetic theology implied or encapsulated therein, the conjunction of the concept of the creative and that of large-scale instrumental music, had a far-reaching influence on Schoenberg's thinking, with the result that in spite of the oblique relationship between aesthetic theory and compositional practice – a practice in which there can be no talk of instrumental music ranking lower or of a secondary role for the texts – we must expect to find traces of metaphysical dogma.

III

It would not be an exaggeration to call early atonality, which Schoenberg embarked upon with 'fear and trembling' and in full awareness of an irrevocable quality which was difficult to bear, a state of emergency in the precise sense that a state of emergency is the opposite of a state of affairs in which the law prevails. Yet the emancipation of the dissonance, which was not so much a qualitative leap logically resulting from what had gone before as an arbitrary act, was not at all the mere abolition of an old law and the introduction of a new one. The critics who raised a hue and cry about anarchy did indeed touch upon an essential aspect of the process, the significance of which they vaguely perceived, even though their aesthetic judgment failed to assess it correctly.

The concept of the state of emergency means that Schoenberg claimed that the suspension of the existing musical order, which he accomplished in the final movement of Op. 10, defined a historical state whose advent would turn out to be irrevocable, no matter how one looked at it. Schoenberg took a decision whose seriousness – and the fact is nothing short of

---

* See below, pp. 172 ff. [Trans.]

self-evident – no one at the time who was musically competent could afford to disregard. Before embarking on an interpretation of history which concerned itself with continuity and discontinuity, one would first of all have to find a reason for the fact that even bitter opponents perceived Schoenberg's decision to be an act of incalculable significance, an event which, even a decade and a half later, could only be circumvented, so it was thought, by countering it with an equally abrupt decision in favour of neo-classicism, the supposedly necessary next step, with which Schoenberg's expressionist atonality was so to speak to be relegated to a past which was of no concern to the present.

To say that Schoenberg owed to the resounding success of the *Gurrelieder* a reputation which could not simply be destroyed by claiming that Opp. 10 and 11 were insignificant sectarian aberrations is of course true to a certain extent, though it does not explain everything. One of the reasons why the transition to atonality was taken seriously at all, that is, in the sense of a catastrophe, was, apart from the respect which was Schoenberg's due, a mode of thought no doubt typical of the nineteenth and early twentieth centuries: the tendency, which ran counter to the dominant belief in progress, to look upon approaching events as being both the road to impending disaster and unavoidable.

Yet the fact remains – and to have to admit this is rather difficult for a historian – that it is, strictly speaking, impossible to give a reason for Schoenberg's decision of 1907. Those who speak of historical necessity, of the dictates of the historical moment which Schoenberg obeyed, make the event appear more harmless than it actually was. The suspension of the existing order, the proclamation of the musical state of emergency, was an act of violence. And thus the theories with which Schoenberg attempted to justify the emancipation of the dissonance are characterised by a helplessness which prevents us from taking them at their word as being motives for compositional decisions. The same holds true, a decade and a half later, for the step to 'composition with twelve notes related only to one another'. Dodecaphony did not acquire the power which caused it to spread irresistibly, even if with some delay, on account of the arguments on which it was based. The reasons for its validity were always rather weak, both in the case of Schoenberg, and later in that of Adorno, who mistrusted it anyway. And even the works in which it manifested itself were, considering its subsequent influence, evidently not the decisive factor, despite their undoubted quality. Either, as in the case of Berg, the technique was unmistakably of secondary importance, one means amongst many with which Berg took precautionary measures within the works themselves. Or, as in the case of Webern, it produced a conflict between latent structure and expressive gesture which led to an open controversy in Webern reception. Or again, as in Schoenberg's late works, dodecaphony remained one of several possibilities, the common and all-embracing principle of which was developing variation.

Apart from this, the attempt to explain in terms of the philosophy of history Schoenberg's power to take decisions, that is, to interpret the diktat of the individual as that of history, is questionable inasmuch as the concept of the 'one' history which the philosophy of history assumes to exist is doubtful and may be suspected of being a myth. What really happens are histories – in the plural: at different places and under diverging circumstances. 'History' in the singular is a fiction.

But insofar as neither a diktat of history, nor the unavoidable logic of apologetic arguments, nor even the compelling evidence that we are dealing with technical preconditions to which important works owe their aesthetic life, is able to provide truthful reasons for the steps to atonality and dodecaphony, then the problem of authority, which arose nonetheless in the case of the one decision as in that of the other, comes to the fore with the clarity it requires, even if a solution is at present hardly in sight.

The authority which Schoenberg claimed for himself and which his contemporaries also accorded him through the tone they assumed, both in their polemics and in their apologias, was rooted in the emphatic awareness of a calling based on the feeling of being a tool. One would not want to deny the obvious fact that Schoenberg's interpretation of himself was determined by a concept of genius which was of Romantic origin, though this is not a sufficient explanation. It is far more the case that the moral pathos which marks Schoenberg's musical poetics, and even technical statements such as those about musical prose – a pathos which was completely foreign to the nineteenth-century concept of genius – bears unmistakably prophetic traits, in the original, authentic sense, that is, that prophecy is directed less at the future and at its impending calamities than at the present and its corrupt depravity. Schoenberg, from a position of extreme vulnerability, is continually sitting in judgment over his contemporaries, whose artistic shortcomings he deciphers as moral ones in an essay such as 'Opinion or Insight?' of 1925.

The fact that anarchical and law-giving tendencies or instincts conflicted in Schoenberg's thinking, forming a complicated configuration which forces one to read him twice if one wishes to understand him, has never been underestimated, and for this reason the phrase 'conservative revolutionary' seemed appropriate. An attempt to uncover the common root from which both the rebellious and the dictatorial traits emanated cannot content itself with pointing to the stereotype of revolutionary dialectics, in which there is a transition or sudden reversal from the one to the other. Rather, the state of emergency which Schoenberg induced with atonality, and the renewed state of legality which he hoped to constitute by means of dodecaphony, were similar in character, in that their substance consisted in an act of decision and not in a systematic web of argument or historical derivation. Schoenberg, if one is not afraid of applying the notorious phrase to him, was a musical decisionist.

The concept of an authority which is prophetic and moral, which judges and which simply decides and does not engage in argument, is so unusual in aesthetics, however, that at first one involuntarily feels that the religious pathos – despite the tradition which sees an artistic genius as a *homo a deo excitatus* – has been assumed illegitimately. The claim that only theological language can enable one to deal with Schoenberg's irritating decisionism in an appropriate manner is in fact based on nothing but the observation that the other languages taken over by aesthetics have failed when faced with this phenomenon. The striking contrast between the compelling fact of Schoenberg's authority and the weakness and inadequacy of compositional–technical or historical–philosophical explanations forces one to have recourse to theological categories, which do at least make some kind of orientation possible. One may then continue to argue endlessly about their logical status – about whether they are legitimate or illegitimate examples of secularisation, whether they are structural analogies without claims to historical origins and continuity, or whether they are merely metaphors whose sole function consists in maintaining the awareness of an unresolved problem.

IV

The analyses of Classical and Romantic works which Schoenberg published and the commentaries which he added to them are based on an unusual concept of tradition which cannot be properly understood as the adherence to an agreed position, nor as the reconstruction of an original state of affairs, nor as the redefinition and appropriation of the ideas of others. Schoenberg offended generally accepted opinion when interpreting the works of others hardly less than when planning his own. He did not think seriously about the possibility or impossibility of understanding the past as it really was; historical authenticity was of little interest to him. The charge that his method of analysis was nothing more than a reflection of his own ideas and problems in the works of others he would rightly have considered narrow-minded and rejected accordingly.

The aesthetics of reception, which in the past few decades have become the scholarly fashion, have made art historians aware of a problem which conveys a feeling of the unfathomable: the problem that the meaning of a work which has come down to us from the past cannot be classified with sufficient exactitude and clarity as the intention of the author or as the embodiment of its contemporaries' views, nor as the result or even the quintessence of reception history, nor yet as an objective substance inherent in the object itself which is independent of the history of its genesis or influence.

An author does not need to know what he is doing; and that he is a privileged interpreter of his own works is a view which was long ago consigned to the scrapheap of outmoded prejudices, with the result that one almost feels provoked to resurrect it a little. The views of contemporaries prove to be a doubtful court of appeal, for what was put in words almost always seems narrow and biased, and the special kind of empathy which contemporaries have and which later generations do not have was either not expressed at all or only expressed inadequately. The documents of reception history are either few and far between and inconsequential, or, if many of them have come down to us, paint a confusing picture; and they seldom permit the abstraction of a result in which inner connections are perceivable, even in the case of unrestrained dialectical interpretation. And finally the idea that a work has an objective, clearly defined meaning *per se* which reception more or less approaches, independent of its author's intentions and the perceptions of the audience, is, as 'substantialism', suspected of being metaphysical. (Of course, the empiricists' premiss that metaphysics are *a priori* unscientific is itself unscientific because it is dogmatic.)

It seems then that Schoenberg shared none of the opposing convictions in the controversy sketched above, but rather that he took his bearings tacitly from a concept of tradition which is far removed from present-day thinking and whose essence can most nearly be elucidated by looking at the theological source contained in the aesthetic transformation, albeit in concealed form.

If one is not afraid of crude simplification one may assume that there is a distinction which is as self-evident in theology as it is initially disconcerting in aesthetics: the distinction between the meaning that a tradition or a work conveys and the substance on which it is based.

The belief that the revelation on Mount Sinai did not put into words a distinct, clearly defined meaning, but that 'meaning' is a category which first constitutes itself in the countless refracted forms in which revelation discloses itself to the human mind – in other words, that an undivided other world of meaning manifests itself in a divided real world of meaning

– belonged, as Gershom Scholem has shown, to the fundamental principles of Torah exegesis in Jewish mysticism of the Middle Ages and the early Modern Age. Revelation is not in itself a comprehensible message, but becomes one only in the reflections which it experiences in human consciousness. And there is no limit to their number.

The changes which aesthetic 'substantialism' (let us not abandon the concept as such) experiences when it is subjected to a theologically-based interpretation are far-reaching. On the one hand, instead of a hard and fast meaning which reception may or may not elucidate, one assumes that there is merely a possibility of meaning which can be updated in various directions. But on the other hand – and this circumvents a dilemma of reception aesthetics – the substratum on which the constitution of meaning is based is not conceived of as a dead letter which only reception can fill with life borrowed from the subject, but appears as an energy which imbues all forms of appropriation.

The mystical exegesis of revelation and the concept of tradition in modern reception aesthetics – which, it is true, do not seem to be aware of the theological implications or structural analogies – share the fundamental assumption that meaning handed down from the past can be experienced only via a third party, and not directly. The utopian dream of a congeniality which provides direct access to it turns out to be an illusion, the reason being an inadequate model, that of a message between subjects engaged in conversation. Furthermore it belongs to the realm of mystical dialectics to accord the same validity to interpretations which are obviously incompatible simply because no one can know whether or not an exegesis unacceptable under certain circumstances will, under quite different premisses, turn out to be true in the near or distant future. And finally the fact that in the case of equally valid but conflicting interpretations we are still dealing with interpretations of one and the same thing forces us to assume the presence of a substance in which is rooted the identity of the object, which in extreme versions of reception aesthetics is on the point of dissolving into thin air; of a substance which can only consist of the mere letter of the text or over and above that in an energy effective therein, though not in an unalterable sense, if, that is, one is prepared to accept the assumptions that form the common feature of the mystical exegesis of a text and modern reception aesthetics.

That the idea of a primaeval energy, which only constitutes itself as meaning or a message in a multitude of refractions, could be turned from theological to aesthetic use was only possible because Schoenberg, in the analysis of the works of others as in the design of his own, proceeded from the concept of a formal idea whose essence lies beyond the real tonal

forms and the connections created between them. In order not to understand Schoenberg too quickly, and that means, wrongly, one has to
become aware of the fact that his method of analysis, if pursued to its
logical conclusion, dissolves musical works into a system of relationships
in which – contrary to hidebound prejudice – not even interval structures
form a clear, unalterable substance. What holds a movement together
from within is intangible and cannot be written down, for – to put it in its
ideal form – it is an embodiment of relationships between variants or
manifestations of thematic material which can be divided into an
unlimited number of constituent parts and whose every feature can be
varied.

But if one now allows that it is on the one hand not enough to speak
solely of relationships and of connections which as it were are suspended
in thin air, and that the substance, in which the inner unity is founded,
cannot on the other hand be pinned down, then there remains only a
single solution: that Schoenberg presupposed as a foundation an energy
which, as we have seen, he determined in theological–aesthetic terms
when at one and the same time stating that it emanated from the 'subconscious' and that it was brought about by a 'miracle'. The idea of
tradition on which his analyses of Classical and Romantic works were
tacitly based thus belongs to the same theological–aesthetic configuration
in which ideas about 'belief' and 'instinctive life', about the latent character of what is structurally important, and about the primacy of the tissue
of relationships over the fashioning of forms were also rooted and where
they found the place which permits their significance as part of the systematic coherence of Schoenberg's thinking to become clearly apparent.

Schoenberg and programme music

I

There is no fixed definition of what programme music actually is. The idea of a 'pure' instrumental music which amounts to nothing more than the functional relationships between the notes is just as much of an abstraction as the notion of programme music as a musical novel, telling a story in detail. The musical reality consists of transitions between the extremes over which there has been so much aesthetic dispute. In addition, the discussion becomes complicated by the fact that opinions concerning the specific nature of programme music almost always get mixed up with value judgments as to the aesthetic merits or faults of the genre: those who defend it tend to regard Schumann's character pieces, whose quality is unquestioned, as programme music, whereas those who reject it define the genre more narrowly.

Only two early works of Schoenberg, the string sextet *Verklärte Nacht*, Op. 4, and the symphonic poem *Pelleas und Melisande*, Op. 5, qualify undisputedly as programme music. That I shall discuss other works as well does not in the least imply that they should be subjected to an all-embracing – or over-flexible – concept of programme music; it is simply that Opp. 16, 34 and 45 demand consideration of problems that are directly bound up with Schoenberg's relationship to the genre.

Schoenberg's aesthetics, the essentials of which must be understood if one is not to misinterpret the programmatic works, are based on two premises which viewed superficially seem to contradict each other. In the first place he subscribed to the maxim, which dates back to the eighteenth century, that a composer expressed himself in a piece of music to the extent that it was 'poetic' and not 'mechanical'. Secondly, he adopted the theory of Schopenhauer and Wagner that music apprehends the essence of the world directly in sounds, whereas verbal language is a mediated, secondary form of expression. When music is linked with a text, therefore – whether a poem set to music or a programme – the music does not illustrate the text, but the text appears as a metaphor for what the music says in the 'true language'.

If the first maxim is to be reconciled with the second, it is essential that the person of the composer who expresses himself through music be defined not in 'empirical', biographically concrete terms, but in terms of the 'intelligible ego' which acts as a mouthpiece for that 'innermost nature'* of things at whose behest Schoenberg believed he composed. Schoenberg's aesthetics of expression should not be equated with the idea that a musical work is a piece of its composer's biography in sound, an idea which is as popular as it is questionable.

A number of aestheticians of the nineteenth and even the twentieth century – most recently Arnold Schering – were obsessed with the notion that it ought to be possible to discover 'secret programmes' in what were apparently works of 'pure' instrumental music. On the other hand, those who despised programme music were concerned to show that verbal headings or programmes were often added after the event. But the conviction that a programme, even a secret one, should nevertheless belong aesthetically to the 'object itself' and not just to the circumstances of its composition, whereas a programme added after composition, even by the composer, should be discounted aesthetically as a mere accessory, is dubious in the extreme. For there is no justification for such a one-sided emphasis on the history of a work's composition, on the biographical element, and for ignoring the composer's intentions – that is, his decision (as expressed in either the suppression or addition of a programme) as to whether the programme should have aesthetic validity or not.

Through its contact with Schopenhauer's philosophy of music, the requirement that a composer must express himself seems in Schoenberg's aesthetics to enter the realm of metaphysics. This implies, on the one hand, that Schoenberg did not regard empirical biography as a matter of aesthetic relevance. (The distinction is important when we come to the interpretation of the String Trio, Op. 45.) On the other hand, he did indeed view literary programmes, such as those on which the symphonic poem *Pelleas und Melisande* and the string sextet *Verklärte Nacht* are based, as constituting a primary element in the creative history of the

---

* Cf. *Style and Idea*, ed. Leonard Stein (London, 1975), p. 141. [Trans.]

work: the subject at least provided the premiss of the music, if not the content. What was primary from the genetic viewpoint is, however, merely secondary from the aesthetic viewpoint: in the finished work, the literary text – even though it may be aesthetically relevant and is intended to be followed by the listener – appears as the mere paraphrase of a music which goes behind the verbal means of expression to convey the true meaning of a drama (*Pelleas und Melisande*) or a poem (*Verklärte Nacht*).

II

Programme music – the method of basing a piece of instrumental music on a text that is an integral part of the work and not just the immediate cause of its composition – has for some decades been in aesthetic disrepute, as if it signified an alienation of music from itself. In the late nineteenth century, with Liszt and the New German School, it represented the 'music of the future', but in the twentieth century it has been consigned to the past or condemned to the realm of light music. (The degree of aesthetic contempt that programme music encounters today, a contempt also expressed in the fact that programmes associated with many of the works that have forced their way into the concert repertoire are almost always ignored, should not be confused with the hostility which programme music aroused in the nineteenth century: what was once attacked as avant garde is now despised as trivial.)

Around 1900, at the time when *Verklärte Nacht* (1899) and the symphonic poem *Pelleas und Melisande* (1903) were composed, the reputation of programme music was still untarnished. In writing programme music Schoenberg joined the company of Richard Strauss in becoming one of the exponents of musical 'modernism' – a 'modernism' which marked a period of transition linking the age of Wagner and the New Music of the twentieth century.

The string sextet *Verklärte Nacht* is based on an (aesthetically dubious) text by Richard Dehmel, from his cycle *Weib und Welt*: a lyric dialogue which determines not only the expressive character of the musical work but also its formal outline, without however the form of the music being externally imposed. Rather, the structure of the poem (comprising five stanzas of unequal length) is itself reminiscent of a musical form, the rondo. A recurring section, representing the walk in the moonlight, alternates with two different, contrasting sections – the woman's confession and the man's reply – on an A-B-A-C-A pattern.

But although the structure of the poem, through its regular alternation of narrative ritornello and stanzas of dialogue, resembles a rondo,

Schoenberg did not simply follow the rondo outline mechanically in the composition. Schoenberg's music, in the early, tonal works just as much as in the late, twelve-note ones, is almost always determined by the principle of 'developing variation': the method of developing themes as far as they will possibly go and of mediating, in the course of a work, between motifs that were first stated separately. The rondo ground-plan, which gives the work formal support, is as it were covered with a web of thematic and motivic relationships, a web which becomes tighter and thicker as the work proceeds.

So while Schoenberg's string sextet can be comprehended and analysed as a closed musical form – the formal rigour seems like a concession to the tradition of the string quartet, of which the string sextet represents a variation in scoring rather than constituting a genre of its own – it is also a piece of programme music; and the programme – the woman's confession of guilt and the man's conciliatory reply – can easily be read in the music, at least in its outlines. The five sections are clearly demarcated and different in character. The prejudice that regards the programmatic tendency as nothing but an attempt to shore up fragile musical forms with extramusical arguments, and, by means of literary associations, to create a (perhaps deceptive) impression of unity where musically there is none, is thus revealed as fallacious. The string sextet is motivated by internal, formal considerations as well as by the external programme.

III

The idea that programme music is nothing but a literary subject translated into sound – so that the music restates what is expressed by the text – is too simple to do justice to a musical reality whose aesthetic principles are not so crude as the detractors of programme music polemically suggest. Regardless of whether one accepts, or dismisses as dubious metaphysics, the theory that the music does not illustrate the text but rather expresses the innermost essence of things, which verbal language cannot reach – that is, regardless of how one views Schoenberg's aesthetics – it should be recognised that, first, it is not the programme itself but the literary subject embodied in the programme that forms the topic of the music (in Liszt's symphonic poem *Hamlet* it is not Shakespeare's text but an idea of the Hamlet figure that the music seeks to 'develop poetically'), and that, secondly, the 'content' of the work is not identical to the subject but results from a mediation between subject and musical form. The content is not pre-given but appears as a function of the form that shapes it.

The symphonic poem *Pelleas und Melisande* – composed with complete confidence in the aesthetic legitimacy of the programme music genre – is on the one hand a work that makes a 'persuasive' effect, through its expressive, sharply defined motifs and through a richness of sound which seems self-indulgent but is actually based on polyphony. But on the other hand it is difficult to grasp aurally, since there are no fewer than four separate conceptions of form interacting with each other.

In the first place the work can be understood as a succession of musical scenes. It is not difficult to recognise the outlines of Maurice Maeterlinck's lyric drama in the symphonic poem: the scene in the wood, where Golaud discovers the mysterious Mélisande; the latter's first meeting with Pelléas; the scene by the well, which provokes Golaud's jealousy; the love scene by the castle tower; the walk (representing an unspoken threat) through the gruesome castle vaults; Mélisande's parting from Pelléas; and the death scene. It is not the scenes as dramatic tableaux, however, but the internal situations of which they are the reflection and visible exterior, that form the topic of the music.

Secondly, the themes which form the basis of the symphonic development are reminiscent of leitmotifs in music drama, both in their melodic–rhythmic character and in the functions they perform. Whereas Wagner made Beethoven's Seventh Symphony one of the significant precursors of music drama, Schoenberg leans on the tradition of the music drama in writing his symphonic poem (whose programme is itself a drama). Either the motifs are used to distinguish a particular scene, or they are associated with a particular character: Mélisande, Pelléas and Golaud are each characterised by two or three motifs. And from the combined effect of the personal and scenic motifs – by varying and transforming the personal motifs in accordance with the changing situations and affects – grows a musical form which resembles a narrative.

Thirdly, the form of the work can be explained as the result of the four movements of the symphonic cycle being compressed into a single span – albeit one that is rather excessive, since it lasts not less than fifty minutes. As Alban Berg recognised, the scene by the well is a scherzo, Mélisande's parting from Pelléas an Adagio; the recapiculation of the themes functions as a finale.

Fourthly, there are the outlines of a sonata form which embraces the entire work. The idea of 'projecting' the four movements of a sonata onto the outlines of a sonata allegro (with exposition of principal and subordinate themes, elaboration and recapitulation)* had already been put into

---

* *Exposition, Hauptthema, Seitenthema, Durchführung, Reprise.* Schoenberg's preferred translations are used: see *Fundamentals of Musical Composition*, ed. Gerald Strang and Leonard Stein (London, 1970), and *Structural Functions of Harmony*, ed. Leonard Stein (London, 1954). [Trans.]

effect by Liszt in his B minor Sonata; and it was taken up by Schoenberg in his First Chamber Symphony, Op. 9, as well as in *Pelleas und Melisande*.

This fourfold planning – as a succession of musical scenes, as a narrative told or suggested by the changing configurations of leitmotifs, as four-movement symphony and as sonata allegro – implies aesthetically that the musical form, by virtue of its complexity, is able to accommodate the literary subject without abandoning its own autonomy. The drama is not forced into an inappropriate musical scheme, nor is the music made dependent on a dramatic plot under whose influence it would become amorphous.

IV

Schoenberg's Orchestral Pieces Op. 16 are one of the documents marking the break in tradition, around 1910, that divides the New Music from the nineteenth century, a century which in terms of music history extends from the *Eroica* to *Das Lied von der Erde*. But the work is also bound up with the tradition of programme music, the very tradition that was the quickest to become obsolete in the twentieth century and which fell into disrepute as representing all that was bad in the nineteenth century. Around 1900, when musical modernism was represented by Richard Strauss – *Ein Heldenleben* and the *Sinfonia Domestica* were composed at roughly the same time as *Verklärte Nacht* and *Pelleas und Melisande* – programme music still stood, aesthetically and from the viewpoint of compositional technique, at the forefront of historical development. Absolute music – and therefore the works of Brahms, not to speak of lesser composers – was regarded as a kind of eroded classicism: an arrogant philosophy of history led the theorists of the New German School to speak of a 'standpoint of the past'. But only a few years later the situation was stood on its head. The symphonic poem seemed like a wellnigh extinct genre; though still in existence it had certainly lost its substance. The works in which Schoenberg approached and then finally crossed the frontiers of tonality belong to genres such as the symphony, the string quartet and the lyric piano piece, in other words those genres which are typical of absolute music.

In Schoenberg's diary for January 1912 we find the entry:

He [the publisher] wants titles for the orchestral pieces – for technical reasons to do with publication. I may give in, since I have thought of titles that are at least possible. Not, on the whole, sympathetic to the idea. For the wonderful thing about music is that one can tell all, so that the educated listener understands it all, and yet one has not given away one's secrets, the things one doesn't admit even to oneself. Whereas titles are a giveaway. . . . The titles I shall perhaps give do indeed give nothing away, being partly technical, partly very obscure.[1]

When the score was first published, in 1912, Schoenberg dispensed with the titles. In doing so he went against the publisher's wishes, which he must have felt had been formulated to accord with the music-aesthetic spirit of the times: the publisher (and the musical public) was not yet aware of the radical change that was taking place as programme music went out of fashion. In the revised score of 1922, the third piece of Op. 16 – in which Schoenberg realised his concept of 'Klangfarbenmelodie' – appeared under the title 'Farben' (Colours), which indeed 'gave nothing away', being 'technical'. But in the version for chamber orchestra of 1925, the word 'Farben' was amplified with the subtitle 'Sommermorgen an einem See' (Summer Morning on a Lake); and as early as 1921 Egon Wellesz had reported that Schoenberg was inspired by the flickering of light on the surface of the Traunsee. By using a title that 'gave something away', in 1925, Schoenberg however found himself no less opposed to public opinion – which in the meantime had changed – than he had done when suppressing the title in 1912. His pupil Richard Hoffmann says that Schoenberg believed he was 'now old enough to be able to afford being called a Romantic'.

Is Op. 16, No. 3 an example of programme music, then? A technically advanced piece of music which is subject to an outmoded aesthetic? A convincing answer is possible only when it is admitted that, as has already been shown, programme music is a category of aesthetics, not of biography. The decisive factor is not whether a composer has been moved by extramusical impressions, be they real or literary, but whether he has decided that the extramusical elements, be they expressed in the form of a programme, a motto or a title, should be part of the object itself, should pertain to the work as a musical entity. Whether or not Op. 16, No. 3 is a piece of programme music, therefore, depends on Schoenberg's aesthetic intention, not on biographical facts. Schoenberg's decision in 1912 was unequivocal. Extramusical premises did indeed exist, but he did not 'give them away'; they did not belong to the work itself, merely to the circumstances of its creation, which were the private concern of the composer. This conviction was typical of the progressive position of music-aesthetic opinion around 1912, but it contradicted the popular aesthetics of the nineteenth century, aesthetics which still prevailed so far as the public was concerned: the idea that music, as long as it did not exhaust itself in mere mechanics, was an expression of the composer's experiences, so that one had to know his biography in order to understand the works, which were their manifestation in sound. And if Schoenberg in 1925, according to the testimony of Richard Hoffmann, said that he could afford being a bit of a Romantic in his old age, he was obviously referring to the concession to the Romantic conviction of the aesthetic relevance of biographical data that was enshrined in the title 'Summer Morning on a Lake'. In defiance of a 'New Objectivity' whose hostility to Romanticism offended him, Schoenberg declared his support for an aesthetic which in the 1920s had been described as hopelessly outdated. Although, strictly speaking, he understood the theory that music was a form of self-expression on the composer's part in the sense of Schopenhauer's meta-physics and thus sought to keep factual and biographical details separate from aesthetics – and, therefore, from the determination as to what constituted a topic for aesthetics – he nonetheless even went so far as to defend the biographical element in his polemical response to the doctrine of 'New Objectivity' that dismissed the principle of self-expression lock, stock and barrel. But whether Schoenberg's aesthetic decision of 1925 must be taken as the decisive one, merely because it came later, is not certain. It was motivated psychologically rather than objectively, whereas in 1912 his aesthetic opposition to the spirit of the age, or public opinion as he saw it, was in accordance with his compositional technique.

V

The *Begleitungsmusik zu einer Lichtspielszene* (Accompaniment to a Film Scene), Op. 34, was composed in the winter of 1929–30, at a time when Schoenberg was preoccupied with ambitious, comprehensive works: one thinks of the opera *Von Heute auf Morgen*, the Orchestral Variations (which represent a sort of compendium of twelve-note technique) and the music drama *Moses und Aron*. Around 1930 Schoenberg felt free and secure enough in his use of the twelve-note technique, which he had developed only a few years earlier, to attempt those large-scale forms which had always attracted him and for the purpose of which the twelve-note technique had always been intended, even though it had first been tested on smaller structures. This tendency to compose in large spans, over long distances as it were, is evident also in the *Begleitungsmusik*, despite its brevity. The piece almost gives the impression of being an excerpt; and that Schoenberg himself thought of it in these terms is suggested by the word 'Szene', which evokes a drama of which the work is part.

The title suggests thoughts of film music illustrating a situation or series of events. But the 'Film Scene' to which it refers is a fiction; the

'Accompaniment', which accompanies nothing, is really an autonomous orchestral piece. The programme which forms the basis of the music was summarised by Schoenberg in a few words – 'Threatening Danger, Fear, Catastrophe' – words which may remind listeners of other, non-programmatic works by Schoenberg. If one were trying to classify the *Begleitungsmusik*, it would be easiest to regard it as a symphonic poem, a genre to which Schoenberg had contributed in his early works (*Pelleas und Melisande* and *Verklärte Nacht*). This tendency to make use of what he had done earlier in his career at a time when musical conditions had changed so much as to make such a retrograde step seem impossible was extremely characteristic of a Schoenberg in whom musically revolutionary and conservative traits cancelled each other out.

It seems that the audience at the first performances, which were conducted by Klemperer in Berlin and Jalowetz in Cologne respectively, sensed the programmatic tendency to be a retrospective feature in the context of twelve-note technique. In a letter to Jalowetz of 1931 Schoenberg wrote: 'People do seem to like the piece: ought I to draw any conclusions from that as to its quality? I mean: the public apparently likes it.'[2] The joke about the 'conclusions . . . as to . . . quality', which could only be negative, was also meant seriously. The alienation between Schoenberg and his public was already so great that Schoenberg distrusted a success as if it were a blemish on his own work. And his suspicion that the programme, which made the work accessible, covered it up at the same time was not without foundation. The success, which was doubtless due to the return to programme music – that is, to the comprehensibility of programme music – was likely to lead to a misunderstanding. The words 'Threatening Danger, Fear, Catastrophe' give a name to what the music expresses. But in the very process of articulating the expressive content they transform it into an illustrative one. The music that depicts fear – total, direct expression – because it has crystallised in a musically illustrative image, is removed to a distance; it loses its sting. The listener feels he has been placed in the role of a spectator instead of being himself directly affected; and since it is film music (albeit only fictitious) he accepts the dissonances he would otherwise not tolerate.

The *Begleitungsmusik zu einer Lichtspielszene* is illustrative music of the utmost constructive rigour; programme music in dodecaphonic technique. The enduring complaint that the twelve-note structure cannot be heard is mindless: it was never Schoenberg's intention to emphasise the technique. Yet from an aesthetic viewpoint dodecaphony is not completely a matter of indifference: the sense of a hidden logic forces itself on a listener even if he cannot understand the construction (which is the technical correlative of the aesthetic impression). Nonetheless a twelve-note structure that is virtually inaudible and may remain so is without significance for the external form, the outline of the whole. And the price Schoenberg paid in this work for making the compositional technique more sophisticated by using dodecaphony was a coarsening of the formal conception. The main constructional element so far as external form is concerned is tempo change: first the tempo gradually increases, from a slow beginning, to Allegro and Presto; then it subsides again, only to increase once more in a second intensification; finally it returns to the original speed, Adagio. As the tempo slows towards the end of the work, the compositional technique becomes simpler, expressing numbness in the face of catastrophe.

VI

Schoenberg's String Trio, Op. 45, is one of the works of New Music most difficult to place: a work of old age in which – just as in Beethoven's late quartets – the esoteric is interlocked paradoxically with ruthlessness, and introversion with an outwardly directed pathos.

The trio was composed in 1946, after Schoenberg had been seriously ill with heart trouble. Thomas Mann reports:

He told me about the new trio he had just completed, and about the experiences he had secretly woven into the composition – experiences of which the work was a kind of fruit. He had, he said, represented his illness and medical treatment in the music, including even the male nurses and all the other oddities of American hospitals.[3]

But although the piece contains autobiographical elements, it would be inappropriate to describe it as programme music. For the decisive factor is not the influences and conditions under which a piece is composed, but simply the aesthetic decision taken by the composer as to whether the extramusical elements should form part of the work itself as a programme shared with the listener; and Schoenberg did not leave any comment on the work for the outside world – his 'giveaway' was a private matter. It would not be appropriate, therefore, to pursue the biographical traits that are 'secretly woven into the composition'; the trio should be understood as autonomous music, as form and structure.

The work realises – albeit in a more complicated form in which the original scheme is hardly recognisable – a formal idea that had already been used by Schoenberg in *Pelleas und Melisande* and the First Chamber Symphony, Op. 9: the idea of condensing the four movements of a sonata – Allegro, slow movement, scherzo and finale – into a single movement, in such a way as to identify the movements of the cycle with the sections of a sonata allegro (principal theme, subordinate theme, elaboration and recapitulation). Schoenberg himself divided the trio into three 'Parts' linked by two 'Episodes'. Part I is the exposition of the principal theme; this exposition is expanded into an entire section, in that the theme is preceded by an introduction in which the motivic outlines first shape themselves and followed by an 'area of liquidation' in which the melody is reduced back to mere sound. The First Episode – the term obscures the true situation – represents the subordinate theme of the sonata form and the slow movement in terms of the sonata cycle (the tempo character of the slow movement matches the cantabile quality which is traditional in the subordinate theme). Part II is the scherzo of the work as a whole, inasmuch as it begins by recalling a waltz or Ländler. Yet there is a paradoxical relationship between the rhythmic gestures and the austere quality of the sound: the waltz character is, so to speak, masked. The Second Episode is an elaboration, not however on account of the motivic material, which derives from neither the principal nor the subordinate theme, but because of the compositional technique: the section seems like an atonal reflection of Baroque counterpoint. But in Classical and Romantic sonata form counterpoint became a technique of elaboration and a feature of the elaboration section. Part III, the finale, is simply a recapitulation; indeed, in stark contradiction to Schoenberg's principle of 'developing variation', a principle which aims at the constant transformation of themes and motifs, earlier groups of bars are recapitulated unchanged or with only slight variations. Even stranger than the literal nature of the reprise, however, is the procedure of patching together what had initially been kept separate, or conversely, of cutting a few bars out of an earlier phrase. This patchwork technique seems like a relapse into formal simplicity or even primitivity. Yet it is just this paradoxical interlocking of extreme complexity and a strange disregard for the postulates of formal 'culture' that is one of the distinguishing features of a late work, a feature which Schoenberg's trio shares with the late Beethoven quartets.

Musical prose

The expression 'musical prose' is used by Arnold Schoenberg in his essay 'Brahms the Progressive' to signify a musical language freed from the straitjacket of 'four-square compositional construction' (Wagner). The term appears unambiguous and also seems to provide a name for a phenomenon which performs a function in the areas of rhythm and melody similar to that performed by the emancipation of the dissonance in the area of harmony. Melodic ideas should be as self-sufficient and meaningful without the support of symmetries and correspondences as are dissonances without their resolution onto consonances.

Independently of Schoenberg, Heinrich Besseler used the phrase 'musical prose' in 1953 to characterise the melodic style of Gregorian chant and of Netherlands choral polyphony, a style said to be distinguished by 'constantly producing something new'. 'Prose is an old Latin word meaning unbound speech [*ungebundene Rede*, usually translated as prose, as opposed to *gebundene Rede* or verse], which proceeds in a simple and straightforward manner: *oratio prorsa* or *prosa*. Everyday prose is free in every respect. It constantly comes up with something new. But the same is also true of literary prose. It generally avoids the regular and the orderly; it avoids verbal repetitions, assonance and rhyme; it even avoids too great a similarity in the construction of sentences, for this could give the impression of an elevated style with rhythmic parallelisms.'[1]

For Schoenberg, however, asymmetry, the emancipation from the rhythmic–metric scheme, is merely a by-product of musical prose. What matters is not the irregularity as such but what caused it: the 'idea' that expresses itself 'in prose', in contrast to the 'formula' that tries to impose itself by means of symmetries and repetitions. When Schoenberg speaks of 'prose', he is thinking of a language which can express an idea directly, without repetitions and circumlocutions: 'This is what musical prose should be – a direct and straightforward presentation of ideas, without any patchwork, without mere padding and empty repetitions.'[2] The concept of the 'musical idea' may be suspected of being either a mere synonym for 'melodic phrase' or a chimera. And it can hardly be denied that it threatens to pale into a phantom of a word when Schoenberg downgrades musical 'logic', together with evenness, symmetry and repetition, to a 'means of presentation' which clarifies the musical idea but contributes nothing to its expressive content or its beauty. 'Evenness, regularity, symmetry, subdivision, repetition, unity, relationship in rhythm and harmony and even logic – none of these elements produces or even contributes to beauty. But all of them contribute to an organization which makes the presentation of the musical idea intelligible.'[3] A musical idea, however – if the concept is to be neither fictitious nor tautological – cannot be understood as anything other than the essence of the relationships by means of which a musical phrase reaches beyond itself and its immediate existence.

I

The F major oboe melody in the last movement of *Das Lied von der Erde*, 'Der Abschied' (Ex. 1), is praised by Schoenberg as a paradigm of musical prose. The individual melodic phrases 'vary greatly in shape, size and content, as if they were not motival parts of a melodic unit, but words, each of which has a purpose of its own in the sentence'.[4] But although Schoenberg insists that the meaning of the words is paramount, the eloquence and power of the music is also determined to a considerable extent by the syntax of the period. The melody is divided irregularly into 3 + 2 + 3 + 4 bars. Yet Mahler adheres to traditional syntax, the correspondence between antecedent and consequent. The asymmetry of musical prose presupposes the symmetry of 'bound speech' so that it can then vary it and achieve eloquence by means of variation.

The unifying element that holds the phrases together is provided not by sharply defined motifs and rhythmic–metrical patterns but by inconspicuous formulas and vague melodic outlines. The third phrase is a varied sequence of the second, a relationship which is half-concealed but impossible to overlook. At the same time it recalls (through its turn and its closing figure [that is, the d^2–a^1–c^2]) the opening phrase and thus acts as a synoptic consequent.

Ex. 1

The syntax, however, is not merely a 'means of presentation' which conveys the musical 'content' without having any effect on it. If the units of melody are 'words', as Schoenberg says, it is impossible to separate their meaning from the context in which they·exist. The sigh of relief that is perceptible in the second phrase seems forced and constricted in the third (the sequence): the highest note is emphasised, by means of the syncopation and the *sforzato*, as if it had to overcome some kind of resistance. The fourth phrase is an epilogue which compresses fragments of the third phrase – the opening figure (g^1–a^1–b^1 flat–a^1–b^1 flat) and the closing figure (c^2–g^1–a^1–b^1 flat traces the outline of d^2–a^1–c^2) – together with one another.

The fact that the third phrase has the effect of a 'word' which expresses a meaning is due to the 'formal' procedure of varied sequence, a procedure to which Schoenberg ascribes a merely 'presentational' function. Put briefly: the 'contents' of the unbound language feed on the 'forms' of the bound. Yet the 'forms' are not eloquent in themselves. In the bound speech of traditional periodic construction, the 'formal' scheme of the descending sequence has a particular quality which remains hidden: it is there but not clearly expressed. In Mahler's musical prose, on the other hand, the same scheme exhibits that particular quality for all to hear: namely, the quality of being exaggeration and retraction at one and the same time.

II

The idea that unbound speech is capable of absorbing bound speech is one of the basic tenets of Romantic literary theory. 'Poetry', according to a fragment by Novalis, 'is the prose among the arts.' And Walter Benjamin[5] drew attention to a letter to August Wilhelm Schlegel in which Novalis declares that the limitations of prose are a condition of the freedom of poetry:

If poetry wishes to expand, it can do so only by limiting itself; by drawing itself together and letting its fiery material so to speak flash and congeal. It acquires an appearance of prose, its constituent parts are not associated so intimately – are therefore not under such stringent rhythmic laws – and it becomes more capable of presenting what is limited. But it remains poetry, and therefore true to the essential laws of its nature; it becomes so to speak an organism, whose entire structure betrays its origins in fluidity, its original elastic nature, its freedom, its omnipotence.

The paradox that Novalis constructs out of poetry and prose, expansion and limitation, implies – prosaically expressed – that prose is a more precise form of poetry; but precision entails both delimitation (that is, restriction) and connection (that is, expansion); for as the definition of an object becomes more accurate so the number of relationships to which it is applied increases.

This digression into literary theory seems an unnecessary ornament in an attempt to define the qualities of musical prose. It is not immediately clear that the connection between precision, wealth of relationships and prose which Novalis suggests is of relevance to music. Yet if we simply sketch out an analysis we will soon be able to recognise in music the distinguishing features of the Romantic concept of prose.

Schoenberg cites the theme of the Andante moderato from Brahms's String Quartet Op. 51, No. 2 (Ex. 2) as a piece of musical prose which outwardly observes the limitations of eight-bar phrase construction without being a regular period. The theme is divided into $1\frac{1}{2}$ + $1\frac{1}{2}$ + $1\frac{1}{2}$ + 1 + 1 + $1\frac{1}{2}$ bars. There is no correspondence between bars 1–5 and 5–8, which function as antecedent and consequent, apart from the fact that they are both divided into three parts. Musical coherence is brought about through motivic development, not as the result of some 'tectonic' scheme.

Schoenberg sees the second phrase as a varied sequence of the first;[6] the fourth-figure e^1–d^1–c^1 sharp–b circumscribes the note d^1. The deviation of the sequence from the model is motivic, not ornamental, in character. On the one hand the fourth-figure is developed out of a motivic remnant of the first phrase; on the other hand, in bar 4 it is split off from the phrase-ending. In the second half of bar 4 it is reduced to three notes, in bar 5 to two. The motivic remnant – the 'feminine ending' c^1 sharp–b – is taken up again in bar 6, but as a descending fourth instead of a descending second; and in bar 7 it is both avoided and suggested – avoided in the upper voice, the phrasing of which contradicts the similarity with bar 6, and suggested in the syncopated figure of the second violin. The rhythmic figure of the closing bar combines a reminiscence of the opening phrase with the 'feminine ending' from bar 5.

Ex. 2

This fragmentary analysis is already enough to show that there is a correspondence between the wealth of rhythmic and melodic relationships generated by the theme and the more precise definition of the motifs. Taken from its context, the last bar would be nothing but a conventional cadential phrase; that it appears as a melodic feature and as a logical culmination, not as a mere conclusion, results from its connection with the endings in bars 3 and 5. The 'musical idea' expressed in the closing bar is the essence of its relationships with what has preceded it.

The theme is prose-like by virtue of its irregular construction. This is not the only element, however, that departs from the norms of musical metre. In order to clarify the metrical structure of bars 1–3, Schoenberg notated them in 6/4.[7] Yet the assumption underlying his analysis – the idea that a melodic correspondence (1½ + 1½ bars) is necessarily bound up with a metrical one – is not self-evident; on the contrary, it is questionable. The original notation of the theme is more precise than the interpretative paraphrase. True, the latter does conceal the fact that the beginning of the second bar is weak, not strong; weaker, even, than the second half of the first bar. But in the second phrase – the sequence of the first – the barline is justified metrically; it indicates that the gradation of stress in the sequence differs from that of the model: that is, strong-weak-weak-weak-strong-weak (Ex. 3).

Ex. 3

The change from strong-weak-weak (bars 1–2) to weak-strong-weak (2–3) is motivated both harmonically and rhythmically: chord I takes priority over chord II, and the undivided note-value over the divided one, a priority that predominates so long as the metre is not firmly established. If, therefore, the theme is a piece of musical prose, as Schoenberg says, it derives its prose character not from the alternation which Schoenberg perceived between 6/4 and 4/4 metre but from a method of grading the stress that cannot be notated undistorted either in 6/4 or in 4/4.

III

The concept of musical prose goes back to the early nineteenth century. Writing about the *Symphonie fantastique* of Berlioz, Schumann praised its 'unbound speech', its emancipation from the 'law of the regular beat', as a model of 'higher poetic punctuation'.[8] In contrast, Grillparzer found in musical prose, as exemplified for him by Weber's *Euryanthe*, a lack of 'inner (musical) logic'. 'No trace of melody, not just of agreeable melody but of melody in general', he noted in 1823. 'But by melody I mean an organically unified sentence whose various parts are mutually linked by musical necessity.' And in 1821 he spoke of 'musical prose-writers', who lacked 'the sense of a whole':

For every true melodic theme has its inner law of structure and development which to the true musical genius is sacred and inviolable and which he cannot give up for the sake of the words. The musical prose-writer can begin anywhere and end anywhere, because the individual fragments and sections can easily be rearranged and put in another sequence; but he who has a sense of a whole can give it only in one piece or not at all.[9]

Grillparzer's loathing for *Euryanthe*, whose music he described as 'contrary to police regulations', may be hypochondriacal; but there is no doubt that Weber breaks through the conventions of 'four-square compositional construction'. In the fractured aria of Lysiart, and even in the cantabile one of Adolar ('Wehen mir Lüfte Ruh'), two-bar phrases alternate with three-bar phrases and downbeat motifs with upbeat motifs, with the result that the listener is forced to adjust quickly to the abrupt changes instead of being able to entrust himself to a regular rhythm. But even in Mozart – who is used as a yardstick to condemn Weber – the 'rearrangement of the individual fragments and sections' for which Grillparzer reproaches the 'musical prose-writers' is not at all unusual. Schoenberg describes the third part of the second *Figaro* finale ('Susanna, son morta') as an example of the procedure whereby phrases of varying length and differing character are joined to one another so loosely that through rearrangement the music can adapt itself to changing dramatic situations.[10] And Thrasybulos Georgiades speaks of a discontinuity of heterogeneous melodic shapes. 'Nothing that is continuous; every section is self-contained, unified, hermetically sealed, a solid body, heterogeneous from the others; the succession jerky, in itself inexplicable.'[11] What holds the melodic phrases together is 'pure metre', 'a referential system which establishes unity only in the mind'.[12]

Such a 'pure metre', set up in opposition to heterogeneous melodic shapes, would thus be the medium whereby, in music, 'bound' rhythms are subsumed into an all-embracing 'prose' rhythm in a manner comparable to that adumbrated by Novalis for poetry. The idea of 'pure metre' and its function seems to derive from a comparison of Mozart's rhythmic practice with asymmetrical structures from the seventeenth century in which there is no distinction between the metre and the rhythmic 'foreground'. Merope's aria from Lully's *Persée* (1682) is composed of dissimilar rhythms, though it would not make sense to talk of a 'change of metre' (Ex. 4). For what defines the rhythm is the declamation of the lines, not the succession of different bars. Lully does not join 4/4 bars onto 3/4 bars but groups lines of different length around focal points which he marks with barlines. What we have between two barlines, however, is not a 'bar' in the sense of a primary rhythmic unit but the almost accidental sum of the end of one line and the beginning of another. (It would be

Ex. 4

Ma ri-va-le jou - it d'un sort trop fa-vo -   ra - ble,   et je souf-fri-rais

trop   si je   ne mou-rais   pas.

possible, without destroying the rhythmic structure, to replace the quaver at the end of the first line [see brackets in Ex. 4] with a dotted crotchet, so creating a 4/4 bar.)

While the bar is a secondary concern and merely a result in Lully, in Mozart it seems to be a premiss, a sturdy framework for the conjoining and support of the individual rhythmic shapes. But the notation is not always clear and unambiguous. The opening section of the last *Figaro* finale is an Andante in 4/4 time; the rhythmic model of bars 1–2 is the pattern ♩♩♩ | ♩. In bar 13, however, the 4/4 bar turns into a 2/4 bar with the basic rhythm ♫♫ | ♩♪, without the change being notated.

In the second section of the finale (Con un poco più di moto) the rhythmic feeling is disturbed by an asymmetrical gradation of the stress. One of the defining elements in the sentence structure is the abrupt change between phrases of different length: that is, between lines consisting of one, one and a half and two bars. The melodic style 'acquires an appearance of prose, its constituent parts are not associated so intimately – are therefore not under such stringent rhythmic laws – and it becomes more capable of presenting what is limited' (Novalis). The construction of bars 65–9 ('Che dita tenerelle') is irregular: 1½ + 1 + 1 + 1½ (Ex. 5). Yet the uniformity of the alternation between strong and weak half-bars seems – in the notation – to be undisturbed; the transition from the downbeat rhythm of the first phrase (♩♩ | ♩) to the upbeat rhythm of the second, third and fourth phrases does not produce a conflict between the one-bar and the one-and-a-half-bar construction of the lines. But in bars 75–7 and 78–80 the third and fourth phrases, now split off from the first two, are notated so as to begin with a downbeat (♩♩ | ♩♩ | ♩) instead of an upbeat (♩ | ♩♩ | ♩♩); the strong half-bars appear weak, the weak strong.

Ex. 5

This contradiction can be explained in any one of three ways. First, the change in notation could be understood as a metrical reinterpretation of the phrases; secondly – in order to avoid the metrical reinterpretation – the barlines could be rearranged so as to introduce bars of 6/4 or 2/4; or, thirdly, the 4/4 bar could be interpreted as a double 2/4 bar, with the result that the notational contradiction would disappear. The third explanation is an illusory one; for the question of whether the uniformity in the alternation of strong and weak is disturbed by whole bars or half-bars makes a difference only of degree, not of kind. On the other hand, it is difficult, indeed almost impossible, to choose between the first and the second interpretations; for in order to be plausible it ought to be possible to draw support from a theory. But the problems involved in making a connection between rhythm, harmony and the gradation of stress have hardly been recognised[13] – they even remain submerged in Hugo Riemann's system of rhythm and metre, though the correlation between harmony and metre forms the (implicit) basis of the system.

For our analysis of the last *Figaro* finale it may suffice to describe the rudiments of a theory for the gradation of harmonic and metrical stress. If we assume a uniform 'harmonic rhythm' (an assumption the finale fulfils – the standard unit of harmonic change is the minim), then the chord progression I-I is strong-weak, I-V-I or I-IV-I is strong-weak-strong, and I-V-I-V or I-IV-I-IV is strong-weak-strong-weak. The I-IV-V-I cadence is mixed; the beginning suggests the gradation strong-weak, the end a reinterpretation as weak-strong-weak-strong.

In the *Figaro* finale the gradation of harmonic stress is unambiguous, since it agrees with that of rhythm and melody. The ending, which appears melodically as both the goal and the focal point of a line, is based harmonically on a 'relative tonic': the A major chord is 'relative tonic' of the line 'che dita tenerelle'. And the 'relative tonic' represents the harmonic focal point except where chords are repeated ('mi pizzica, mi stuzzica'). The lines 'mi pizzica, mi stuzzica' and 'm'empie d'un nuovo ardor' are therefore notated 'incorrectly' in bars 67–9, 'correctly' in bars 75–7 and 78–80.

This distinction, unnoticeable in bar 67, becomes perceptible when different notations of a phrase are juxtaposed (Ex. 6). The metrical displacement of the oboe melody is the result of a half-bar overlap. The second half of bar 87 is at once the conclusion of the first three-bar phrase and the beginning of the second. And the half-bar acts – in contradiction to the notation – as a strong downbeat. The reinterpretation, however, is not abruptly enforced but is prepared in bars 86–7, whose harmonic scheme, I-IV-V-I, establishes the change from ♩♩|♩♩ to ♩|♩♩|♩.

Ex. 6

Tut - to Su-san - na   pig - lia

Va tut - to a

ma - ra - vig - lia

Bars 85–90 are divided latently into 2 + 3 + 2 + 3 + 2 minims. Yet it would be going too far to talk of a change in metre; and according to Thrasybulos Georgiades even the concept of overlap is 'inadmissible'.[14] Georgiades distinguishes between a background, comprising 'pure metre' and 'homogeneous harmonic current', and a foreground in which heterogeneous melodic and rhythmic shapes present themselves. The distinction seems abstract. For the concept of the bar already includes a differentiation between strong and weak half-bars which is dependent on the harmonic and rhythmic content of the bar: in the *Figaro* finale the emphases occur when the end of a line coincides with a 'relative tonic'. On the other hand, there exist contradictions between harmonic–rhythmic metre and notated metre, contradictions whose outward sign is the displacement of phrases within the bar. And it seems that the theory of 'pure metre' has to be understood as an attempt to cling to the notated bar as a musical reality while avoiding the consequence of this, namely that the gradation of stress within a phrase may vary on repetition. If the gradation of stress is ascribed to the harmonic–rhythmic 'foreground', rather than to the 'background' metre, then the metre, as 'pure metre', is not affected when the harmonic–rhythmic emphasis is displaced to the second half of a bar. Conversely, the emphasis of the phrase is not suppressed by that of the bar, but is retained despite the contradiction, though at the same time the emphasis does not lead to a change of metre. The 2 + 2 + 2 + 2 + 2 arrangement of 'pure metre' and the 2 + 3 + 2 + 3 scheme which results when we take the intervals between the focal points of the phrases exist as background and foreground simultaneously, without cancelling each other out.

Disconcerting though it may be, this split within the concept of metre is no chimera. But it is in order to ask on what the phenomenon that Georgiades calls 'pure metre' is based. If one compares the *Figaro* finale with the quotation from Lully's *Persée* (see Ex. 4), it becomes clear, on the one hand, that in Mozart the primary grouping of the beats – the alternation between strong and weak crotchets – is not affected by the discrepancy between harmonic–rhythmic metre and notated metre, whereas in Lully it is. On the other hand, the rhythm of chordal change is irregular in Lully, regular in Mozart, where the norm of chord duration is the minim. The regular crotchet 'pulse' and the uniformity of chordal change create the impression of unbroken musical progress. And although they do not directly affect the discrepancy between harmonic–rhythmic metre and notated metre – the contradiction between the half-bar groupings $2 + 2 + 2 + 2 + 2$ and $2 + 3 + 2 + 3$ – their indirect influence is nevertheless decisive. For they explain why the change from 2/2 to 3/2 rhythm does not crystallise in a change in time signature: the latent regrouping that results from the harmonic–rhythmic structure appears as a minor and merely momentary disturbance of the uniformity, since the crotchet 'pulse' and the rhythmically undifferentiated harmonic progression override it.

IV

In the theory laid down by Wagner in *Oper und Drama*, the concept of musical prose performs the function of the antithesis in a dialectical construction:

> The melody which is complete in advance, and which has taken its character from the dance – the only way in which our modern musical hearing is able to understand the essence of melody – will never accommodate itself to the spoken accent of verse. This accent emerges now in one, now in another, element of the verse, and it never returns at the same place in the verse-line.[15] . . . So if the musician who was only concerned with a reproduction of the natural expression of speech – melodically heightened yet essentially accurate – clung to the accent of speech as being the only thing capable of forming a natural and illuminating bond between speech and melody, he was obliged to overcome verse completely. . . . In doing so, however, the musician dissolved not only the verse in prose but also his melody, for musical prose was all that remained of the melody which only emphasised the rhetorical accent of verse dissolved into prose by means of musical expression.[16]

The logic of this is not infallible. The lines 'Die Sónne hébt sich noch einmal . . . und zéigt mir jéne Stélle' in Heine's poem 'Die Stadt' are irregularly stressed. But Schubert has done justice to the shift of accent from the third to the second metrical foot by means of an analogous displacement of the highest note, without being obliged to alter the position of the line in the bar (Ex. 7).

Ex. 7

In Hugo Wolf's 'Jägerlied' (Mörike) the procedure is more complex. The five-foot line corresponds to a 5/4 metre divided into 2 + 3 crotchets (Ex. 8). The accent on 'Brieflein' – and thus on the second foot – seems to necessitate a dissolution into musical prose, a regrouping of 2 + 3 + 2 + 3 into 2 + 4 + 3 + 1. The shift of accent is supported by the harmony: the six-five chord on A sharp, as an alteration of the sixth-chord on A, is an upbeat to the six-four chord on B. If, however, one interprets the crotchet extended by a fermata as a 2/4, it becomes clear that while the 5/4 rhythm has been interrupted by an interpolated 'spare' upbeat, it is not completely suspended: 2 + 3 (+ 1) + 3 + 2.

Ex. 8

The goal towards which Wagner's argument in *Oper und Drama* strives – in dialectical terms, the negation of the negation – is verse in the shape of *Stabreim*. It is supposed to 'redeem' the prose which is the result of the negation of false poetry[17] by turning it into true poetry. Through *Stabreim* the rhythmically irregular, 'logical' accents of the verse that has been dissolved into prose are 'made accessible to emotion';[18] it provides the transition to the music. Wagner's mania for alliteration is thus an attempt to justify musical prose, the irregularity of the intervals between the accents. But the rhythm itself does not change. The negation of the negation – the idea that by means of *Stabreim* the 'logical' accent is transformed into the 'emotional expression', in other words, that prose is transformed into poetry – is musically irrelevant. Musically, Wagner writes prose. In this quotation from the closing scene of *Das Rheingold* (Ex. 9), the alliteratively related syllables appear in irregular alternation

Ex. 9

Zitt' - re und   za - ge,   ge-zähm-tes   Heer!

on the different beats of the bar. And in his *Mitteilung an meine Freunde* Wagner also describes his own melodic style as being similar to prose. 'Every time the expression of poetic speech urged itself on me so forcefully that I could not justify the melody to my feelings except by reference to it, this melody – if it was not to stand in forced relation to the verse – had to lose almost all rhythmic character.'[19]

One has only to analyse Schoenberg's *Das Buch der hängenden Gärten* to see that when Wagner declared the shift of stress in the verse line to be the source of musical prose he had recognised something of crucial importance. In song XIII ('Du lehnest wider eine Silberweide') it is not the recurring poetic metre but the varying arrangement of the stresses _ _ ⌣ _ ⌣ and _ ⌣, ⌣ _ _ that determines the musical rhythm of the lines 'Ich bin im Boot, das Laubgewölbe wahren / in das ich dich vergeblich lud zu steigen' (Ex. 10). The correspondence between the lines is abolished, and the verse is dissolved into musical prose.

But Schoenberg does not always ignore the correspondence between lines. In song VIII ('Wenn ich heut nicht deinen Leib berühre') the final lines, 'Kühlung sprenge mir, dem Fieberheissen, / der ich wankend draussen lehne' (Ex. 11), are composed in rhythmically parallel manner, despite the change in stress from _ ⌣ _ ⌣ _ to _ ⌣ _ _ ⌣.

V

In 'Brahms the Progressive' Schoenberg hesitates to characterise Mozart's technique of asymmetrical grouping as musical prose; instead, he claims,

Ex. 10

Ich bin im Boot,__ das Laub-ge-wöl-be wah-ren,   in das ich dich ver-

- geb - lich lud__ zu stei - gen.

Ex. 11

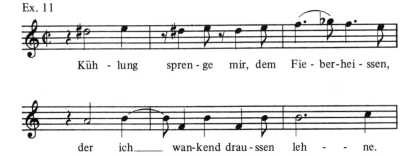

Küh - lung   spren - ge   mir, dem   Fie - ber-hei - ssen,

der   ich___   wan-kend drau - ssen   leh - - ne.

the combination of heterogeneous structures betrayed a baroque sense of form. 'But it is not yet what deserves to be called "musical prose". One might rather be inclined to ascribe such irregularity to a baroque sense of form, that is, to a desire to combine unequal, if not heterogeneous, elements into a formal unit.'[20]

On the other hand it seems that those features which distinguish Mozart's procedure from the musical prose of Schoenberg are not dissimilar to the differences between Mozart and Lully. For the regular 'pulse' of the beats and the uniformity of 'harmonic rhythm' which mediate between heterogeneous melodic phrases in the *Figaro* finale are lacking in Schoenberg's musical prose just as they are in Lully. Thus one might say that Schoenberg is closer to the 'baroque sense of form' than Mozart.

Yet it went against the grain with him, as opposed to Lully, to leave contrasts as they are. In the quotation in Ex. 12 from song IV ('Da meine Lippen reglos sind und brennen') of *Das Buch der hängenden Gärten*,

Ex. 12

Noch war viel-leicht mir mög - lich   mich zu   tren - nen

accompaniment and vocal line are rhythmically heterogeneous. The
accompaniment – syncopations notwithstanding – clearly defines the 5/8
metre: the chords represent a 'relative dominant' and a 'relative tonic',
which act as upbeat (2/8) and downbeat (3/8) respectively. The declama-
tory stresses of the vocal line contradict the 3/8 + 2/8 + 3/8 pattern
(accompaniment) by means of the 3/8 + 3/8 + 2/8 grouping. Yet Schoenberg avoids defining the difference as a contrast. The accent on the third
foot of the line ('möglich'), the 'beginning of the bar' in the vocal line,
coincides with a syncopation in the accompaniment, with the result that
the discrepancy between the 3 + 2 + 3 and 3 + 3 + 2 patterns dwindles
into a nuance.

Schoenberg's procedure can be described as a 'mediating' one. But
'mediation' is a word that means many things, and the idea of an inner
affinity with Mozart's technique which it might suggest would be mere
illusion. Schoenberg 'mediates' in that he reduces contrasts to the level of
the smallest possible differences. But in Schoenberg's music the neutral
medium that held together the heterogeneous musical shapes in Mozart –
the medium consisting of the regular 'pulse' of beats and the uniformity
of 'harmonic rhythm' – has disappeared.

Emancipation of the dissonance

I

Arnold Schoenberg found the word 'atonal' offensive, as indeed it may originally have been intended to be. What mattered was not the negative element, the lack of tonality, but the reason why tonality had been renounced: the 'emancipation of the dissonance'. And to justify this emancipation – the procedure whereby dissonances are treated in the same way as consonances[1] – Schoenberg argued that the difference between consonance and dissonance was a matter only of degree, not of kind. 'They are no more opposites than two and ten are opposites, as the frequency numbers indeed show; and the expressions "consonance" and "dissonance", which signify an antithesis, are false.'[2]

The grouping of sonorities [*Zusammenklänge*, also 'chords'] into consonances and dissonances was one of the premises of contrapuntal theory. A consonance can exist on its own; a dissonance must be resolved. In harmonic theory this distinction became a problem as early as the eighteenth century. In his article 'Dissonanz' in Sulzer's *Allgemeine Theorie der schönen Künste*, Johann Philipp Kirnberger wrote: 'But just as consonance is not something that is absolute, but rather something that gradually diminishes the perfect harmony of two strings tuned in unison, until finally one senses more conflict than agreement between the notes, so it is impossible to be precise about where the consonance of two notes ends and the dissonance begins.' Similarly Gottfried Weber, in his *Versuch einer geordneten Theorie der Tonsetzkunst* (1824), remarked: 'For I would indeed like to see the dictator who would be willing to draw the line between where the more euphonious ends and the less euphonious

120

begins – which combinations of notes are to be regarded as lying on this side of the line and which on the other.'[3] Schoenberg's claim that a dissonance is nothing but a more remote consonance has its basis, therefore, in a music–theoretical tradition. It can be refuted neither on acoustical grounds nor on the basis of the psychology of sound.

The differences in degree between intervals, with gradations ranging from the octave as the highest degree of consonance to the semitone or major seventh as the lowest, are natural phenomena. They are not denied even by the composers of atonal or serial music, whether Schoenberg, Krenek or Pierre Boulez.[4] The idea that 'emancipation of the dissonance' means that degrees of consonance and dissonance are obliterated, and that intervals are transformed into mere distances, is based on a misunderstanding. All that is abolished is the specific distinction between consonance and dissonance, the division of the intervals into two contrasting groups – a division which was based on compositional technique, not on the unalterable nature of the thing. (Since it depended on compositional technique, the decision as to which intervals were consonances and which dissonances, together with value judgments such as the evaluation of the fourth on the one hand and of the third and sixth on the other, varied throughout history.)

If the phrase 'emancipation of the dissonance' is taken literally, it is directed against the need for resolution. Unresolved dissonances were not rare even in tonal music, but they were interpreted as ellipses. The suppressed note of resolution was simply to be assumed, and its absence explained as a special quality of the dissonance. The emancipation that Schoenberg had in mind, on the other hand, means that dependent dissonances are to be reinterpreted as sonorities in their own right. The exception becomes the rule, the characteristic deviation a neutral norm, the ellipsis a closed structure.

According to Schoenberg, the emancipation is the consequence of a development in which the more remote and complex tonal relationships, as well as the simple and close-lying ones, gradually became directly comprehensible. 'What distinguishes dissonances from consonances is not a greater or lesser degree of beauty, but a greater or lesser degree of comprehensibility . . . The term "emancipation of the dissonance" refers to its comprehensibility, which is considered equivalent to the comprehensibility of the consonance. A style based on this premiss treats dissonances like consonances and renounces a tonal centre.'[5] Schoenberg regarded the traditional antithesis between consonance and dissonance as an element of compositional technique – as a method of presenting musical ideas in comprehensible form. And as a mere procedure it was to be measured according to the purpose it was supposed to fulfil; if it proved to be superfluous or useless, it could and should be abandoned.

To be sure, the term 'comprehensibility' is not unambiguous. The functions of notes in a tonality are to be distinguished from immediate tonal relationships. As a tonal relationship, a tritone is more difficult to comprehend than a sixth; yet the dominant function of a tritone is, in general, easier to grasp than the subdominant function of a Neapolitan sixth.

Thus if confusion is to be avoided, the notion of comprehensibility must be refined; but at the same time it is difficult to define the connection that, according to Schoenberg, exists between the degree of independence or dependence of sonorities and the degree to which they can be comprehended. True, it seems as though the theory and practice of counterpoint were based on a firm and unambiguous relationship between the treatment of intervals and their degree of comprehensibility: simple, directly comprehensible tonal relationships create independent sonorities, the more complex ones dependent sonorities. But the correlation is not all-embracing. The fourth above the bass is treated as a dependent sonority, even though as a tonal relationship it is simple and directly comprehensible. (Conversely, many augmented and diminished intervals, which are complex as tonal relationships, are used in place of consonances in the counterpoint of the seventeenth and eighteenth centuries: the diminished fifth appears as a resolution of the dissonant fourth, the augmented sixth as a resolution of the dissonant seventh. In 1739 Johann Mattheson concluded that the diminished fifth and augmented sixth should be regarded as consonances; what determined the nature of an interval was not the mathematically definable tonal relationship but its contrapuntal use.)[6]

On the other hand, the distinction between independent and dependent sonorities has not been linked with the definition of the tonal function of the notes and intervals in any satisfactory way. If one accepts the functional theory of Hugo Riemann as a fitting description of tonal harmony, one is forced to draw a distinction between the comprehensibility of the tonal functions and their meanings, on the one hand, and contrapuntal technique, the treatment of a note as consonant or dissonant, on the other. According to Riemann, the question of whether the note F in C major appears as the root of a triad, as a suspended fourth resolving onto the third of the tonic triad or as the seventh of a chord on the dominant has no bearing on the note's significance; for in C major, irrespective of the immediate context, the note F always represents the subdominant. Functional theory, taken to its extremes – extremes which Riemann himself avoided – is indifferent to contrapuntal technique.[7] (This made it possible for Hugo Leichtentritt to base an analysis of Schoenberg's Piano

Pieces Op. 11 on Riemann's theory of tonality without contradicting the letter of the theory.[8] From the lack of mediation between the rules of contrapuntal technique and the definition of tonal meanings Leichtentritt concluded that tonal comprehensibility was not affected by a change in contrapuntal technique, even one so profoundly radical as the emancipation of the dissonance. The analysis may be considered arbitrary or even absurd; that it was possible without a breakdown in logic is a sign of unresolved difficulties.)

The idea that emancipated dissonance should be comprehensible implies nothing other than this: that with sufficient effort even a very complex sonority becomes transparent with regard to its tonal relationships and can be understood as a structure in its own right. Yet it is uncertain whether comprehensibility in itself is the decisive factor. To be sure, the fourth-chord C-F-B flat-E flat is immediately comprehensible as a structure of tonal relationships; judged by the norms of the Pythagorean tonal system it is even simpler than the six-four-three chord C-F-A-E flat upon which in a tonal composition it ought to be resolved. The emancipated dissonance, however, in contradistinction to the dependent one, is an event without consequences, an isolated sonority. The chord is not deprived of comprehensibility, but it no longer leads anywhere.

II

The literal meaning of dissonance is a 'sounding apart'; and it seemed appropriate to link the notion of the emancipation of the dissonance with a theory of counterpoint, that is, of regarding the ungainly sonority dividing the notes as the correlative of a polyphony which is primarily concerned with the clear differentiation and contrast of the voices.[9] Yet the idea of a polyphony that is dissonant in principle should not be confused with the misunderstood concept of 'linear counterpoint'.[10] Dissonance should be understood as the way the notes move apart, and therefore as an effective element, not as the chance result of an uncompromising use of counterpoint in which the sonorities are incidental.

The explanation may be attractive in its simplicity, but it is inadequate. Schoenberg's earliest atonal works are less polyphonic than the preceding tonal ones,[11] and as a theorist he was more concerned to find a harmonic justification for emancipated dissonances than he was to find a contrapuntal one. He even linked the theory of the emancipation of the dissonance with a polemic against the concept of 'non-harmonic notes' [*harmoniefremde Töne*];[12] and a 'non-harmonic note' is nothing but a dissonance produced exclusively by melodic or polyphonic means.

The term 'non-harmonic note' derives from Gottfried Weber.[13] According to Weber, 'harmonies' are sonorities that can be used without reference to melodic movement: for example, triads and seventh chords. By contrast, 'non-harmonic notes' – passing notes and suspensions – must have a melodic or polyphonic basis. But the concept of 'harmony' embraced not only the structure of chords but also their interconnection and coherence.[14] Thus a dissonance is 'harmonic', according to Weber, if the resolution necessitates a change in the root of the chord and so brings about a harmonic progression. If the root stays the same, the dissonance is regarded as 'non-harmonic', in other words as an ornamental addition without influence on the harmonic development.

The claim that passing notes and suspensions are without influence was denied by Schoenberg. He analysed some passing notes in a Bach motet to show that they performed a harmonic function and thus were not 'non-harmonic': they interrupted the monotonous repetitions of the tonic chord and suggested the subdominant.[15]

The aesthetic motive behind this attack on the concept of 'non-harmonic' notes was the abhorrence of ornament and padding which Schoenberg shared with Adolf Loos. Schoenberg saw a flaw in splitting up the texture into essential and ornamental notes, in the search for a harmonic basis for some dissonances and a melodic basis for others.[16] The idea that lay behind his polemic was that of a texture in which every note could be justified on harmonic as well as on melodic or polyphonic grounds.

According to Schoenberg, whether a dissonance was treated as a suspension or as a passing note – the technique which motivates Weber's concept of the 'non-harmonic note' – was just a matter of presentation. The essence of the matter was the dissonance itself, the immediate phenomenon;[17] and in the emancipated dissonance, which no longer sought to justify itself as a suspension or passing note by means of a resolution, it came to the fore undisguised.

The argument is flawed by a contradiction. On the one hand Schoenberg emphasises the function of the dissonance, on the other the phenomenon as such. On the one hand he stresses the influence which notes that have incorrectly been considered as 'non-harmonic' can have on the harmonic development; on the other it seems as if he regards the dissonant sonority, since it is an isolated fact, as a phenomenon which is legitimate and meaningful in its own right. The contradiction indicates that Schoenberg recognised the isolation of emancipated dissonances as a problem whose solution by means of an expanded theory of harmony was as necessary as it was difficult. The idea of a counterpoint that was dissonant in principle did not in itself suffice to justify the emancipated dissonance.

Characteristic is the attempt to supply 'hidden roots' for 'non-harmonic' notes in order to demonstrate that they are in fact 'harmonic'.[18] In traditional harmonic theory – the theory of scale degrees developed by Rameau and Simon Sechter – the hypothesis of 'hidden roots' was a means of explaining connections between chords. Thus Schoenberg's experiment implies that the proposition that what appear to be 'non-harmonic' notes are actually 'harmonic' only seemed to him to be valid when it explained the connections between the chords as well as their structure. That the 'hidden roots' are imaginary and – as speculative hypothesis – dubious is immaterial. What matters is the problem that motivated the attempt to explain it: the problem that emancipated dissonances lacked consequence.

III

In some atonal works or sections of a work the dissonant sonorities, unwieldy in themselves and with respect to each other, are related through the use of complementary harmony – through the method of letting a first chord be followed by a second one which supplies the missing notes of the chromatic scale.[19] In music of the early atonal period the procedure is still tied to the tradition of chromatic harmony, being the ultimate consequence of the technique of transforming one chord into another by means of leading-note movement in the individual voices, a technique which goes back to Wagner and Liszt. (Later, in dodecaphonic music, complementary harmony appears in the shape of a principle to which Milton Babbitt gave the name of 'combinatoriality': here, the first half of the basic form of the row and the first half of one of the transpositions of the inversion together provide the complete twelve-note range.[20] The parallel with the trope technique of Josef Matthias Hauer is obvious.)

A second procedure that took up the compositional implications of the emancipation of the dissonance was the technique of the chord centre,* which had already been sketched out, at least in outline, by Debussy and Scriabin.[21] In this technique, a dissonant sonority, which gradually

---

* See below, pp. 203f. [Trans.]

evolves or else is stated at the beginning and then sustained, forms the harmonic framework of a movement. The chord centre is a harmonic ostinato; and it is no coincidence that it is in a passacaglia, the fifth of the *Altenberg-Lieder*, that Alban Berg presents a complex of notes first as a melodic succession and then as a chord: the development of the chord centre from the ostinato is, so to speak, spelt out. To be sure, the technique of the chord centre was more ephemeral. It had the effect of reducing pieces to the utmost brevity, and one suspects that Schoenberg's scepticism with regard to the ostinato style was carried over to the chord centre.

What mattered was not the harmonic ostinato technique as such but the premiss on which it was based: the idea that chords, by analogy with sequences of notes, could be motifs. 'This occurred to me', Schoenberg wrote, 'even before the introduction of the basic set, when I was composing *Pierrot lunaire*, *Die glückliche Hand* and other works of this period. Tones of the accompaniment often came to my mind like broken chords, successively rather than simultaneously, in the manner of a melody.'[22] Already in one of his first atonal works, the Piano Pieces Op. 11, sequences of notes were sometimes transformed or inverted into chords.

The seemingly paradoxical concept of the harmonic motif, the idea that chords could be motifs, is a consequence of tendencies or earlier forms already present in Wagner and Liszt. Ernst Kurth saw in the *Tristan* chord an 'independent chord structure', even a 'leitmotif';[23] and Alfred Lorenz analysed the motivic functions of the *Tristan* chord, which he described as a 'mystic chord', in *Parsifal*.[24] (That the chord is 'independent', as Kurth maintains, implies that it appears in different enharmonic interpretations and in changing contexts without losing its identity.)

If chords are understood as motifs, as individual, self-justifying constructs, the problem of the emancipated dissonance – its harmonic lack of consequence – is not removed; but it does appear in a different light. To be justified in the context of a movement, motifs do not need to have any immediate consequences; it is enough that they fit meaningfully into a context of variants and contrasts.

The principle with which Schoenberg sought to create a coherent set of links between motifs was dodecaphony, 'composition with twelve tones related only to one another'. It has been explained by Adorno and others as a generalised form of thematic–motivic work.[25] This interpretation is undoubtedly correct, but it must be qualified by adding that the concept of the motif in Schoenberg's musical thinking included chords as well as sequences of notes; and it even seems as if the difficulty of relating emancipated dissonances to one another was one of the driving forces behind the development of twelve-note technique.

In dodecaphony, the immediate consequence of a chord conceived as a motif became a secondary matter. 'But as such progressions do not derive from roots', Schoenberg wrote, 'harmony is not under discussion and evaluation of structural functions cannot be considered.' On the other hand Schoenberg was convinced that a later theory would discover functional connections between the chords. 'One day there will be a theory which abstracts rules from these compositions. Certainly, the structural evaluation of these sounds will again be based upon their functional potentialities.'[26] As for the harmony that 'is not under discussion', Schoenberg believed that one day it would prove amenable to analysis. It was not sufficient for him, then, to find a reason for chords in dodecaphonic terms, that is, in their derivation from the row. The difficulty occasioned by the fact that emancipated dissonances could not create progressions remained unresolved; to be sure, it had become less pressing, by virtue of the fact that chords could be treated as harmonic motifs, but it had not completely disappeared or become irrelevant.

That Schoenberg left the solution to a future theory should not be misconstrued as an expression of uncertainty. Schoenberg saw the difficulty as a problem of theoretical presentation, not of compositional thought. 'Evaluation of (quasi-) harmonic progressions in such music is obviously a necessity, though more for the teacher than for the composer.'[27] 'Idea' and 'presentation' are the fundamental categories in Schoenberg's aesthetics or poetics, an aesthetics of genius whose principle can be summarised in the formula that the idea alone is decisive and the presentation secondary. Presentation, for Schoenberg, meant everything that could be analysed: the form, the functional connection of the parts,[28] and also the tonal or dodecaphonic structure. It would be incorrect to think that Schoenberg had a low opinion of tonality because he regarded it merely as a means of presentation.[29] He spoke in much the same way of twelve-note technique; attempts to analyse the row structure of dodecaphonic works seemed to him a waste of time.[30] The law-giving authority in the case of musical phenomena is the formal instinct of the genius; theory, which lags behind, may or may not follow.

What is 'developing variation'?

The concept of developing variation, one of the central categories in Schoenberg's musical thinking, has received so much attention in recent decades that the essence of the term has been put at risk and allowed to be forgotten: namely, that it is not just the name of a technique, but that of an idea, even though Schoenberg himself could not decide whether to define it as a 'technique', a 'style of presentation' or the 'development of a [musical] idea'. But if one attempts to trace the outlines of what Schoenberg had in mind, the most direct approach is to take what seems the roundabout method of sketching a few of the problems one can get caught up in when making considered use of this category.

I

The difficulty caused by the fact that in Schoenberg the terms 'theme', 'basic shape' and 'idea' tend to overlap cannot be solved by the arbitrary use of definitions in order to ensure the establishment of clear distinctions between them. Rather, it should challenge one to look into the objective reasons *why* the language is so unclear. The same applies to those categories which correlate to 'theme', 'basic shape' and 'idea': as a concept 'developing variation' is complementary to 'theme', 'abundance of shapes' to 'basic shape', and 'presentation' to 'idea'.

In 1925 Schoenberg noted: 'The more primitive a musical idea and the piece that is based on it, the greater is the regard for comprehensibility, the slower the tempo in which it is presented, the fewer the shapes and the fewer the more remote shapes that can be made use of in this context.'[1] The 'shapes' that emerge from developing variation, then, serve to

128

'present' the 'idea'. On the other hand, in an article written in 1931, 'Linear Counterpoint', Schoenberg equated the terms 'theme' and 'basic shape': 'Whatever happens in a piece of music is nothing but the endless reshaping of a basic shape. Or, in other words, there is nothing in a piece of music but what comes from the theme, springs from it and can be traced back to it; to put it still more severely, nothing but the theme itself.'[2] Finally, in his essay 'J. S. Bach', written in 1950, Schoenberg dropped the terms 'basic shape' and 'theme' in favour of 'idea' and 'basic unit'; and the method of generating 'thematic formulations' from a 'basic unit' he called 'developing variation'.[3]

In 1930, in the article 'New Music, Outmoded Music, Style and Idea', 'idea' was defined both as the whole of a form and as a 'method' of creating 'balance', without wholly excluding the colloquial equation with the concept of theme. 'In its most common meaning, the term idea is used as a synonym for theme, melody, phrase or motive. I myself consider the totality of a piece as the idea: the idea which its creator wanted to present.'[4] Now, the ambiguity that turns the concept of the idea into a category that eludes definition – a category whose significance extends from the initial motif of a movement, through the method of mediating between the various shapes, to the form as a whole – is certainly not a meaningless coincidence but rather the linguistic manifestation of an ambiguity within the concept itself. For the relationship between idea and presentation, theme and developing variation, basic shape and abundance of shapes, is in a strict sense dialectical, and the exaggerated assertion that the substance of a movement is already implicit in the theme should be avoided just as much as the opposing one-sided view, that the idea of a work is nothing but the sum of the relations between the shapes through which it leaves its mark, without any priority being given to the material stated at the beginning. An exaggerated appeal to substance is as misleading as an extreme functionalism, and any discussion of whether a basic shape is the 'germ' of a work or a formula for a system of connections between interrelated shapes would miss the point; for the one is just as possible as the other. The relationship between what a theme 'contains' from the outset and the features that it later 'acquires' from the context would be distorted if it were generally discussed only in terms of a substance which is not generated by developing variation but which is merely brought up to date by it. Instead of complicating the concept of the theme, one should keep open the choice among the various possible ways in which the theme may be related to the form as a whole, for this connection cannot be determined in terms of a general principle – that is, by applying a doctrine – but only in respect of each case, that is, with regard to the unique quality of a work. And, in turn, our understanding of what is actually meant by theme, basic shape or idea is dependent on the nature of the total form, and the mediation between theme and total form that is established by developing variation.

II

The correlation between theme and total form may be illustrated by reference to the problem of determining the appropriate level of abstraction when defining the 'basic unit' of a work. And by considering levels of abstraction we can also shed light on the difference between developing variation and thematic work, a difference often lost in the common parlance of music theory.

Developing variation differs from thematic–motivic work above all in the higher level of abstraction which it permits and perhaps even requires. If one compares Schoenberg's analysis of the theme of the Andante from Brahms's String Quartet in A minor, Op. 51, No. 2, with the results of the method dictated by musical common sense, the difference is obvious. A conventional analysis would proceed from a four-note motif in which diastematics and rhythm have 'coalesced' as a 'concrete' structure; then, through the use of concepts such as the addition and subtraction of notes, the sequence and inversion of phrases, the delimitation of motifs and the displacement of metrical stress, it would make the way in which the following bars are derived from the first two more comprehensible. Compared with this, Schoenberg's method of deducing all the motifs from the interval of an ascending and descending second is abstract, inasmuch as it ignores rhythm and articulation with a thoroughness which flies in the face of ordinary listening habits derived from tradition – and thus reduces the results of the analysis to a statement about merely latent processes.

It would be misguided, however, to make a judgment on the advantages and disadvantages of the analytical method dependent on a psychological experiment with listeners, the choice of whom always predetermines the result of such an experiment. The decisive factor is not whether a level of abstraction falls short of the historically determined limits of audibility but whether it must be assumed in order for us to be able to comprehend and analyse the inner unity of a work: the overriding principle should be the idea that the work is perfectly consistent, an idea which naturally constitutes just as much of a 'prejudgment' in Hans-Georg Gadamer's sense as the experimental psychologists' recourse to the *vox populi*.

The abstraction with which Schoenberg the analyst operated consisted as a rule in the fact that intervals or complexes of intervals appeared as the true substance of music, whereas the other features of the composition, from rhythm through harmonic and metrical function to the delimitation of motifs, were treated as the mere 'surface', more a matter of 'presentation' than of 'idea'. In an analysis of the first of his Orchestral Songs, Op. 22, Schoenberg defines the semitone and the minor third as being 'always the same' substance, regardless of rhythm and articulation. And in *Fundamentals of Musical Composition* the concept of motivic content is used to refer exclusively to diastematics, not to rhythm and harmony. 'Common content, rhythmic similarities and coherent harmony contribute to logic. Common content is provided by using motive-forms derived from the same basic motive. Rhythmic similarities act as unifying elements. Coherent harmony reinforces relationship.'[5]

Not that rhythm is ignored on principle. But when Schoenberg, in analysing the subordinate theme of the first movement of Brahms's E minor Cello Sonata, Op. 38, claims a rhythmic analogy between the first and third bars yet ignores the difference between a motivic interval and a 'dead' one, the problem of determining the appropriate level of abstraction is not solved, merely emphasised in a slightly different manner.

It seems, therefore, as though diastematicism was the true substance of music for Schoenberg. Yet it can hardly be denied that he sometimes – as in the first of the Five Orchestral Pieces, Op. 16 – composed motivic connections which can be explained only if one starts out from the concept of a diastematic 'outline', a concept which implies that the intervals are, on the contrary, anything but precisely fixed. All that is certain is that, for example, a small interval is followed by a larger one and the larger one, in turn, by a smaller one. The technical concept of the outline corresponds to the aesthetic fact that it is often an expressive gesture which provides the starting-point for a work.

The need sometimes to regard a mere outline as the primary musical element is moreover not the only circumstance that prevents a one-sided concern with interval structure. The idea of diastematics proves especially precarious in twelve-note music, to which from another point of view it is central. In 'My Evolution' (1949) Schoenberg described 'all self-contained units of a piece' as being 'derivatives of the tonal relations' in a 'basic set of twelve tones'.[6] Strictly speaking, however, it is virtually impossible to understand what he meant by 'tonal relations', if in the vertical dimension the grouping of notes can remain open and if in the horizontal dimension motivically effective intervals can arise from the movement of the row between the voices – intervals which are not contained in the row at all.

Irritating though it may be at first sight, the imprecision of the expression 'basic shape' – whose meaning can vary between an actual theme defined in all its parameters, an abstract interval structure and a still more abstract basic pattern reaching back behind the intervals to mere outline and expression, is unavoidable to the extent that the degree of abstraction on which an analysis is based either depends or should depend on the specific character of the work. Whether it is appropriate to start out from an interval structure, a melodic outline or a specific rhythmic–diastematic shape can only be decided from case to case, not on the basis of a general principle. When, as in Beethoven's *Diabelli Variations*, diastematic, rhythmic and syntactic elements (syntactic in the sense of the form of a sequence abstracted from its content) are separated from a theme one by one and elaborated in isolation, it would be inappropriate merely to follow Rudolph Réti's method of reconstructing a 'basic shape' or 'cell' which consists of nothing but a structure of intervals. Where form as a whole is concerned, it is much more likely that the complete theme with all its features acts as the 'basic shape'. On the other hand, in other works, such as the first movement of Beethoven's *Les adieux* Sonata, it may well be useful to speak of a 'subthematic' structure which exists as an abstract, diastematic entity without the defining features of rhythm, metre or harmony. For it is a structure at a high level of abstraction – the chromatic progression of a fourth or third in the form of direct or indirect tonal relations – that mediates between introduction, principal and subordinate themes and elaboration, and thus determines the unity of the whole; and it is only as the correlative of this unity that one can determine a suitable level of abstraction for defining elements such as theme, basic shape and idea.

III

In the compound term 'developing variation', the word variation denotes a (to a certain extent) tangible aspect of compositional technique; the word development, by contrast – a word which Schoenberg equated with 'growth' – denotes a form of aesthetic interpretation. Moreover the implications contained in the concept of development derived from Aristotle are by no means unproblematic.

In the first place, the process whereby a second motif derives from a first, and a third from the second, does not always imply that the third is still connected with the first by means of some common feature. But while one may sense a derivational unity, it is not always possible to speak of a uniform substance as posited by a concept of development reminiscent of growth from a seed.

Secondly, the custom of labelling motifs alphabetically and variants numerically is unclear inasmuch as it remains an open question whether the numbering refers to a temporal proximity or distance or to a substantive one; and the concept of development misleadingly suggests that the one coincides as a matter of principle with the other – whereas the most cursory analysis of a sonata movement by Haydn, Beethoven or Brahms is enough to show that what comes earlier chronologically is by no means always the more closely related with regard to content.

Thirdly, the technique of introducing motifs or themes without any initial substantive connection between them and then drawing them closer together cannot be understood in terms of the concept of development and has therefore been neglected in analytical practice. The concept of development merely denotes the process whereby an idea stated at the outset is differentiated in order to generate various later shapes; it does not apply to the opposite process whereby heterogeneous motifs subsequently grow together, though it is just this process that characterises the beginning of the period of thematic–motivic work as represented by the first movement of Haydn's String Quartet Op. 33, No. 1.

Fourthly, in addition to temporal and substantive proximity or distance there is a third aspect at work in developing variation, an aspect which can be described as formal context. A motivic relationship that is remote substantively may of course be recognised without difficulty when it links formally analogous passages – the beginnings of antecedent and consequent, or corresponding bars in a set of variations. The same applies to the principle of contrasting derivation, which is assumed to be effective between the principal and subordinate themes of a sonata movement but not between the rondo and the episode sections of a rondo.

The concept of entelechy – the goal-directed process of development – and the notion of musical space in which all the motivic shapes and relationships that serve to present an idea are collected together in imaginary simultaneity: these two concepts, even though they contradict each other or seem to contradict each other, were in a similar way constitutive elements of Schoenberg's musical thinking; and this indicates the direction in which a resolution of the difficulties outlined above must be sought. To put into practice and make manifest in composition the dialectical unity underlying these divergent concepts is the idea which – as the perfect example of a problem that admits of no definitive solution – forms the substance or hidden basis of the principle of developing variation.

Schoenberg and Schenker

The dispute between Arnold Schoenberg and Heinrich Schenker – witness Schoenberg's ironical remarks in the *Harmonielehre*[1] and Schenker's vigorous polemics in the second volume of *Das Meisterwerk in der Musik*[2] – was in the first instance a controversy concerning the significance of non-harmonic notes, a subject which appears harmless enough. The dispute as such would be hardly worth examining if it revealed nothing beyond each antagonist's lack of understanding of the other and the failure of both to do justice to the subject about which they claimed to be speaking. But beneath the surface of a discussion about technical details is concealed a conflict of fundamental principles concerning modes of musical thought – modes of thought which cannot simply be reduced to the clichés of 'progressive composer' and 'conservative theorist'.

According to traditional music theory, which is of eighteenth-century origin, non-harmonic notes – suspensions, passing notes, changing notes and anticipations – differ from chordal dissonances in that their resolution does not involve a change of harmony, that is, the movement of the fundamental; so that in Ex. 1a the dissonant c^2 is a non-harmonic dissonance, but in Exx. 1b and 1c a chordal dissonance. Chordal disson-

Ex. 1

ances, which influence the progression of the fundamental, are considered 'essential' dissonances, whereas non-harmonic notes are 'incidental' dissonances. Whether a dissonance belongs to the harmony or not thus depends less on the structure of the individual chord than on its function within the context of the progression. A non-harmonic dissonance does not impinge on the harmonic progression; it is melodically motivated and has a momentary colouristic effect, without being of harmonic conse- quence – of consequence, that is, to the progression as a series of related individual chords.

Traditional theory was rejected by both Schenker and Schoenberg, but on opposite grounds: Schenker denied the concept of the 'essential' dis- sonance and Schoenberg that of the 'incidental'. In Schenker's theory of structural levels the passing note is a basic category: the system of linear progressions to which he reduced a musical work is a system of passing notes. According to Schenker the consolidation of a seventh or ninth into a chordal dissonance is merely an illusion, a foreground phenomenon, the nature of which a listener who is capable of grasping the middleground and background will recognise as being a passing note.[3] In Schenker's theory passing notes are non-harmonic notes in the most extreme sense of the term: 'It is as if a vacuum existed between the dissonant passing note and the stationary cantus firmus note.'[4] The acoustical fact of dissonance has no musical relevance.

Schoenberg on the other hand attempts to show exactly the opposite, namely, that the term 'non-harmonic' is a misnomer.[5] He maintains first that, in a musical masterpiece at least, no note is without influence on the harmonic progression.[6] Its harmonic consequence – that is, its conse- quence within the context of the harmonic progression – may admittedly be at times difficult to discern, but is never wholly absent. Secondly, the dissonant harmony resulting from a suspension or passing note must be understood in itself as being a chord: as an essential and not an incidental phenomenon.[7] Calling a dissonance a suspension or passing note is simply an attempt at justification; the dissonance itself, however, represents the real end at which the composer was aiming.[8] And thus legitimation by means of contrapuntal considerations can be dispensed with as soon as one is able to grasp the dissonance in itself, as an 'emancipated dissonance'.

Both Schenker and Schoenberg disregarded the evidence of normal listening. Schoenberg was possessed by the idea that no musical occur- rence is, or should be, without significance for the context, for the musical logic. Taken strictly, his assertion that non-harmonic notes, notes with- out harmonic influence, do not exist is an aesthetic postulate, rooted in the opposition to all things ornamental and without function, rather than a description of musical reality. Schenker, on the other hand, used the fact that the vertical element in the case of some passing notes is almost imperceptible and of no consequence[9] as the basis for the speculative conclusion that all passing notes are to be heard exclusively horizontally, whether they belong to the foreground, the background or the middleground of a musical work. Thus while Schoenberg demands that the consequence for the harmonic progression of even the most fleeting dissonance must be taken account of, Schenker postulates the exact opposite: that the dissonant nature of even the harshest vertical combinations must be disregarded in order to penetrate the musical surface and arrive at the horizontal progressions upon which coherence depends.

Schoenberg and Schenker were arguing at cross purposes: neither tried to understand the motives and intentions of the other, and each strove to ridicule individual contentions of his opponent taken out of context. Schoenberg reproaches Schenker for reducing the concept of harmony to the triad and dwells with irony on a digression into mysticism of numbers,[10] without taking into consideration the function performed by the restricted concept of harmony within a system of categories whose aim it is to explain coherence in music: to present an answer to the question of why a musical process stretching over hundreds of bars should be experienced as a self-contained unity and not as a series of disjointed and heterogeneous moments. Schenker, on the other hand, using his own concept of the passing note, has little difficulty in showing that Schoenberg had not grasped the true nature of the passing note – the discovery of which he, Schenker, had been the first to make.[11] Schenker's conviction that his own theory matches the nature of the matter is so absolute that he expects any sensible musician to recognise a phrase with a sequential progression of fifths as its fundamental bass (G–C–F–B flat–E flat–A–D–G) as having a falling fourth (G–F–E flat–D) as its framework, the remaining notes being merely passing notes.

Viewed methodologically, Schoenberg's and Schenker's contentions regarding non-harmonic notes really result from the questionable procedure of using extreme instances as typical examples. Schenker's observation, that passing notes in Palestrina are almost imperceptibly dissonant, is just as indisputable as Schoenberg's point of departure, that in the *Tristan* chord, quite to the contrary, the 'justification by the melodic element' – through the suspension – is simply a means to the end of presenting the dissonance as a chordal sonority. (This is not to deny, of course, that the suspension's urge for resolution – an historical implication of the chord – is an integral constituent of its expressive character.) From such phenomena, however, whose perception they share with the normal listener, both Schoenberg and Schenker quickly proceed to speculation. And to the objection that the empirical foundation of their theories was too weak they might well have replied that such a charge amounted to an attempt to establish in the realm of music theory a dictatorship of mediocrity.

On the other hand Schoenberg's and Schenker's reference to extreme instances is by no means mere exaggeration which could be put right by taking a middle course; their method is part of the substance of the two opposing theories. Schenker had no alternative but to deny that he was elevating a peripheral phenomenon to the status of a musical norm; the admission that his empirical concept of the passing note had become, in the course of a few steps in his argument, a speculative concept would have radically altered the sense and logic of the whole system. Schenker persists in his contention that the middleground and background are not merely artificial constructs but matters of perception – intuitive perception. As a speculative hypothesis the system of linear progressions in the middleground and fundamental structure in the background served as a means of explaining and making comprehensible a fact of perception – the impression of compelling musical coherence over long stretches – without, however, itself claiming to be a matter of perception. But Schenker considered his theory as instruction in musical listening: the depiction of musical reception as implicitly predefined in musical masterpieces and as a challenge to the listener.

Schoenberg's counterthesis, that the term 'non-harmonic note' is a misnomer, since even the most transitory passing note has some influence on the harmonic process, however slight, is at once plausible and questionable: plausible, because it corresponds to a musical feeling; questionable, because by 'harmonic process', traditional theory, in reducing the perceived to the demonstrable, understood exclusively the progressions of the fundamental bass and the resolution of dissonances in relation to it. This limitation of the concept was by implication accepted by Schoenberg when he attempted (albeit without success) to justify non-harmonic notes by means of latent fundamental progressions.[13]

According to Collingwood, the understanding of a text implies the reconstruction of the question to which it represents an answer. And with regard to the chapter on non-harmonic notes, one might contend that the problems of Schoenberg the composer in the period around 1910 must be taken into account in any attempt to do justice to the ideas of Schoenberg the theorist, speaking apparently of an aspect of the dead past. The expression 'non-harmonic note' reveals itself on closer analysis to be a cipher.

At first sight it might well appear that after the abandonment of tonality Schoenberg would be more likely to emphasise the motivic and contrapuntal foundations of dissonance rather than its harmonic function. For Schoenberg, however, 'justification by the melodic element' was something he took for granted, not a problem that occupied his mind. What he was attempting to find – without knowing whether he would succeed – was the possibility of demonstrating, and not merely feeling, the harmonic importance of non-harmonic notes. And when he speaks of the non-harmonic notes of traditional theory he is also referring to the emancipated dissonance of his own atonal compositional practice; otherwise the emphasis of his argument is inexplicable.

The difficulty in which Schoenberg had landed through the emancipation of the dissonance is concealed by the vagueness of the contention that emancipated and unresolved dissonance is immediately comprehensible. The expression 'comprehensibility' is ambiguous. It implies either that a dissonant chord can function plausibly in itself, without the support of a consonance, or that even outside the traditional system of fundamental progressions and resolution of dissonance it can have a real function in the harmonic context, instead of being merely transitory in effect. For Schoenberg, the harmonic plausibility of emancipated dissonance was an established fact about which he had no doubts; its harmonic function, however, was a problem which, at least for the time being, he was unable to solve.

The concept of the non-harmonic note in Schoenberg's argument is consequently a code name for that of emancipated dissonance. When he maintains that a non-harmonic note must be regarded as impinging on the harmonic development, what he means primarily is that an emancipated dissonance is neither purely melodic in function nor its harmonic effect merely transitory, but that it may also bring about harmonic coherence. And however questionable Schoenberg's thesis, that the dissonance is the purpose of the passing note and the melodic procedure only a means and justification, when applied to the past, it shows distinctly that in his attempts to demonstrate the harmonic functions of non-harmonic notes, which traditional theory – and Schenker above all – interpreted exclusively in melodic terms, he was privately thinking of emancipated dissonance, whose significance for harmonic coherence represented a problem which beset him during the free atonal period. It was this problem that he later – incorrectly – believed to have been solved by dodecaphony.

Schoenberg, though he dissolved tonality, nevertheless strove against abandoning the function which it had performed.

Schoenberg, who detested being called a revolutionary, would doubtless have found offensive the suggestion that he fell short of Schenker in his reverence for the masterpieces of the past. He considered himself a perpetuator of tradition, and the theoretical projects left unfinished at his death revolve about a problem which Schenker too recognised to be of central importance: the problem of how musical coherence is to be established. But between the answers that Schoenberg and Schenker gave to the same question lies a gulf which could hardly be imagined deeper. One could of course simply dismiss one of the two theories as false, or alternatively maintain that music is nothing but a substratum of acoustics, which may be stamped arbitrarily with categorical formulations of differing extremes. But a historian who does not wish to surrender either to dogmatism or to scepticism must attempt to explain how it is possible for Schoenberg's and Schenker's interpretations of musical tradition to coexist.

It is manifest that Schenker, when speaking of coherence, meant primarily tonal coherence, whereas Schoenberg thought of motivic coherence. The conflict of opinion is reduced if one views the matter in historical perspective: it appears less marked when one takes into account the fact that in the instrumental forms of the eighteenth and nineteenth centuries, although tonal and motivic development were closely related, the accent gradually shifted from tonal to motivic structure. Schenker and Schoenberg, while ostensibly talking about the same thing, were therefore directing their attention to different stages of musical history. Schenker's fundamental structure is a formula for the passage from the tonic to the dominant and back to the tonic. In Schoenberg's musical thinking, on the other hand, the central category, whether the aim is to explain coherence in the work of other composers or to establish coherence in his own, is the concept of developing variation. This is to be understood as an extension of the principle of thematic–motivic work, in that besides derivations from clearly defined themes or motives it also embraces intervallic and rhythmic relationships which remain partly hidden instead of being immediately recognisable by their motivic profile.

For Schoenberg musical coherence, the principles of which he endeavoured to establish, meant logic in sound. A musical work, whether in the process of composition or as experienced by the listener, appeared to him as a discourse which emerged with compelling consequence from the particular and individual quality of the material presented at the beginning, a discourse in which even the smallest detail carried in itself the necessity of its own existence. On the other hand the fundamental structure, on which Schenker based his theory, is an unchangeable law which demands fulfilment if the internal unity of a work is to be preserved. Musical coherence in Schenker's theory, unlike Schoenberg's, is not an embodiment of the consequences extracted from unrepeatable material, but an unalterable *nomos* which governs the varying formations of the foreground. Schenker, for whom the nature of a matter is contained in its origin, seeks the law concealed behind the manifestation. Schoenberg on the other hand, aspiring more to ends than to origins, follows the consequences that emerge from a musical idea. His traditionalism consists less in the discovery of the past in the present than in the discovery of the future in the past.

Schoenberg's Orchestral Piece Op. 16, No. 3 and the concept of *Klangfarbenmelodie*

Schoenberg's Orchestral Piece Op. 16, No. 3 has become famous for its connection with a term which is as memorable as it is difficult to understand. This is the term 'Klangfarbenmelodie', which Schoenberg coined in 1911 at the end of his *Harmonielehre*. He postulated that it should be possible to create progressions out of tone colours, 'progressions whose relations with one another work with a kind of logic entirely equivalent to that logic which satisfies us in the melody of pitches. That has the appearance of a fantasy of the future and is probably just that. But it is one which, I firmly believe, will be realised.'[1] The connection between Op. 16, No. 3 and the concept of *Klangfarbenmelodie* became suspect, however, because it was at first misinterpreted and then disputed.

The fact that the orchestral piece begins with a five-note chord repeated for three bars in varying instrumentation, but otherwise unchanged, encouraged the simplistic explanation that a *Klangfarbenmelodie* must be the varied coloration of a single sustained pitch.[2] This excessively narrow definition of the concept meant, however, that there could be no question of a *Klangfarbenmelodie* in Op. 16, No. 3.[3] For in the first place it was undeniable that although the pitches in the piece changed slowly, they changed nevertheless. Secondly, Schoenberg described *Klangfarbenmelodie* in 1911 as a 'fantasy of the future': Op. 16, No. 3, however, had already been composed in 1909. The first argument shares with the hypothesis it challenges the assumption that a *Klangfarbenmelodie* is to be understood as the varied instrumentation of the same pitches. But just as a change in pitches need not necessarily present itself in a single tone colour in order to be a melody, so a change of instrumentation, in order to appear as a *Klangfarbenmelodie*, need not necessarily be confined to a single sustained pitch. Instrumentation becomes *Klangfarbenmelodie* not because the pitch melody dwindles to monotony but because a balance is achieved between instrumentation and pitch melody in place of the usual predominance of the latter. Schoenberg achieves the balance in Op. 16, No. 3 by reducing the melodic element, not by abolishing it. The second argument – the objection that is bound up with the words 'fantasy of the future' – seems more convincing but is, however, not indisputable. According to Schoenberg, it is 'probably' a 'fantasy of the future' that alternating tone colours should 'work with a kind of logic' which is 'equivalent' to the logic of pitch melody. The sentence is not unambiguous. Either it means that *Klangfarbenmelodie* is a utopian dream, a piece of 'music of the future'; or it signifies that it already exists in embryo but without its logic having as yet been recognised. The second interpretation can draw on the argument that the discussion of *Klangfarbenmelodie* occurs in a chapter devoted to chords of which the same is true, that they were written at a time when it was not yet possible to explain and justify them theoretically. Thus Schoenberg himself was not sure whether Op. 16, No. 3 demonstrated the logic of alternating tone colours, in the possibility of which he believed; but in any case the piece was meant to be a first attempt on those lines. And so he was able to say of *Klangfarbenmelodie* – whose existence becomes apparent only when its logic is comprehended – that it was 'probably' a 'fantasy of the future'.

Schoenberg's *Harmonielehre* closes with the words: 'Tone-colour melodies! How acute the senses that would be able to perceive them! How highly developed the spirit that can find pleasure in such subtle things! In such a domain, who dares ask for theory!'[4] By 'ability to perceive' and 'subtlety' Schoenberg cannot have meant merely the perception of alternating tone colours, on the one hand, or an analytical appreciation of the overtone structures on which the tone colours are based, on the other: the one would be too simple to justify Schoenberg's emphasis, the other too illusory for his certainty to be comprehensible. It seems, rather, that Schoenberg was thinking of a feeling for the 'logic' of a series of tone colours, a feeling which was as yet undeveloped but which had the capacity to be developed. One can base an attempt at a more precise definition of what Schoenberg had in mind on Helmholtz's *Die Lehre von den Tonempfindungen*, a book which Schoenberg, for all his pretended lack of erudition, had presumably studied before writing his *Harmonielehre*; for he shares with Helmholtz two striking ideas that depart from the general run of music theory: first the view that the difference between consonance and dissonance is one of degree, not of kind,[5] and secondly the conviction that tonality is not a natural law of music but merely a formal principle.[6] Thus, if one assumes that Schoenberg had at least a cursory acquaintance with *Die Lehre von den Tonempfindungen*, it is clear that he could have deduced the idea of a 'logic' of *Klangfarben-melodie* from what Helmholtz says about the 'logic' of the melody of pitches. According to Helmholtz, the 'feeling for the melodic relationship between consecutive notes' is based on the unconscious 'sensation of similar overtones in the sounds in question'.[7] A corresponding 'logic' of *Klangfarbenmelodie* is indeed more complicated than the logic of pitch melody, inasmuch as the coincidence of overtones on which it is based is more involved. But it is not inconceivable. Certainly Schoenberg did not postulate by this that one could listen to the overtones analytically; as Helmholtz did with regard to the relationship between pitches, he thought simply of a 'feeling' for tone-colour relationships, a feeling rooted in an unconscious 'sensation of similar overtones'. The feeling for a systematic connection of tone colours analogous to that of pitches is still undeveloped; but again it was Helmholtz who was convinced that the capacity for hearing tone colours could be increased,[8] thus enabling Schoenberg to derive support from him for his 'fantasies of the future'.

'The Obbligato Recitative'

The title Arnold Schoenberg gave to the last of his Five Orchestral Pieces, Op. 16, 'The Obbligato Recitative' [*Das obligate Rezitativ*], seems puzzling and self-contradictory if the words obbligato and recitative are taken to mean what they do in ordinary usage; for the obbligato, strict style is hardly compatible with the form of the recitative. The paradoxical wording is however no mere caprice, which it would be unnecessarily and inappropriately pedantic to brood over, but an attempt to express a specific idea of form – and the more firmly convinced Schoenberg was of the importance of this idea, the more agonising was the difficulty he experienced in finding words to convey exactly what he meant.

On 22 January 1912 he noted in his Berlin Diary, concerning a lecture he had given without a script: 'All the same I managed to present and justify my idea about the "obbligato recitative" (oddly enough I forgot to call it by this name) reasonably clearly. But not quite. The idea is more profound: one expresses the inexpressible in free form.'[1] Schoenberg therefore regarded recitative as the perfect example of a free form (though it should be added that the use of the word 'recitative' in the title of Op. 16, No. 5 would not be sufficiently explained by accusing him of indulging in a simple inversion: that is, of calling a free form recitative because a recitative represented a free form). And it was precisely in a free – asymmetrical as well as athematic – form that he wished to make a binding, 'obbligato' statement, instead of relying on the formulas of traditional recitative. That he took the musically binding statement as an expression of the 'inexpressible' is to be understood in the light of Schopenhauer's metaphysics of music, to which Schoenberg subscribed in his essay 'The Relationship to the Text' (also 1912):[2] the more rigorously

144

music becomes committed to itself as a language in its own right, instead of relying on a text or programme, the more clearly it 'reveals the innermost essence of the world', which the language of words cannot reach.

It is not that music is eloquent in a verbal sense, as in traditional recitative, but rather that music itself constitutes a language and does not exhaust itself merely in being a structure. This is the essence of the obbligato – musically binding – recitative as realised in Schoenberg's Op. 16, No. 5: it is a question of eloquent music, music that 'speaks', without the *Hauptstimme* of the piece bearing the least resemblance to recitative in the usual sense of the word.

In a diary entry of 28 January 1912 Schoenberg considered, as variants of the concept of 'obbligato' recitative, the wordings 'worked-out' or 'endless' recitative,[3] wordings to which however he did not return. (The Five Orchestral Pieces were composed in 1909; but the titles over which Schoenberg was reflecting in 1912 – undecided about whether or not to give in to the pressure of the publisher, who wanted titles – were not included in the score until 1922.) 'Worked-out' is weaker than 'obbligato', for the concept of the obbligato includes the idea of the binding statement as well as that of rigorous construction – and 'binding' in a sense which reaches beyond the tonal phenomenon. The word 'endless', on the other hand, when associated with a musical term, inevitably recalls Wagner's 'endless melody'. It is uncertain, however, whether in Schoenberg's case a precise understanding of the Wagnerian term can be assumed, or whether he understood it in its imprecise, popular sense – one which borders on misunderstanding. In the common parlance of music aesthetics 'endless melody' meant a stream of music which seemed unstructured and formless to the listener. And the supposition that using the word 'endless' in 'endless recitative' implies that Schoenberg as it were translated a piece of (dubious) Wagner criticism into compositional practice could find support in a letter Schoenberg wrote to Richard Strauss on 14 July 1909, in which he described the Orchestral Pieces as 'not at all symphonic, the absolute opposite in fact, no architecture, no structure. Just a colourful, uninterrupted alternation of colours, rhythms and moods.'[4]

The atectonic, caesura-less, asymmetrical style is however the mere exterior manifestation of an aesthetic idea which Schoenberg shared with Wagner and which was expressed by both the principle of endless melody and that of obbligato (or endless) recitative: the idea that music, in order to satisfy the metaphysical claims formulated by Schopenhauer, must at every moment be 'significant' – 'eloquent' in a sense reaching beyond the limits of verbal language. Nothing should be tolerated that does not justify itself as a musical idea: formulas, padding and ornaments are judged empty and insignificant, and are thus excluded from the binding, musically compelling style which both Schoenberg and Wagner had in mind.

According to Wagner[5] a musical structure is 'melodic' to the extent that it is eloquent. (The term 'endless melody' was misunderstood because people, preoccupied with thinking about the word 'endless', failed to appreciate that it was first and foremost the expression 'melody' that required interpretation.) And a melody (in the emphatic sense of the word) is endless when every note 'says' something, when, that is to say, the melodic development – the meaningful discourse in sound – does not constantly break off to make room for 'unmelodic' interpolations which have the empty, insignificant quality of formulas. The technical features – that is, asymmetry and the avoidance of formal cadences – are a mere consequence of the aesthetic principle: symmetries are barely conceivable without padding, and cadences are liable to be regarded as mere formulas, that is to say, as insignificant. The aesthetic postulate – that the melody (in the emphatic sense) should not be allowed to break off – mediates between the technical aspects and the metaphysical claim that is inherent in the terms 'endless' and 'obbligato' (or 'binding'): the claim that music, whether as endless melody or as obbligato recitative, expresses 'the innermost essence of the world'.

For Schoenberg around 1910, the difference between vocal music and instrumental music seemed a secondary concern, as the essay 'The Relationship to the Text' shows: even in vocal works it is the music that constitutes the 'real language', the text being a mere illustration or translation. Yet the metaphysics of music that Schoenberg borrowed from Schopenhauer hardly seems consistent with the assertion that in the atonal works of the pre-dodecaphonic period the music either shrank to extreme brevity or had to rely on a text as its primary form-building principle. But the contradiction we are dealing with is not an incapacitating one; it is a dialectical contradiction that describes the problem of which the obbligato recitative must be seen as the solution. In Op. 16, No. 5 – a piece which is 136 bars long, so that it can hardly be called aphoristic – Schoenberg drew all those conclusions from atonality which around 1910, before he invented or discovered twelve-note technique, he found compelling, even if they endangered the form: the syntax is asymmetrical, the melodic and polyphonic structure athematic and the form non-repetitive, without the inner coherence of the work being determined by a text or programme. Rather, the *Hauptstimme* unfolds freely, as a chain of constantly new musical ideas. The Fifth Orchestral Piece is therefore obbligato in an emphatic sense: it demonstrates that music can be fashioned in a binding manner without the support of a text, even when it assumes the consequences of atonality. At the same time the instrumental piece is a commentary on *Erwartung*: it shows that the atonal, asymmetrical and athematic structure of the opera does not force one to see the text as being the primary aesthetic factor. In the terms of Schopenhauer's metaphysics, even the opera is 'absolute' music.

The characteristic features of the orchestral piece may, as we have seen, be deduced from the idea that every note – 'indeed, every rhythmic rest', to quote Wagner – must be eloquent: Schoenberg was not prepared to tolerate lack of substance for the sake of the formal function which a phrase performs.[6] But to eschew padding leads inexorably to asymmetry, for a 'four-square' metrical structure can hardly be composed without a certain amount of patchwork and flourishes which in themselves are 'empty and insignificant'. And along with symmetry which seemed to him artificial in the bad sense Schoenberg abandoned repetitions which he felt superfluous: it belongs to the essence of recitative that it constantly says something new, and to the essence of obbligato that it expresses ideas instead of mere clichés.

In any case, the features that characterise obbligato recitative were later summed up by Schoenberg in his article 'Brahms the Progressive' (1933) under the concept of musical prose. (The connection was recognised by Jan Maegaard,[7] though the way he expressed it was not unambiguous.) Musical prose is asymmetrical. It is the antithesis of 'four-square' structure, of the principle of musical verse; it expresses musical ideas without embellishment, patchwork or empty repetitions;[8] it tends constantly to say new things, instead of submitting to a formal scheme which uses repetitions and correspondences to create a piece of tonal architecture;[9] and it is 'absolute' inasmuch as a text is of secondary aesthetic importance compared to music, the 'real language'. (Schoenberg allowed a free musical utterance to pass as musical prose in the narrower sense only when the asymmetry was not externally imposed, through dramaturgical necessities,[10] but grew internally, out of the music itself.)

In addition to the features that obbligato recitative has in common with musical prose, the obbligato in Op. 16, No. 5 also includes among its qualities or defining characteristics unusually full, dense polyphony (ranging from three to six voices): the traditional idea of the obbligato, strict style is connoted in Schoenberg's concept. On the other hand, the *Nebenstimmen*, like the *Hauptstimme*, are examples of musical prose and therefore of 'recitative': they are asymmetrical, athematic and non-repetitive. According to this view, the paradox of the Fifth Orchestral

Piece, as the title suggests or paraphrases, would consist in this (among other things): that the densest polyphony, which inevitably evokes the traditions of canon and fugue, and thus the principles of imitation and repetition, is bound up with a rigorous avoidance of melodic and polyphonic restatement. The piece is free and strictly organised at one and the same time.

Expressive principle and orchestral polyphony in Schoenberg's *Erwartung*

I

Schoenberg's *Erwartung* has been understood by contemporaries and historians in two ways: on the one hand – regarded from the perspective of *Geistesgeschichte** – as the musical epitome of Expressionism, on the other – seen in terms of the history of composition – as the realisation of the idea of a music that is athematic and not definable by formal categories.[1] These judgments are clearly based on the idea that expression and form or structure are mutually opposed, as if one principle predominated at the expense of the other. Theodor W. Adorno, by contrast, who distrusted rigid oppositions and thus preferred to perceive and emphasise the interdependence of extremes rather than the way they diverged, described Schoenberg's *Erwartung* as 'case study and construction in one'.[2] 'The seismographic registration of traumatic shock becomes, at the same time, the structural law of the music. It forbids continuity and development.'[3] The lack of 'continuity and development' should not be taken as a negation of form, but as a 'structural law' in itself. To borrow a phrase from Adorno's *Ästhetische Theorie*, expression and form are conveyed through one another: 'When works are not properly con-

---

* There is no English equivalent for this term. Mary Whittall has written: ' "Geistesgeschichte" can be translated literally as "history of spirit", "Geist" being understood in the Hegelian sense which is similarly implied in the notion of "Zeitgeist" or spirit of the age. As a concept adopted by cultural historians (predominantly in Germany during the period 1920–50), Geistesgeschichte thus refers to the way in which cultural phenomena become subsumed under, and thereby seen as direct manifestations of, a single, all-pervading Zeitgeist peculiar to the epoch in question.' Translator's note to Dahlhaus, *Realism in Nineteenth-Century Music* (Cambridge, 1985), p. vii. [Trans.]

structed, properly formed, they lose that very expressiveness for the sake of which they dispense with formal rigour.'[4] An analysis of *Erwartung* – an interpretation which does not accept the premiss that the work cannot be analysed – ought therefore to try to describe those structural elements which form the basis of the expressiveness; and it ought to try to make that sense of form which Adorno defined exclusively in negative terms – as an absence of 'continuity and development' – comprehensible in terms of compositional technique.

The use of historical categories tends to obscure what is new and unique. But if it may be permitted for just a moment, Schoenberg's *Erwartung* can be seen in two ways: on the one hand, as a *recitativo accompagnato* expanded for the length of an entire musical drama, in other words as musical declamation supported by expressive or descriptive orchestral motifs, and on the other hand as the work of a composer whose musical thinking was influenced first and foremost by the tradition of chamber music. The result is an orchestral texture which is athematic in the manner of accompanied recitative but polyphonic in the chamber music sense, a texture, therefore, which forces heterogeneous premisses together into a paradox: in the nineteenth century excessive counterpoint in a *recitativo accompagnato* was as unthinkable as athematicism in polyphonic chamber music.

The instrumentation is characterised by an avoidance of mixed colours. It is true that the bassoon is sometimes doubled, either at the unison or at the octave, by contrabassoon, violins by violas or – in the woodwind family – oboes by flutes and clarinets; but mixed colours, which are almost the rule in Strauss and Schreker, are avoided by Schoenberg, whose technique of instrumentation derives from that of Mahler. Tone colour is a means of clarification and therefore a function of the polyphony, rather than the polyphony being a function of the richness of orchestral colour. This use of unmixed colours to bring polyphonic structures into prominence is a feature reminiscent of chamber music.

Orchestral polyphony as Schoenberg understood it does not cancel out the expressiveness of the monodrama but on the contrary supports and even generates it. This would hardly need to be emphasised if the prejudice that expression and counterpoint are mutually opposed had not proved well-nigh indestructible, despite frequent refutation; so persistent is the conception, indeed, that it even haunts the thoughts of those whose musical instincts on the whole convince them of the opposite. To talk of mere 'pseudo-polyphony', as soon as contrapuntal writing becomes expressive instead of contenting itself with the expressive poverty of the archaic, is absurd in the light of *Tristan* and *Parsifal*.

From the technical point of view, expression can indeed be understood as a function of polyphony, for the more 'eloquent' a contrapuntal voice is – and the more significant what it has to say – the more emphatically it impresses itself on the consciousness of the intelligent listener as part of the contrapuntal discourse. The *espressivo* is a means of clarification and not – as detractors of Romanticism would have it – of obfuscation. And conversely the expressiveness of a contrapuntal voice is not diminished through being combined simultaneously with other 'eloquent' voices; rather – through contrast, through being thrown into relief or through some process of complementation – it is highlighted, at any rate for listeners who are capable of perceiving contrapuntal structures in general and who are not satisfied with merely registering the fact that different things have been superimposed. In expressive polyphony expression and construction are, as Adorno would say, 'conveyed through one another'.

II

The attempt to define more precisely the relation between expression and orchestral polyphony in Schoenberg's *Erwartung*, and to find some concrete analytical basis for the dialectical formula of how the different elements are conveyed through one another, requires some prior qualification of the theory that the musical structure of the work is athematic. It is surely beyond dispute that the monodrama is not based on themes or leitmotifs, and that both the Brahmsian and the Wagnerian traditions of 'musical logic' have therefore been suspended; and it seems pointless to search for 'leading chords'. But it is still an open question to what extent one can speak meaningfully of motivic connections and even of motivic (as opposed to thematic) work.

If one assumes that Schoenberg understood Webern's orchestral pieces to be symphonic movements compressed into the smallest possible space of time, it is not absurd to interpret the sections of 1–5 bars into which *Erwartung* is divided as contracted Wagnerian periods – those 'poetic–musical periods' which in the *Ring* generally extend to roughly 20–30 bars[5] (or at least, it is not absurd to suppose that Schoenberg saw them in this way). And the sections in *Erwartung* – not unlike Wagnerian periods – are not infrequently defined by means of a characteristic musical idea, which constitutes the predominant motif, albeit not the only one. Particularly striking, though by no means unique, is the motivic work in bars 245–7. At the words 'Wie kannst du tot sein?' the vocal line is based on the three-note figure e^2–d^2 sharp–a^1; this figure is extended, by means of a sequence which overlaps with the model, into e^2–d^2 sharp–a^1–

g^1 sharp–d^1. The motif is anticipated by the horns in double diminution and imitated by the woodwind, first in simple diminution and then in double diminution and inversion. The double basses counter the principal motif with a figure, d^1 flat–c^1–a, which could be a variant of it (resulting from the contraction of the tritone to a minor third) but which, when one analyses the context, proves to be the true basic motif, from which conversely the characteristic motif of bars 245–7 is derived.

Of course, the expression 'basic motif' may well be suspected of being a terminological error or at the very least an exaggeration. For while the musical idea in bars 245–7 emerges unmistakably as a motif, it is uncertain whether, to what extent and in what passages the figure D flat–C–A, which appears to be the basic substance of bars 235–49, constitutes a motif with unifying effect or whether it can merely be regarded as a pre-motivic, diastematic element.[6]

The hypothesis that it is a motif could find support, first, in the fact that the three-note figure permits a semantic interpretation and thus performs a musico-dramatic function. It appears in an exposed register of the voice in bar 415 at the words 'Wo bist du?', creating an analogy with bars 235–49 – in which the woman is presented as struggling, when faced with her dead lover, to evoke the image of the living man.

Secondly, if one assumes that the figure is a motif the way is clear to a meaningful interpretation of the form. The central compositional problem of a work whose 'structural law', as Adorno puts it, forbids 'continuity and development' is to establish reasons why the sections follow one another in the order they do. And one means of imposing unity on sharp contrasts is to interlock the end of one section with the beginning of the next. From the textual point of view, bar 242 – 'Und dann winkten wir beide' – is a conclusion (in the sense that the character is lost in recollection). Musically, however, 'a tender thought . . . [is] expressed by a quick and violent theme', as Schoenberg wrote in the *Blauer Reiter* (1912), 'because the following violence will develop from it more organically'.[7] Vehemently explosive figures in the orchestra anticipate dynamically – though not melodically – the singer's 'Nein, nein, es ist nicht wahr' in the next bar. Yet the contrasts do not remain unmediated. Rather, the counterpoint of the horns and trombones in bar 242 is a *fortissimo* variant of the figure that was played 'sehr zart' by the oboe in bar 241 of the previous section. The dynamic and expressive contrast is conveyed motivically – to the extent that one can speak of a motif at all, for what is involved is none other than the three-note figure D flat–C–A, whose motivic status is not entirely clear.

It would be fruitless to try to make the question of whether these are motifs or pre-motivic linguistic elements dependent on psychological tests to establish the audibility of connections which may or may not be interpreted as motifs. On the other hand, it is not enough that a motivic relationship can be deduced from the notes. Rather, the essential criterion must be whether the connection is form- or structure-building, and that in a sense which accords with the form and structure of the work as a whole; the individual relationship only becomes what it is through the system in which it is subsumed.

Whether the three-note figure D flat–C–A, which appears in bars 235–49 of *Erwartung* in varying degrees of clarity and definition, is essential or – in part, at least – merely an accidental feature depends, therefore, on its relationship to the constitutive features of the work: to the characteristic configuration of expression and orchestral polyphony.

III

The principle that forms the basis of Schoenberg's counterpoint – in *Erwartung* as in the orchestral works – is not the textbook ideal of the equality of voices but the idea that the voices should be clearly separate in function. Vocal line, instrumental *Hauptstimme*, *Nebenstimme* and accompaniment – to use a crude classification – form a hierarchy and are distinguished from one another according to the differing importance of their role in the polyphonic discourse. Bach's polyphonic technique may be recognised as the historical model as soon as one abandons the preconception that fugal texture is the central and paradigmatic type of Bachian counterpoint and acknowledges that the figured-bass polyphony of the cantatas and oratorios, with its hierarchical functions of vocal line, concertante instruments, continuo bass and supporting parts, is the prime manifestation of polyphony in an age which in musical terms can be named after the figured bass or concertante style.

But if functional differentiation of the voices is the principle both of Schoenberg's counterpoint and of Bach's, then the motivic technique in *Erwartung* – a hierarchical technique dependent on the degree of clarity – coincides exactly with a central structural feature of the work, which is its fundamental orchestral polyphony.

The process of linking motifs together – even when it is barely perceptible, and the motifs recede into the inconspicuousness of pre-motivic linguistic elements – helps to constitute both the connection between the polyphonic voices and the shaping of the individual lines. In bars 248–9 of *Erwartung* the three-note figure D flat–C–A appears in one form after another: basic shape (English horn g^1–f^1 sharp–d^1 sharp, flute c^2–b^1–g^1

sharp), inversion (cello a sharp–b–d^1 and C sharp–D–F), retrograde (cello c–e flat–e) and retrograde inversion (vocal line c^2–a^1–g^1 sharp). This dense network of relationships cannot be dismissed as a chance accumulation of the same diastematic element; at the same time it can only with difficulty be perceived as motivic work, since the diastematic connection is not reinforced by a rhythmic one. Nevertheless the semi-latent motivic technique creates a coherence among the polyphonic voices which one senses even if one is unable to define it in terms such as inversion and retrograde. On the other hand – and this is crucial – the motivic technique provides a means for the formulation and clear articulation of musical ideas.

Of course, in order to understand what Schoenberg meant by a musical idea one has to remember that he – in stark contrast to tradition, at least to the tradition of theory – regarded tonality, or the meaning of notes, simply as a means of presentation and not as the substance of musical ideas. For Schoenberg, who insisted emphatically on the principle of expression, the primary, essential element in an idea was its expressive content or gestural outline; the tonal functions and connections were secondary defining features – the means to a comprehensible formulation of the idea, not the nucleus of the original conception. Schoenberg denied that the idea was dependent on language – or else he scorned it – and clung to the notion that language could be shaped by the ideas expressed in it.

On the other hand, the substance of the idea needed to be structured tonally or in some alternative way in order to develop from a vague expressive gesture in the composer's mind into a sharply defined shape; and the other means of formulation, which competed with tonality – a means the possession of which gave Schoenberg the technical confidence to abandon tonality – was motivic technique in its polyphonic form, a technique which featured even in an 'athematic' work like *Erwartung*.

Even those latent or semi-latent relationships whose motivic status is not clear thus perform a structural function, though they are not form-building in the narrower sense; and this is closely connected with the underlying principle of the work, the idea of an expressiveness unfolded polyphonically. Musical expression that has broken away from conventions; the formulation of expressive, gestural musical ideas by means of recurring motifs or intervals (instead of tonal functions); the hierarchy of voices in the polyphonic texture based on the model of Bachian counterpoint; the gradation of motivic relationships, which range from obvious, form-building connections, counteracting the tendency of the music to break up into expressive moments, on the one hand, to semi-latent interval structures, conveying the feeling that the polyphonic voices are connected, on the other: these are the constitutive features of Schoenberg's monodrama, and they form a configuration which can be said to constitute the work's 'musical poetics'.

Schoenberg's late works

I

By common consent, an authority that is certainly not to be despised, Arnold Schoenberg is on the one hand the composer of the *Gurrelieder* and *Verklärte Nacht*, also of *Pierrot lunaire* and the George songs, and on the other the inventor or discoverer of twelve-note technique – a procedure which is regarded as esoteric and puzzling, even though the features that establish it as a method, a set of rules or a 'preformation of the material' can be explained in a few sentences which one does not even have to be able to read music to understand. The problems, which lead to all sorts of difficulties, begin only at the point where the method is translated into composition.

The connection between the early works, which became integral parts of the concert repertoire at a time when there was a revival of interest in Jugendstil and the Secession, and the dodecaphony of the 1920s – the object of enquiry of a circle of initiates, whose efforts concentrate on the philological, philosophical and compositional problems inherent in Opp. 23–5 – is disrupted or even broken completely by the image of Schoenberg we have created for ourselves. And if it seems an almost hopeless undertaking to mediate between what the public knows of the early works and what it has heard about twelve-note technique, it is still possible to sketch out some of the reasons why our view of the continuity of Schoenberg's oeuvre has been distorted.

First, the fact that the early works have become associated with Jugendstil, whose second existence has already lasted longer than its first, is more a matter of reception history than of the history of composition.

The philosophical context in which the works have been perceived for the last decade and a half* contrasts markedly with their origins. Schoenberg regarded himself as an ally of Adolf Loos, the opponent and antagonist of the Vienna Secession, not only because of personal affection but also because of their profound agreement over aesthetic convictions: Schoenberg's concept of musical prose implies, among other things, a similar hostility towards ornament to that proclaimed by Loos. We do not wish to get tangled up in a controversy as to whether these ideas, which seem to have been absorbed by later critics in such a way as to suggest an affinity with Jugendstil, should be accorded an independent aesthetic legitimacy. Nonetheless, we can see that the categories upon which an analysis or interpretation of the early works must be based – the concepts of 'musical idea', 'presentation of the idea', 'developing variation' and 'musical prose' – do not merely allow us to make a compositional connection with dodecaphony but positively demand it, thereby suggesting that we should revise our ideas about the division that has opened up between early and late works as a result of their contrasting subsequent histories.

Secondly, as the reception history of Beethoven's late works shows, one must begin by expecting that the continuity of an oeuvre which at first was apparent only to the contemplation of a small number of initiates later becomes accessible to the intuition of the public as well, that is, that the break which was initially perceived seems gradually to close. Meanwhile, the idea that it is possible to reconstruct a logical development in Schoenberg's compositions, leading from tonality to atonality, has to a certain extent been assimilated aesthetically by listeners, inasmuch as the abyss separating *Verklärte Nacht* and *Pierrot lunaire* has long since ceased to be as deep as a reading of critical works which claim that the New Music began with the emancipation of the dissonance would suggest. And by analogy it cannot be ruled out that a sense of aesthetic continuity on the part of the public, a feeling for the inner unity of Schoenberg's oeuvre, might ultimately result from the analytically ascertainable level of rigour that provided the basis for the creation of dodecaphony. As far as the reception history of his works is concerned, Schoenberg's dictum that the composer's sense of form must correspond with an as yet unrecognised logic may be inverted into the prediction that when this logic is recognised the public will at last develop a sense of form that no longer has any need of conscious reflection.

---

* Dahlhaus is writing in 1983. [Trans.]

II

Although dodecaphony appears as the object of theoretical exertion it has also attracted the questionable kind of fame that is founded on no more than hearsay. Nonetheless, the late works, which were written in the American period and which marked a partial return to tonality, have fallen victim to a neglect which has scarcely been affected by occasional performances of the String Trio, Op. 45, or of *A Survivor from Warsaw*, Op. 46. Irritated by the juxtaposition of dodecaphonic and tonal works – by the alternation between an esoteric element by which they feel repelled and a conciliatory element which they distrust – listeners have avoided the late works. Their strong confessional character – the emphasis on the Jewish aspect, which was bound to leave an indelible impression on Schoenberg's music since he never drew a distinction between person and work – has been hard to reconcile with the cosmopolitan character of the way twelve-note technique has spread, almost epidemically, since the Second World War.

Even a fragmentary attempt at a historical interpretation, one undertaken in full awareness of its inadequacies – an attempt to reconstruct some of the problems to which the late works can be understood to represent the solution – is scarcely possible in any meaningful way if we fail to consider the reasons that led to their being almost completely ousted from the general consciousness. And the fact that the reception of the philosophy of Adorno has just reached a low-point – as Adorno himself noted a few decades ago, not without bitterness, in the case of Martin Heidegger, who has in the meantime come to the fore again – should not prevent one from seeing in Adorno's interpretation (which, in fact, Schoenberg himself rejected) all the motifs collected together which for years – and in this respect Adorno's exegesis of Schoenberg may be compared to Nietzsche's criticism of Wagner – both partly blocked the way to an understanding of the late works and partly paved the way for it.

To cite simple mistakes and faults of interpretation is, to be sure, pedantic and a little churlish but is nevertheless unavoidable when they are mixed, sometimes in a convoluted way, with insights that are still worth discussing. First, Adorno's claim (in his *Philosophie der neuen Musik*) that *Die Jakobsleiter* and *Moses und Aron* remained fragments because Schoenberg was prevented from completing them by an 'unconscious distrust' regarding the possibility of producing 'major works' is pure conjecture which, by using the word 'unconscious', makes rational discussion impossible. At any rate, Schoenberg never consciously abandoned any of these works, which he worked on or was resolved to work on until his death. Secondly, Adorno assumes (though not without show-ing some scruples) that there is a distinction between dodecaphonic major works and non-dodecaphonic minor works or 'parerga', a distinction which shows itself to be utterly untenable with regard to the Second Chamber Symphony, Op. 38, *Kol Nidre*, Op. 39, the Variations on a Recitative for Organ, Op. 40, the Variations for Wind Band, Op. 43A, the Prelude, Op. 44, the *Survivor from Warsaw*, Op. 46, and the *Drei Volks-lieder*, Op. 49. Even the distinction between works with opus number and those without does not, it seems, permit any conclusions to be drawn: it would be arbitrary to see a profound categorical difference between the Suite for String Orchestra, to which Schoenberg did not assign an opus number, and the Variations for Wind Band, Op. 43A.

Thirdly, Adorno's attempt to interpret Schoenberg's late works as the expression of a 'renunciation of material' – and by material Adorno meant nothing less than the objective spirit and the way it is manifested in music – is precarious inasmuch as the dialectics he employs ultimately get lost in a jungle in which the various strands of thought are seemingly impossible to disentangle. On the one hand Adorno believes he ought to 'rescue' what he wrongly classifies as the 'minor works' by means of the argument that the historico-philosophical truth that manifests itself in the twelve-note works is confronted by a kind of 'human right' 'which is nothing more than a matter of negative necessity'.[1] In other words: it would be inhuman to condemn the present time, however wretched it may be, exclusively by the standards of a utopia whose realisation is almost unattainably remote; instead one must allow it – if only with historico-philosophical reservations – the music it needs in order to survive aesthetically. On the other hand, the 'renunciation of material' is supposed to mean that 'subjectivity finally extends incommensurably beyond the consequences and correctness of the structure':[2] the abandon-ment of dodecaphony seems like an escape to freedom. To put it in undialectical and trivial words, Adorno cannot decide whether he should praise the abnegation and dodecaphonic construction in a large pro-portion of Schoenberg's late works as a liberation from the constraints of the method or dismiss them as a patronising concession to the existing situation. His inability to decide – and he cannot extricate himself from it simply by dividing the non-dodecaphonic works into the aesthetically successful and the unsuccessful – is no coincidence, for Adorno had always regarded dodecaphony as a historical necessity and an aesthetic misfortune at one and the same time: the element of compulsion in the method was suspect to him. That does not mean that the repressive trait which he sensed it contained could be equated with existing society in a facile and non-dialectical way (according to the popular Marxist method of analogy): dodecaphony 'designs a picture of total repression but, by no means, the ideology thereof'.[3] And as a picture it is criticism, not affirmation. At the same time, however, it shares in the rationality of the modern European age, a rationality that has degenerated into falsehood: in the dialectics of enlightenment, in whose historical development man's dominion over nature ultimately resulted in the oppression of mankind by the very instruments that had been created to serve the dominion over nature. In dodecaphony the 'self-fashioned system of rules in the subjugated material' stood opposed to the subject as an 'alienated, hostile, and dominating power'.[4] The hope that in some future time, which at present cannot be foreseen, the constraints of the twelve-note method will be subsumed in a new spontaneity of free composition[5] remains an empty utopian dream, even though Adorno cautiously hints at the possibility that the postulate could provide the starting-point for a justification of Schoenberg's late works.[6] The 'objective spirit' which – so he believed – dictated his philosophy also blocked the escape-route suggested by his piety towards Schoenberg. Slowly but surely, Adorno manoeuvred his dialectics into a cul-de-sac.

On the other hand, he falls into a trap whenever he thinks he can see a way out. The term 'context of meaning', one of the basic categories in Adorno's aesthetics, is an ambiguous concept inasmuch as it remains an open question whether the context as such already guarantees meaning or whether the expressive or gestural meaning associated with a musical motif fits into a context which then defines and modifies it – similarly to the way a word fits into a sentence. In his interpretations of Schoenberg's late works Adorno decides in favour of a simple equation between meaning and consistency, albeit with traces of an uneasy philosophical conscience which is betrayed by the quotation marks placing the word 'meaning' at a distance: 'The "meaning" of music, even in free atonality, is determined solely by its inner relationships'.[7] But this crude simplification means that, in order to speak of the expressive quality of the late works, Adorno has to assume a 'destruction of "meaning"' (that is, of context) and then characterise their expressive quality as 'inlaid' (that is, as destroying consistency), a concept reminiscent of Walter Benjamin.[8] The historical model on which this thought-process is based – it is not stated but can be reconstructed from Adorno's contributions to Thomas Mann's *Doktor Faustus* – is the music of Claudio Monteverdi, which owed its expressiveness in part to its infringement (censured by Artusi) of traditional contrapuntal rules. Adorno's interpretation of Schoenberg's late works as a restoration of expression beyond the constraints of the system is the exact correlative of the comparison Adorno makes elsewhere, with reference to Ernst Krenek, between the discipline imposed by twelve-note technique and exercises in the style of Palestrina.[9] But since Adorno does not make explicit the historical analogy he has in mind, he neglects to justify it, and the argument remains to a certain extent suspended in mid-air. The problem of how the expressive quality of the dodecaphonic works may be distinguished from that of the non-dodecaphonic works – as it must if Adorno's theory is to convince – is not even touched on in passing.

III

An attempt to interpret Schoenberg's late works from the standpoint of compositional technique as well as that of the philosophy of history was made in 1955–6 by Dieter Schnebel, who described them as 're-tonal'.[10] The premiss from which he began was the surprising claim that the concept of voice was 'a category of tonal music'. And since Schoenberg never stopped thinking contrapuntally – that is, in voices – he was obliged to return to tonality. But in this return, which was thus nothing less than a chance occurrence, Schnebel believes he sees a transformation not only in historical awareness but in history itself as a process. 'But then it becomes clear that history ceases to progress only in one direction, only forwards. It can now evolve not only forwards but also backwards. This fact shows that the composer has history itself at his disposal.'

Schnebel's assumptions are partly faulty and partly incomprehensible. The concept of voice – is it really necessary to say this? – is by no means tonally founded; and since there was a form of counterpoint that existed before tonality, it is hard to go along with the hypothesis that a post-tonal counterpoint is a contradiction in terms. Conversely, there is nothing inherent in the concept of tonality – that is, the concept of functional connection between chords – that obliges one to think in terms of voices. The relationship of a dominant to a tonic is in principle independent of the register in which the notes appear; a disruption or fragmentation of the musical texture does not mean that the tonality is abolished.

Moreover, the idea that the direction of history can be reversed is incomprehensible without an explicit philosophy of time – which Schnebel fails to provide. Schnebel's fragment of theory is an aphorism which breaks off without opening the way to an advance in thought.

IV

In 1976 Heinz-Klaus Metzger sketched out an explanation of 're-tonal' music – a term he took over from Schnebel – in the form of a criticism of the criticisms that had been made of Schoenberg from a serialist standpoint.[11] Schoenberg's music contained an unresolved contradiction between the atonal–dodecaphonic pitch structure and a rhythmic–syntactic order which bore the ineradicable traces of its origins in the tonal forms of the eighteenth and nineteenth centuries. This contradiction formed the *topos* that, on the one hand, justified extending row technique to cover duration in the 1950s and, on the other, was supposed to explain why Schoenberg returned to tonality in some of his late works: by regressing in this way, it was thought, he was following the implications of the rhythmic–syntactic structure instead of those of the pitch structure.

In contrast to this, Metzger insists that in late tonal works such as *Kol Nidre*, Op. 39, the decisive factor in atonality, namely the emancipation or dissociation of the individual sound from the hierarchy of sounds, is preserved, while at the same time one of the destructive characteristics associated with twelve-note technique, the element of compulsion in the method, is avoided. Nonetheless, Metzger is reduced to the aporia of describing every sound as a 'unique individual example' while simultaneously having to maintain that the 'material that has been reduced to the same level' is 're-qualified' by tonality. It remains unclear how it is supposed to be technically possible for chords to be qualified without a hierarchy and for a tonal connection to be established if all the sonorities are strictly individualised. In the meantime, the idea that tonal functional connection can exist without it being possible to substitute one chord for another – which is to say, without sacrificing the individuality of the chords in any way – seems at present to be an empty utopian vision. And a theory of tonality which gets by without the concept of chordal hierarchy does not even begin to emerge from Metzger's attempt at an explanation. It has all the appearance of a sudden flash of intuition without any theoretical foundation.

It is possible and even likely that Metzger was thinking of a state of affairs which René Leibowitz hinted at, without describing it in detail – though the connection is not explicit. In order to explain the tonality of the post-atonal period, Leibowitz proceeds on the assumption that the declared aim of a new tonality that was supposed to be reached via dodecaphony – Schoenberg spoke of 'pantonality' – was not, in the 1920s, achieved: 'The problem of new tonal functions has remained in the balance: it has been avoided but not resolved'.[12] And in the late tonal works – Leibowitz refers, as Metzger subsequently does, to *Kol Nidre*, Op. 39 – Leibowitz believes he can recognise a tonality whose wealth of chords and chord-relationships shows the influence of compositional experiences that are indebted to dodecaphony:

Here we may find many of the tone-row principles incorporated into a freely handled tonality. All possible aggregations of the total resources of chromaticism are tried. . . . The most distant, unheard-of tonal relationships are established; there is a systematic effort not to let a single possibility of such tonal relationships go unused.[13]

Actually, however, it is not the row principle that returns in a tonal trans-formation, but a tendency which always dominated Schoenberg's musical thought and which therefore left its mark on dodecaphony in a number of essential ways: the tendency to make the most of the full chromatic stock of notes or chords within the narrowest space and – in a tonal com-position – to delay repeating a chord for as long as was possible without breaking the musical thread.

V

In order to do justice not only to dodecaphony and its apparent inner inconsistency but also to the initially irritating succession of dodeca-phonic and non-dodecaphonic works in the American period, one must start out from the simple fact that Schoenberg never abandoned the modes of thematic–motivic thinking that he had inherited from the eighteenth and nineteenth centuries. His conviction that dodecaphony was the means of continuing a tradition that stretched back to Bach and Brahms was by no means a mere 'ideology of legitimation' (to use the denunciatory jargon of sociology). Nor can Schoenberg's habit, when it came to teaching composition, of analysing works exclusively from the eighteenth and nineteenth centuries, instead of discussing the presuppo-sitions and problems of twelve-note technique, be dismissed as mere caprice on the part of a pedantic teacher who never managed to draw the conclusions that his pupils really expected of him from the premises which he believed he was obliged to present in such detail.

The idea that Schoenberg owed his twelve-note rows to intuition and not to construction, as though they were themes or melodies, is credible enough. The expression 'basic shape' – strictly speaking an inappropriate phrase in an abstract twelve-note theory, since all forty-eight forms of the row are, as Adorno says, 'equidistant . . . from a central point' – thus expresses, in Schoenberg's concrete musical poetics, a compositional reality. As 'musical idea' the 'basic shape' is more than just the first form chronologically in which the row – the embodiment of forty-eight distinct versions, all with equal rights – appears in a movement. Between the original and the retrograde inversion there exists – secretly, tacitly and contrary to the theory – a hierarchical relationship.

At the same time, Schoenberg radically transformed the concept of motif, which derived from the tradition of Beethoven and Brahms. To be sure, the idea of a vertical or harmonic motif was anticipated vaguely and sporadically in Wagner's late music dramas; but in the form that Schoenberg gave to it, it signifies a qualitative leap in musical thought. The principle of explaining and treating chords as motifs, as if they were sequences of notes projected in another direction, appears as the solution to a problem which had been caused by the emancipation of the dissonance. The decision no longer to resolve dissonances meant that chords which had hitherto been linked to each other through the necessity of progressing from dissonance to consonance were left isolated and unrelated in such a way that the whole musical structure was in danger of collapsing. One way out of this difficulty – which Schoenberg, who was rigorous where musical coherence was concerned, must have found especially serious – lay in the idea that chords, like note sequences, were or could be motifs, that is, that the vertical plane belonged to the same motivic pattern as the horizontal.

Of course, the reverse of the theory which Schoenberg called 'the unity of musical space' was an emancipation or breaking away of the diastematic element from rhythm (which cannot be a constituent element of a motif on the vertical plane); or, to be more precise, it explains the way the concept of motif is split up into its diastematic and rhythmic components. Traces of this procedure – that of establishing diastematic relationships independently of rhythmic ones and, conversely, rhythmic connections separately from diastematic ones – may be observed in composers of the nineteenth century: the former notably in Beethoven and later in Liszt, the latter above all in Schubert. Schoenberg, however, takes the separation of the elements to the extreme (and it is only because of this that one notices the historical background to the method in the nineteenth century). It is characteristic of atonal works – dodecaphonic as well as non-dodecaphonic – that rhythms function to a certain extent as themes whose diastematic element is interchangeable, and that, conversely, diastematic structures establish a connection which remains beneath the surface of the rhythmic–syntactic compositional texture. (That 'sub-motivic', rhythmically indifferent diastematic configurations guarantee the latent inner coherence of a movement can already be demonstrated in works of Beethoven; and Rudolf Réti evolved out of this fact a theory of 'thematic cells' which, because it was claimed to be universally applicable, and was unfortunately taken to sectarian lengths, has therefore become partially discredited.)

VI

If now, working on the assumption that Schoenberg never abandoned motivic thought but radically transformed it, one tries to understand the succession of dodecaphonic and non-dodecaphonic works in the American period from the standpoint of compositional technique, the expanded concept of motif we have just outlined turns out to be the decisive factor. For to the same extent that a motif can be not only a diastematic–rhythmic structure but also a structure that is either diastematic or rhythmic, without losing its unifying function, the distinction between dodecaphonic and non-dodecaphonic atonality – and even between atonality and tonality – becomes secondary, because it is simply the way a motivic connection works that has changed and not the crucial fact that it exists at all in the first place.

It is possible, though not essential, for chords to function as motifs in tonal works. On the other hand, a dodecaphonic texture in which the chords are not the direct result of the row but emerge from the notes of different, melodically based row forms requires special precautions if the chords are to be justified on contrapuntal grounds, that is, with respect to the voice leading that brings about the transition from one chord to another. The fact that the harmony is only partly based on dodecaphony means that it has to be given – as if by way of compensation – a polyphonic legitimacy.

In those theories of harmony, influenced by the model established by Moritz Hauptmann and Hugo Riemann, which are based on the concept of function, the contrapuntal implications of harmony are generally neglected: what functional theory registers in a chord is largely independent of voice-leading tendencies. Schoenberg, however, grew up in the Viennese tradition of scale-degree theory, not the Leipzig one of functional theory; and the less chords are explained functionally, through their direct or indirect relation to the tonic, the more significant the contrapuntal connections that lead from one chord to another seem to be. But a harmony which has always been permeated with counterpoint is more likely, in principle, to permit modifications of the chord structure – provided that they are contrapuntally compelling – than is the case with a functional harmony whose theory demands that every note be justified as the root, third or fifth of a tonic, dominant or subdominant.

Thus, a contrapuntal way of thinking that can explain the most remote harmonies, together with a concept of motif that embraces exclusively diastematic or rhythmic structures in addition to those that combine the two, forms the precondition that permits the constitution of tonal, dodecaphonic and (non-dodecaphonic) atonal works in equal measure and without any change in the fundamental musical thought patterns as a context of musical meaning.

VII

What Adorno calls a 'growing indifference of the material'[14] is connected in Schoenberg's late works with a return to the 'artwork of ideas' which manifests itself as unmistakably in his intention to finish *Die Jakobsleiter* after an interruption of a quarter of a century as it does in the conception of *Moses und Aron*. The latter is a confessional opera [*Bekenntnisoper*] intended as a 'major work' in the emphatic sense, whose first and second acts (1930–2) marked the conclusion of a period which – apart from a few choruses and *Von Heute auf Morgen*, the opera with the divided aims of being a conversation-piece in twelve-note technique – had been dominated exclusively by instrumental music ever since Op. 23.

The concept of 'artwork of ideas' includes, if only peripherally, programmatic instrumental music, which is not uncommon among Schoenberg's late works, starting with the *Begleitungsmusik zu einer Lichtspielszene*, Op. 34, composed in 1930, at the same time as *Moses und Aron*. There is no reason to doubt Thomas Mann's report that in the String Trio, Op. 45, Schoenberg had expressed in music the course of an illness from which he scarcely hoped to recover. And that the programme note Schoenberg jotted down for his Piano Concerto, Op. 42, is staggeringly ingenuous, direct and naive is no reason to deny its authenticity: 'Life was so easy / suddenly hatred broke out (Presto) / a grave situation was created (Adagio) / But life goes on (Rondo)'.

The supposition that Schoenberg later changed or rejected the aesthetic of programme music that he had sketched out in the 1912 essay 'The Relationship to the Text' cannot be supported, it seems, by documentary evidence. According to this aesthetic idea, a programme constitutes – in varying degrees of literary, pictorial or biographical detail – the basis for a composition and the way it is received but never the actual content and substance of a musical work. In 1912, rather, Schoenberg was convinced that it was music that expressed the 'innermost essence of the world', in the sense of Schopenhauer's metaphysical world view as transmitted through Wagner. It depicted the interior, whereas a text – in vocal music as well as in programme music – depicted merely the exterior.

The relationship between music and language that forms the basis of the dramaturgy of *Moses und Aron*, coupled with Schoenberg's return to the Jewish faith, one of whose characteristics is to take language emphatically at its word, caused the Schopenhauerian aesthetic, which was accepted unquestioningly by those German composers who preserved the Wagnerian tradition around 1900, to become suspect. The programmatic elements in instrumental works, but above all the dominance of vocal music and the character of the texts, which are invariably burdened with philosophy or biography and whose verbal form may sometimes be questionable (though their confessional seriousness places them above criticism), force us to come to an interpretation other than the one suggested by Schopenhauer's metaphysical world view, a world view which was created as a philosophy of absolute music and in which texts, programmes and scenic events appear as interchangeable surface phenomena for the music – which alone can penetrate to the profundity of the world. In Schoenberg's late works, the significance of the content has grown in proportion to the degree that the distinction between the musical means has become irrelevant. It seems that Schoenberg, in the last decades of his life, moved away from the absolute music which later became exclusively predominant in the serialism of the 1950s.

VIII

To talk of the topicality of a phenomenon that belongs to the past – and indeed to an almost forgotten past – is unquestionably a precarious exercise. For the idea that history does not repeat itself is a *topos* whose validity was not even seriously threatened by structuralism, which everywhere strove to replace the living protagonists of the history of events with anonymous structures. Nevertheless the attempt to trace the broad outlines of the parallels which suggest themselves spontaneously between Schoenberg's late works and some of the tendencies of the 1970s may count as one of those risks that historians must be permitted to take from time to time if they are not to suffocate under the mere accumulation of data and facts.

The 'growing indifference of the material' that Adorno, as we have seen, discerned in Schoenberg's late works means, first, that atonality and tonality as well as dodecaphonic and non-dodecaphonic atonality are able to exist alongside one another without the one denying the other's right to exist, and, secondly, that history – represented in Adorno's aesthetic theory by the material – had lost the power to dictate to composers what was allowed and what was forbidden. And bound up with the 'growing indifference of the material', so Adorno believed, was a restoration of musical expression, which was in danger of disappearing under the domination of dodecaphony and its systematic constraints.

The question whether or to what extent it is admissible to draw a distinction, as Adorno does, between an 'authentic' expression, which characterises one part of Schoenberg's late work, and a so to speak 'borrowed' expression, which manifests itself in the classicistic works from the Suite, Op. 25, to the Piano Concerto, Op. 42, must be left open – not because Adorno's distinction would have been disputed angrily by Schoenberg himself, but because it is impossible to make a coherent statement about the complex relationship between dodecaphony and expressive quality in a few sentences. More relevant is the circumstance that in general a connection seems to exist between emphatic expressiveness, an uninhibited alternation between atonality and tonality and a state of mind which Arnold Gehlen, writing a few years after Adorno's *Philosophie der neuen Musik*, was later to call 'post-history': a connection which came unmistakably to the surface in the 1970s in the musical phenomena that were given the absurd label of the 'New Simplicity', to the horror of the composers concerned. To keep the choice between tonality and atonality open on principle, to evade what Adorno proclaimed as the diktat and compulsive logic of history and to strive for a frankly subjective, individual expression instead of for 'objective correctness', the idol of the 1950s – in other words, all the impulses that emerged in the last decade were already present (albeit under different historical conditions) in Schoenberg's late works, without, it seems, the younger composers being aware of the connection. The fact that there is no documentary evidence that confirms this direct link need not, however, disconcert the historian: for him it is not a decisive factor. For that historical continuity or affinity can be discussed even when the protagonists of the events know nothing about it is one of the maxims without which the writing of history would not be possible – and one, therefore, to which a historian must cling if he does not wish to abandon the whole point of his profession.

The fugue as prelude:
Schoenberg's *Genesis* composition, Op. 44

In his (second) article entitled 'Composition with Twelve Tones', which probably dates from 1947,[1] Arnold Schoenberg wrote:

> I believe canonic or other imitation should serve only to create a more intimate relationship between the accompanying voices, which make the sonority fuller, and the main voice. Even the writing of whole fugues is a little too easy under these circumstances [that is, the circumstances of twelve-note composition]. Composition in those forms in which the highest achievement has already been reached by composers whose mode of expression was that of contrapuntal combination – composition in those forms should only be undertaken for some special reason. For instance, if a composer feels he must still a sort of nostalgic longing for the beauty of the past; or if he wants to demonstrate his all-round technique; or because in the course of a large-scale work – an opera, an oratorio, a cantata, etc. – one of the sections must be in the old style.[2]

The composition of fugues, which is in a way 'too easy' using twelve-note technique because there is neither some form of tonal foundation nor a regulated use of dissonance to stand in the way, may nevertheless be justified by 'some special reason'; and one of the reasons Schoenberg gives is the necessity, arising out of the idea of a work, to go back temporarily to the 'old style'.

It hardly needs saying that when Schoenberg refers to the composer who brought the fugue to its 'highest achievement' he means no one other than Bach. So when in September 1945 Schoenberg wrote his *Prelude*, Op. 44, for mixed chorus and orchestra as the introduction to a cantata on the biblical Creation story, and gave the main section the structure of a fugue or fugato, the archaising form, even though the work is dodecaphonic, must be taken as a reference to Bach, and indeed as a reference which the listener will understand as such.

169

The *Prelude* forms the beginning of a series of works on Genesis commissioned by the composer and publisher Nathaniel Shilkret; the other parts were written by Shilkret himself (The Creation), Alexander Tansman (The Fall), Darius Milhaud (Cain and Abel), Mario Castelnuovo-Tedesco (The Flood), Ernst Toch (The Promise) and Igor Stravinsky (The Tower of Babel).

That Schoenberg depicts the state of things before the Creation by means of a fugue (with introduction and coda), and so to some extent interchanges the contrasting and complementary categories of prelude and fugue, is an initially rather puzzling paradox which can only be resolved when the German tradition of Bach exegesis – that is, the tradition in which Schoenberg grew up – is taken into account. (Willi Reich's conjecture[3] that the 'extraordinarily complex structure of the work' symbolises the 'technical difficulties' involved in the creation of the world has little basis in fact. In the first place, the twelve-note structure can be analysed without much trouble; secondly, far from describing the dodecaphonic composition of fugues as complex, Schoenberg actually felt it was 'too easy'; and thirdly, the subject or idea of the work is not the Creation itself – whether or not it is 'technically difficult' – but the state of things before the Creation.)

Bars 1–24 of the *Prelude* appear as a kind of introduction to the introduction which the work as a whole represents. From the various forms of the row Schoenberg builds up melodic shapes which function like themes (basic shape in tuba and violins, bars 2–7; retrograde inversion in violins, bars 12–15); but he does not develop the implications inherent in the 'themes' – which are therefore not themes in the strict sense – in any way. The technical element, which according to Schoenberg's own criteria is like a broken promise, contains a violation of the basic tenets of Schoenbergian aesthetics or poetics, a violation which scarcely permits any explanation other than that it is meant to represent a 'Pre-Condition' in which nothing is yet decided.

The fugue or fugato (bars 25–76) consists of six entries of the subject, the last two of which are fragmentary stretti (the last of all is vocal without a text) which split up the polyphony into its thematic and motivic elements. Fugue subject and twelve-note row do not correspond; rather, the row wanders to and fro between the subject and the rhythmically complementary, strict counterpoint, which share out the dodecaphonic supply of notes between them (Ex. 1).

The subject comprises basic set and retrograde inversion, the counter-subject inversion and retrograde; and if one accepts the premiss that 'composition with twelve notes related only to one another', regarded as

Ex. 1

'pantonality', is a kind of 'substitute tonality', this arrangement, which departs from the traditional scheme, can be understood in the sense that the dodecaphonic complementation of the thematic shapes is meant to represent a substitute for the tonal complementarity of tonic and dominant.

That the fugue, despite the transformation into dodecaphony, should remind us of Bach is unavoidable and would almost go without saying even if Schoenberg had not claimed, provocatively, that Bach was 'the first composer with twelve notes' – a claim which 'was a joke, of course',[4] but which contained an element of seriousness. And the paradox that a fugue figures as prelude, indeed as a prelude depicting the moment before the creation of the world, discloses its meaning when one thinks of what is probably the most famous remark about Bach as fugue composer, a remark which every German musician, no matter how well-read or ignorant he may be, knows and treasures in his consciousness as a literary relic: Goethe's comment about Bach:

At this point I was reminded of the good organist of Berka; because it was there, while I was completely calm and without outward distractions, that I first formed an opinion of your great composer. I said to myself: it was as if eternal harmony were communing with itself, just as may have happened in God's bosom shortly before the world's creation; so in the same way my inner emotions were moved and it seemed to me as if I had neither ears nor eyes and as if I neither possessed nor needed any other senses at all.

These words occur in a letter to Zelter of 21 June 1827 (to be more precise, in a supplement to the letter). The 'good organist of Berka' – of whose playing of Bach Goethe was reminded when Zelter, prompted by mentioning a new edition of Shakespeare, came round to speak of Bach, another of the 'impenetrables' – was the Inspector of Baths and organist Johann Friedrich Schütz, whom Goethe mentions in his *Annalen* of 1814 and 1816. 'Musically cheered up by Zelter's presence and by Inspector Schütz's performance of Bach sonatas'; 'Dined at the Inspector of Baths'. After dinner, sonatas by Sebastian Bach'.[5] One must not be misled by the word 'sonatas'; Goethe obviously used it as a synonym for 'instrumental pieces'. That it was really a question of fugues is testified by a guest who was present: 'After dinner Schütz played some fugues by Sebastian Bach, which gave Goethe great pleasure. He compared them with luminous mathematical problems: their subjects were so simple and yet produced such great poetic results.'[6]

In a controversy between Rudolf Smend and Walter Wiora, which revolved around the question of whether Goethe's remarks revealed a profound understanding of Bach, based on a long tradition of musical exegesis,[7] or whether they represented no more than an impressive formulation of ideas casually picked up from Zelter,[8] one not unimportant difference has not been considered: the fundamental distinction of whether the expression 'eternal harmony' refers to the tonal system, which according to an ancient and unbroken philosophical tradition mirrors the structure of the cosmos, or whether (as with Goethe) it refers to a musical work of art whose aesthetic significance is transformed into a metaphysical one by the self-forgetting listener. The passages that Wiora cites from Johannes Kepler, Andreas Werckmeister and Johann Gottfried Herder in order to show the historical profundity of Goethe's remark[9] do indeed speak of an eternal harmony which God carried within himself before the Creation; but they use the word 'harmony' exclusively to refer to the structure of the tonal system, not to that of a work of art. (Kepler: 'Prius sunt in Archetypo, quam in Opere, prius in mente divine, quam in creaturis'; Werckmeister: [The simple proportions to which the consonances correspond] 'can reflect God's nature for us, albeit in a shadowy way, as it has always been from eternity to eternity, even from before the world was created'; Herder: [The dreamer of Kalligenia hears] 'one sound in everything, the hymn of Creation'; 'Worlds circled around me; it was as if I sensed God's thoughts here, the rule of Creation which was explained to me in harmonies by Kepler.') On the other hand, Goethe, who was thinking of Bach's fugues when he put his feeling for the metaphysical substance of music into words – words which were to have an immeasurable historical effect – used the term 'harmony', in full accordance with the theoretical usage of the eighteenth and early nineteenth centuries, to denote a polyphonic texture. The word 'conversation', which, in another context, he used to characterise the relationship between the voices in a string quartet – borrowing a *topos* which can be shown to go back to the sixteenth century – similarly refers to the relationship between the voices in a composition and not to the relationship between the notes in the tonal system.

But whilst harmony, endowed with metaphysical dignity, is to some extent reified by Goethe and brought down from the spheres of 'musica mundana' to the tonal phenomenon represented by a Bach fugue, Goethe also allows musical perception to be dissolved almost completely into some form of mystical contemplation: ' . . . it seemed to me as if I had neither ears nor eyes and as if I neither possessed nor needed any other senses at all'. It was this very tendency towards abstraction, however, this 'countermovement' of ideas whereby the 'musical' mechanism of heaven was given a new meaning in the earthly work of art, that was of fundamental and revolutionary importance for Schoenberg, who in *Moses und Aron* and the *Modern Psalm*, Op. 50C, spoke of God as the 'Inconceivable', 'of whom I cannot and should not make for myself an image'. For the justification of symbolising God's thoughts before the Creation with a fugue in the spirit of Bach lay in a form of aesthetic contemplation which was removed from concrete reality by its emphasis on the metaphysical and the mystical, with the result that the fugue Goethe was talking about ceased to be something that Schoenberg shunned and was obliged to shun on religious grounds: namely, an 'image'. Schoenberg's *Prelude* is music about a remark about music.

Rhythmic structures in Webern's Orchestral Pieces, Op. 6

In order to explain the subordination of rhythm – or the parameter of duration – to the twelve-note technique, and to justify this historically, apologists of serial music argue that in both atonal and dodecaphonic music rhythm remained, so to speak, 'tonal'. It adhered to principles that had evolved together with tonal harmony, with the result that an advanced pitch structure had come to contradict a retrospective and obsolete rhythmic usage – a contradiction which only the serial method, in extending the twelve-note principle to all elements of the structure, had resolved.

Yet the claim that there was a discrepancy between the parameters in atonal and dodecaphonic music is too crude to do justice to historical reality. Although it may be true for certain twelve-note works, such as the Third and Fourth String Quartets of Schoenberg, it seems dubious when applied to the early atonal period, in which the individual elements of composition were still always developed to the same extent: this was in accordance with the principle of homeostasis, which for Schoenberg was a matter of aesthetic conscience. The 'floating' [*schwebende*] or 'suspended' [*aufgehobene*] tonality which Schoenberg had described in his *Harmonielehre* corresponds in works like Webern's Op. 6 Orchestral Pieces to a 'floating' or 'suspended' metre in which the decline of tradition is, so to speak, spelt out. And in their details the rhythmic structures are no less complex and sophisticated than the tonal ones. It is hardly possible to speak of any inner lack of simultaneity between the individual elements of composition (the parameters, to use the terminology of serial music).

I

The fourth orchestral piece of Webern's Op. 6, an alienated, as it were, fragmented and distanced funeral march, is based rhythmically on a slow, heavy 4/4 metre, which the tamtam and low bells ('of indefinite pitch') mark emphatically with regular strokes. But within this metrical pattern, which has the character of a quotation, the rhythms are related to one another on the basis of principles that do not derive from metrical tradition (Ex. 1).* The wind chords in bars 8–9 enter one semiquaver

Ex. 1

after the beat each time, on the first, fourth and second crotchets of the bar respectively. Thus the delay of a semiquaver is always the same, whereas the placing of the beats [that is, the beats on which the chords enter] within the bar varies. However, in the wind chords of bars 10–11, which are based on the same rhythmic figure, the position within the beats changes to the exact opposite: the chords enter on the fourth, second, third, second and fourth semiquavers respectively. (It would be an exaggeration to draw attention to the retrograde in the number sequence 4–2–3–2–4.) For each chord entry two rhythmic elements – the position within the individual beat and the position of the beat in the bar – are therefore distinguished from one another, in order to be varied separately. The fact that we are concerned, nevertheless, with different elements within one and the same chord entry ensures an inner connection between bars 8–9 and 10–11.

It would be difficult to deduce the analytical mode of thought whereby a rhythmic phenomenon is divided into its constituent elements from the tradition that lasted from the seventeenth to the nineteenth centuries. On the other hand, this mode of thought shares with serial methods (though one could not say it anticipates or prefigures them) the basic principle of abstraction: elements that had grown together in traditional rhythmic usage are split up.

The rhythmic sophistications in bars 8–11 presuppose the simplicity of a regularly accented beat. And a similar intermingling of archaic and

---

* Dahlhaus refers to the revised (1928) version of the score. [Trans.]

modern characterises other rhythmic techniques in Op. 6, No. 4 as well.
The piccolo part in bars 12–13 is based rhythmically on modified
repetition (Ex. 2). A rhythm consisting of seven notes is immediately

Ex. 2

repeated, but with different ties across the beat. To interpret this as varied
repetition – an interpretation which does not reveal any kind of inner
coherence or regularity until the apparent rhapsodising of bars 12–13 –
assumes that syncopations within a beat differ in rhythmic significance
from ties across a beat: the latter should be regarded and perceived as
mere modifications or transformations of the rhythm, not as fundamental
alterations of it. And although the demands on musical listening may
seem exceptional, in Op. 6, No. 4 they can be satisfied, because the beats
of the bar are clearly marked by tamtam and bells. A traditional element
of rhythm, the stereotyping of the beat, forms the premiss for unexpected
consequences.

In bars 19–21, similarly, inner coherence is primarily based on rhythm
(Ex. 3). The horn phrase is nothing but a slightly modified rhythmic

Ex. 3

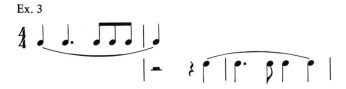

imitation of the clarinet melody, with two quavers compressed into a
crotchet. To be sure, the phrase is displaced by one crotchet in the bar.
This procedure may recall metrically displaced imitations in music of the
seventeenth and early eighteenth centuries, but must be understood
differently. In contrast to irregular entries of the subject in Baroque
fugues, Webern's metrically modified rhythmic imitations do not contradict the regular barring but, on the contrary, presuppose it. For Webern,
who avoided straightforward repetition, variation by crotchet displacement is a fundamental constitutive feature and not an accidental, dis-
ruptive element.

II

Any attempt to reduce the rhythmic structures of the Orchestral Pieces Op. 6 to an all-embracing formula would be pointless and inappropriate. The significance of the individual elements of rhythm, quantity and barring is variable. True, the bar, which is the foundation of traditional rhythmic usage, still represents a musical reality, but to varying degrees and with differing functions.

In the fourth piece, the funeral march, the bar provides, as we have seen, a firm framework and setting for the rhythm. When towards the end of the movement, in bars 31 and 34, a striking syncopated rhythmic figure, consisting of five quavers, is transferred from the position of second-to-sixth quavers in the bar to that of first-to-fifth quavers, the displacement can indeed be recognised as metrical variation because of the clear articulation of the time signature provided by the percussion. The barring is not suspended but emphasised.

Not so in the third piece, in whose eleven bars the time signature changes no fewer than eight times (between 4/4, 6/8, 3/4 and 2/4). In addition, the metre is blurred by numerous *ritardandi* and by the rests at the beginning of bars. One could speak of a 'floating' rhythm, a metrical parallel to 'floating' tonality. However, bar and time-signature changes, even though they can scarcely be perceived as such, are by no means redundant; there is no question of quantitative rhythm (Ex. 4). The

Ex. 4

rit.

change from 6/8 to 3/4 in bars 5–6 may at first sight appear nonsensical, since the chord on the fourth quaver of bar 6 stands at odds with the 3/4 time and conforms rather with the 6/8 that the 3/4 has just replaced. The change of time signature is however to be understood as indirect notation: on the one hand, as a tempo direction (dotted crotchet in 6/8 = crotchet in 3/4), and on the other as an instruction concerning articulation. The chord appears on the unstressed part of a 3/4 bar – instead of on the stressed part of a 6/8 bar – because it should be played in a hesitant, not an accented, manner: the reticent attack corresponds to the *ritardando*. It is not the change of time signature, as an alteration of the basic metrical pattern, but the articulation resulting from it that makes sense of the apparently absurd notation.

In the fifth piece the metre is reduced to musical prose. Sixteen of the twenty-six bars begin without anything happening on the downbeat, that is, with ties or rests. (As a result of the accumulation of so many irregularities the metrical sophistication results in the time signature becoming unrecognisable.) This suspension of regular metre is, however, less a premiss from which Webern starts than a process which he follows through. The opening of the movement (bars 1–5) is based on the principle of fragmentation and liquidation, as if it were an ending (Ex. 5). In

Ex. 5

bars 1–2 a group of five notes, b flat–c^1 sharp–d^1–c^1–b, is introduced; in bars 3–4 it is repeated, but without its central note, d^1; and in bar 5 it is reduced to a motivic remnant, the single note c^1. The diastematic decay is matched by a rhythmic one: when the group of notes is repeated, the marked rhythm of the opening is dissolved in floating syncopations, and the time signature becomes blurred.

Whether Webern, who was not exactly ignorant of musical history, turned to quantitative rhythm as a counter-principle to metrical rhythm is virtually impossible to decide. In bar 15 of Op. 6, No. 2 a harshly dissonant pair of chords is repeated immediately with one slight rhythmic variation: instead of five semiquavers (4 + 1) it comprises four (3 + 1) (Ex. 6). The fact that the second chord of the pair falls initially on an

Ex. 6

unstressed semiquaver and then on a relatively stressed one is of no importance, for the difference is outweighed by the *sforzato* accent. The articulation is thus not affected by the rhythmic variation, with the result that the difference in duration seems a mere matter of quantity. On the other hand, the syncopation of the first chord caused by the semiquaver rest at the start of the bar must, from a rhythmic point of view, be taken seriously; for the association of a dynamic outburst with a syncopation was a rhythmic *topos* dating back to the eighteenth century, a *topos* which unquestionably still influenced even Webern's musical thinking. The semiquaver rest is not just an interruption, then, but does indeed represent the strong beat of the bar.

At the centre of the sixth and last piece, which by and large has the character of an epilogue, there is a written-out *ritardando*. In bars 11–17, two pairs of chords, *a* and *b*, alternate almost regularly (according to the pattern *a a b b a b b a a*) (Ex. 7). The repetition is linked with a continuous

Ex. 7

rhythmic expansion: the duration of the chords increases from quaver triplet through regular quaver, crotchet and dotted crotchet to minim. The pairs of chords are almost always at odds with the metre: they cut across the triplet rhythm or create syncopations. But it is unlikely or even impossible that the contradictions between actual grouping and notated metre are to be perceived as musically ambiguous. Only the start of the passage, with its opposition of quaver triplets and pairs of chords, may be interpreted as differentiation. Later the metrical rhythm turns undeniably into quantitative rhythm. The position in the bar is indiscernible and a matter of indifference, and rhythmic values are reduced to mere duration.

III

The idea that in dodecaphonic music it is precisely through its backwardness, its dependence on tradition, that rhythm contributes to form is a *topos* of Schoenberg criticism. The theory may have a certain validity, but as a general proposition – when applied to works of the early atonal period such as Webern's Op. 6 – it is inappropriate and even wrong. In the first of the Orchestral Pieces it is primarily rhythm that constitutes the musical form, though Webern makes no concessions to established and familiar patterns in order to make his structural ideas comprehensible.

The piece divides into four sections: exposition (bars 1–4), continuation (bars 4–7), intensification (bars 8–14) and recapitulation (bars 15–19).

The exposition is reminiscent of a closed period, though the historical premiss for such a thing – namely, metrical rhythm – is dissolved in musical prose. A rhythmic and tonal parallel – a principal and subordinate group (bar 1 and bars 2–3 respectively) each consist of a semiquaver phrase (flute), a sustained note (trumpet or horn) and chords (celesta or muted lower strings) – is enough to suggest the outline of an antecedent-consequent scheme. And the syntactic structure corresponds to the formal function in creating a clearly defined beginning.

The second section, the continuation, is based on rhythmic complementation. Three voices (clarinet, trumpet and cello) are intertwined in dense yet clearly perceptible counterpoint, and this against a background of regular semiquaver movement, which provides a frame of reference and a support for the rhythmic complications. Although thirty-two notes in all are sounded by the three *Hauptstimmen*, only twice do two of them, and only once do three of them, coincide. The listener is reminded of Bach's method of associating rhythmic complementation and thematic development. As in the exposition, then, the contrapuntal texture, in which a historical model is subsumed, arises out of the formal layout.

In the intensification Webern pushes the principle of rhythmic complementation to its limits. Different ways of dividing up the 2/4 bar – crotchets, crotchet triplets, quavers, quaver triplets, semiquavers and semiquaver triplets – are superimposed one on top of the other, giving the impression of a dense rhythmic and tonal network or trellis. The polyphony of the continuation section suddenly becomes diffuse, though in a highly sophisticated manner.

The recapitulation appears as a variant of the exposition, though there is no diastematic correspondence. The individual elements of the exposition – the melodic phrase *a*, the sustained note *b* and the chords *c* – are rearranged according to the pattern *b c a*, but not to the extent that they obscure the connection with the opening. Diastematically, the second group in the recapitulation, by contrast with the exposition, is a simple restatement of the first; and this repetition, combined with the slowing down of the rhythm, seems like a way of stopping the music, a substitute for an ending based on harmonic resolution.

Analytical instrumentation: Bach's six-part ricercar as orchestrated by Anton Webern

Listeners who confuse New Objectivity, in the spirit of which they interpret Bach's music, with fidelity to the work have accused Anton Webern's instrumentation of the six-part ricercar from the *Musical Offering* of being 'late Romantic'. What they mean by this is that the orchestral colour is decorative: that is, it has been added to the music as a superficial embellishment instead of developing out of its structure. The abstract polyphony of the original becomes dissolved in its opposite: in blobs of colour.

This wilfully ignores the fact that, although the instrumentation calls for an orchestra of six woodwind, three brass, timpani, harp and strings, it is in every respect as transparent as chamber music and is conceived with clear presentation of the lines rather than a full sound in mind. Certainly, Webern does not restrict himself to a straightforward transcription of the contrapuntal voices, which, taking a simplistic view, seems to be the ideal way of presenting polyphony. Nowhere except at the end, which stands out oddly against the rest, does one find a solid tutti with doubling of the voices. In the string parts, contrary to tradition, one player to a part is the rule, more than one the exception. Even the timpani, whose roll is used by Webern for pedal points, are treated as an obbligato, independent part.

Of course, to say that Webern's method is analytical and that its aim is the clarification of the contrapuntal structure and not colour for its own sake – to say this, however convincing it may be, is not enough to refute the charges that have been brought against the instrumentation. For what matters is not the fact that it is analytical but the manner in which it is so.

In a letter of 1930 concerning his orchestration of Bach organ works,

Arnold Schoenberg wrote to the conductor Fritz Stiedry:

Our modern conception of music demands clarification of the motivic procedures in both horizontal and vertical dimensions. That is, we do not find it sufficient to rely on the immanent effect of a contrapuntal structure that is taken for granted, but we want to be aware of this counterpoint in the form of motivic relationships. Homophony has taught us to follow these in an upper voice; the intermediate phase of the 'polyphonic homophony' of Mendelssohn, Wagner and Brahms has taught us to follow several voices in this manner. Our ear and our powers of comprehension will not be satisfied today if we do not apply the same yardstick to Bach.[1]

Schoenberg sensed – and this is the justification for his orchestrations – an inner proximity or affinity between his own contrapuntal style of writing and the polyphony of Bach. Both appear, in contrast to the homophony of the Classical period and the 'intermediate phase . . . of Mendelssohn, Wagner and Brahms', to constitute a third phase in which not just one or several but all of the voices were constructed and bound up with each other motivically. Polyphony as Schoenberg imagined it would therefore be the ultimate form of a kind of thematic–motivic work in which all the voices participated at every moment. But Bach's polyphony differed from the modern type – to enlarge upon Schoenberg's idea – in that it lacked a clear instrumental presentation of the motivic structure, an explicit manner of orchestration which first emerged in the homophonic and semi-polyphonic phases. Schoenberg does not, however, claim to understand Bach better than Bach understood himself; rather, he was referring to the development of musical listening. The experience gained from having the motivic structure clarified by the orchestration – an experience which the listener owed to Mahler – could not be forgotten when listening to Bach, in spite of all efforts to think historically.

What Webern, who agreed with Schoenberg on the principles of orchestrating Bach's music, understood by motivic construction can be seen from his instrumentation of the ricercar subject (Ex. 1). The subject is broken down into no fewer than seven fragments, which are distinguished from each other by changes in tone colour. And though the analytical character of the instrumentation is undeniable, the claim that connections are being clarified appears tenuous. It only begins to seem justified when one realises that the way the melody is divided up supports rather than endangers its internal dynamic.

The six notes of the chromatic fourth-progression g^1–f^1 sharp–f^1–e^1–e^1 flat–d^1 take up three bars (if one includes the crotchet rest that separates the fourth-progression from the opening phrase), with the result that, if the rhythm remained constant, as in the case of the subject's opening phrase, every note would occupy a minim. The regular measure of a

Ex. 1

forward movement in minims can still be felt as a premiss or background, as a pattern which forms a foil for the individual rhythmic profile of the fourth-progression.

The essential feature of the rhythmic differentiation which distinguishes the fourth-progression from the opening phrase is the progressive extension of the upbeats from crotchet through minim to dotted minim – a retardation which is the counterpart of the rhythmic acceleration that takes place when the chromatic progression continues beyond the interval of a fourth. The extension of the upbeats is like a kind of congestion, which is cleared up with the sudden change to crotchets; this change does not follow abruptly, therefore, but is prepared through the internal dynamic of the upbeats. But in order that the upbeat character of the notes g^1, f^1 and e^1 flat can still be recognised, the fourth-progression has to be broken down into two-note motifs; and at the same time the way the melody is divided up is justified, in that it heightens the upbeats whose progressive extension constitutes an essential feature of the melody's internal dynamic. The analytical procedure of dissolving the music into blobs of colour, for which Webern has been criticised, proves to be a means of establishing connections.

On the other hand, it cannot be ruled out that Bach would have felt that the stressing of the rhythmic difference between the upbeats and the dividing of the fourth-progression into two-note motifs was an exaggeration of a subordinate element. For while there is no doubt that Bach must have been aware of the dynamic nature of the rhythmic differentiation, one can at the same time sense that he maintains an inner distance vis-à-vis the dynamic element in the music.

And indeed the sense that Bach is keeping the musical events at a distance is not merely a vague impression in the mind of the modern listener, who is divided by centuries from the time when the music was composed, but an experience that can be defined by referring to the object itself. The underlying musical phenomenon is the constant and unfailingly regular progress of the music. The individual musical shapes do not appear with their own peculiar rhythmic impulse, as they would in Haydn and Mozart, but adapt themselves unobtrusively to a rhythm that is established in the very first bar and the regularity of which is not disturbed by anything that happens subsequently. One may resist the temptation of offering a metaphysical interpretation of the pervading basic movement, which is manifested in the form of the figured bass. But it can hardly be denied that this basic movement cancels out the modern, dynamic features of Bach's music: that is, they are preserved, but relegated to the status of secondary elements and so to speak removed to a distance where they become indistinct.

At the same time, nothing would be further from the truth than to conclude that, because the differentiations are subsumed in a basic rhythm, they are inessential; one of the mistakes made by those critics of Bach who consider themselves to be objective when assuming a rough-and-ready attitude is to emphasise the regular progressive movement in the music and ignore the differentiations.

Certainly, the challenge of making the details of these distinctions audible without letting them interfere with the basic rhythm is hardly one that can be met completely. Any attempt to give an adequate description of the ricercar subject lands us in a dilemma. If we emphasise the way it is divided into motifs and the difference between the upbeats, we are in danger of breaking up the basic movement; but if we suppress it so as not to endanger the regular progress, the chromatic movement seems stiff and lifeless. And it almost appears as if the contradictory interpretations to which the catchwords 'New Objectivity' and 'Romanticism' have become attached are antithetical ways of evading the difficulty, or the insoluble nature of the problem, without wishing to speak of a compromise, a timidity anxious to avoid extremes.

Webern's decision is unambiguous. His instrumentation divides the chromatic progression into two-note motifs which are distinguished from each other by means of the different upbeats and which are at the same time – insofar as the progressive extension represents a dynamic element – interrelated. What distinguishes them and what binds them together are one and the same thing. The rhythmic differentiation between the upbeats, expressed by a change in tone colour which emphasises the upbeat character of the notes g^1, f^1 and e^1 flat and with it the difference between the upbeats, is additionally emphasised by a change in articulation from *portato* through *legato* to *marcato*. To quote Moritz Hauptmann, *portato* should be understood as the 'accent of the beginning', *marcato* as the accent of syncopation which results from the anticipation of the downbeat. The regularity of the basic rhythmic movement is forced into the background, as the marking *poco rubato* over the chromatic progression indicates (Ex. 2); but it is not totally suppressed, for Webern thought that the first five notes, the subject's opening phrase, should be performed – as he wrote in a letter to Hermann Scherchen – in a 'very steady, almost stiff' manner.[2] The basic movement is intended to be presented clearly before it is modified.

Ex. 2

But though it may seem reasonable to split up the subject into motifs on the basis of the premises on which the analysis is conducted – motifs whose distinguishing features are the same as those which bind them together – it is difficult to make musical sense of the fact that the subject is divided among the three instruments according to the scheme 1–2–3–2–1–2–3 (trombone–horn–trumpet–horn–trombone–horn–trumpet; for the second entry, flute–clarinet–oboe–clarinet–flute–clarinet–oboe; etc.). To assume that Webern was guided by the character of the motifs on the one hand and by the character of the instruments on the other and strove for a close correlation between the two is obvious and almost trivial. Yet it turns out to be flawed if we analyse the entire piece. What we do find is that Webern gave equal emphasis to each of the nine wind instruments that take it in turns to present the subject entries and that the distribution of instruments is based on a principle of permutation which bears a remote similarity to twelve-note technique. Each subject entry is assigned to three instruments on the basis of the same 1–2–3–2–1–2–3 pattern and without the slightest variation in articulation. And in the eleven solo entries (the twelfth and last is presented with voices doubled) each of the nine instruments appears once in slots 1 and 2 of the 1–2–3–2–1–2–3 scheme; two instruments are used twice, trumpet and bass clarinet in slot 1, horn and trombone in slot 2. (Only in slot 3 is there a slight deviation from the principle: flute and english horn remain unused.) To underline the affinity with twelve-note technique, we could even talk of eleven tone colours alternating with each other at the beginning of the eleven subject entries; for the trumpet is used once *con sordino* and once *senza sordino*, the bass clarinet at first on its own and later with the support of the double bass.

If, therefore, the way the instruments are distributed among subject entries throughout the whole piece is determined by an abstract variation scheme rather than by the character of the instruments (though Webern does not entirely ignore this), we may observe something similar in the arrangement of the instruments within the subject as well. As he wrote to Scherchen in the letter mentioned above, Webern felt the subject to comprise four groups of five notes (he included the final note [c^1] in the countersubject that continues the subject). Indeed, he felt it was possible to divide the chromatic progression, which seemingly consists of only nine notes, into two interlocking five-note groups: the note e^1 flat, which as a syncopation combines minim and crotchet, forms the 'point of overlap', the end of a five-note group in minims and also the beginning of one in crotchets. The subject is therefore divided symmetrically into 5 + 4 + 1 + 4 + 5 notes. And the principle on which Webern based the instrumentation – in order to draw attention to and enrich the symmetry without being pedantic – is that of complementary contrast. The undivided five-note group in the trombone at the beginning corresponds to a five-note group divided between the two other instruments – horn and trumpet – at the end; and conversely the four-note group divided between horn and trumpet in slot 2 corresponds to an undivided four-note group in the third instrument, the trombone, in the penultimate slot. Division and non-division are held in the balance.

The intention behind Webern's instrumentation, which may be described as being dialectical as well as analytical, is to divide up the melody in order to bring out the various connections – and not only short-term connections but longer-term ones as well. This can be demonstrated with reference to the episode that separates the first exposition of the subject from the second. The episode is divided into two sections, which together comprise no less than thirty-eight bars. The first is based on the fourth-progression g^2–f^2–e^2 flat–d^2, which is unfolded in stretto between upper and inner voices. The structuring of the upper voice, however, is ambiguous (bars 57–60) (Ex. 3). On the one hand it seems as though the chromatic passing note (d^2 flat) inserted between the fourth-progression (g^2–f^2–e^2 flat–d^2) and its sequence (c^2–b^1 flat–a^1 flat–g^1) is just a subsidiary note without motivic significance. But on the other hand the note

Ex. 3

sequence e^2 flat–d^2–d^2 flat–c^2 recalls the ricercar subject; and the impression that the chromaticism has a motivic significance – that is, also the impression of a reminiscence – is all the more compelling for being supported by chromatic contrary motion in one of the inner voices.

The element Bach holds in the balance – the relation between the diatonic fourth-progression and the chromatic reminiscence – reaches a point in Webern's instrumentation where all ambiguity disappears. Webern splits up the fourth-progression into two-note motifs (the first played by clarinet, the second by trumpet) and thus breaks up what belongs melodically together in order to stress the thematic reminiscence: the direct relationship is subordinated to the indirect – the connection between exposition and episode – though not sacrificed to it. Only the fact that the trumpet, supported by second violin pizzicato, lifts the four notes e^2 flat–d^2–d^2 flat–c^2 out of their melodic context by virtue of a common tone colour means that they combine to become a motif; and in being perceived as a motif, their relationship to the ricercar subject becomes clear to the listener.

The chromatic quality is the result of the unobtrusive insertion of a passing note rather than of a conscious derivation from the subject. This, and the fact that it was only the possibility of reminding the listener of the subject that prompted Webern to divide up the fourth-progression in this way – a procedure that could scarcely be justified on melodic grounds – is evident from the continuation of the bars cited, a slightly varied sequence (bar 66ff.). Here the chromatic passing note is absent, and Webern leaves the fourth-progression undivided, since to dissect it would no longer be justified as a means of bringing out the chromatic reminiscence.

The fact that the chromatic element is secondary is certainly not beyond dispute. It could be objected that, despite its non-appearance in the sequential continuation, it was intended primarily as a reminiscence and did not come about as an accidental by-product created by the insertion of a passing note. In support of this it might be argued that the second section of the episode is also based on a motif that refers to the chromaticism of the ricercar subject (bars 79–81) (Ex. 4). Webern underlines the similarity to the subject by dividing it analogously into two-note groups: the notes e¹ flat and d¹ flat act as upbeats, d¹ and c¹ as endings. Going by the

Ex. 4

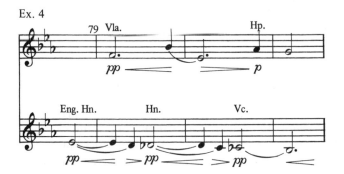

criteria of strict counterpoint, however, this division is questionable. The note d¹ flat (more precisely, the interval d¹ flat–f¹) has two meanings: as a consonant resolution of the preceding dissonance (e¹ flat–f¹) and as a consonant preparation for the following one (d¹ flat–e¹ flat). It may look as if it is to be understood simply as a consonant preparation – and thus, as in Webern's instrumentation, as an upbeat – since the preceding dissonance (e¹ flat–f¹) has already resolved onto the note d¹. But this is an illusion. The note d¹ (and similarly c¹) is not a consonant resolution of a crotchet dissonance but an anticipation of the consonant resolution of a minim dissonance. The basic form (a) is modified by means of anticipation (b) and chromaticism (c) (Ex. 5). In order to further stress the relationship between the ricercar subject and the episode motif through similar articulation, Webern passes over the dissonance–consonance connection – which he emphasises, somewhat pedantically, in the orchestration in other places (for example, bar 49ff.).

Ex. 5

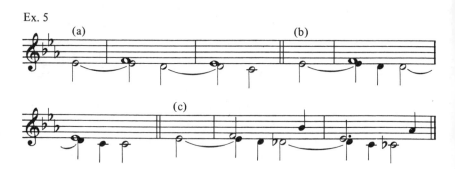

To put it succinctly: Webern regards Bach's polyphony as a form of counterpoint that is primarily motivic rather than linear. Just as the principle of split sonority, the tendency to distinguish the voices from each other, seems to correspond to and demonstrate tonally the idea that the autonomy of each voice constitutes the essence of polyphony, so the method of dividing the melody into sections is based on the notion that the concepts of motif and motivic connection are basic categories of counterpoint. But while analytical instrumentation is based on a theory concerning the nature of counterpoint, it is not heteronomous in the case of the ricercar – that is, imposed on it from outside – but is developed out of the structure of Bach's compositional technique. It is characteristic that the first and second countersubjects to the ricercar subject, however different they may be, do not contrast with one another but are closely linked through the similarity of the motifs; to split the sonority, and so distinguish the voices from each other, would be inappropriate. Both countersubjects consist of superimposed fourths (a), lyrical syncopated figures (b), leaps of a fourth with stepwise passing motion, both 'direct' and in inversion (c), and fifth-progressions in quavers (d) (Ex. 6). And inasmuch as Webern's instrumentation splits up the voices into their con-

Ex. 6

stituent parts and underlines the differences between the motifs through changes in tone colour, it also stresses the connections between the voices, whose linear aspect is retained only in a fragmentary way. Clear contrast, characteristic colouring and close, obvious interlinkage are correlative aspects. The one is both the condition and the support for the others: the relationship between the lyrical syncopated figures – that is, an element which links the countersubjects – would remain hidden if both motifs were not made to stand out from their melodic contexts by a change in tone colour and if at the same time they were not played by similar instruments (solo viola and solo cello).

The unity of the individual voices is subordinated but not sacrificed to the clarification of the motivic structure. Subject and countersubjects remain distinct from each other, more clearly at the beginning, less obviously so later. All the subject entries, except for the very last, are played by wind instruments, the countersubjects primarily (to begin with, exclusively) by the strings. But the difference becomes blurred as the number of voices increases; and as the piece progresses Webern does not hesitate to join fragments of different voices together in one instrument (second violin bars 38–41, horn bars 50–7), though certainly without making such an excessive use of pseudo-voices as Stravinsky does in *Monumentum*, his arrangement of madrigals by Carlo Gesualdo.

The result is paradoxical: while Webern emphasises the motivic connections between the voices through his orchestration, the voices themselves – whose relationships he is supposed to be clarifying – disintegrate. And one might well ask whether the concept of voice is the dominating category in instrumental counterpoint that it seems to be in a theory based primarily on vocal composition. Indeed, the emancipation of the motivic structure from the division of the texture into voices – the net result of Webern's instrumentation – means that a connection is broken that was still taken for granted in Bach, though as a tendency it is prefigured in Bach's music.

At the same time, it is impossible to ignore the difference between the compositional style and the instrumentational style; to deny it would be a useless apologia which compromises what it seeks to justify. The instrumentational capabilities of Bach's time scarcely sufficed to make clear in terms of tone colour (that is, on the surface of the work) what was happening musically (on an internal level). Similarly, it would be wrong to think that one could complete with twentieth-century techniques what was lacking in the less sophisticated technique of the eighteenth century. Contrary to one of the prejudices of the philosophy of history, not every period has at its disposal the means to express everything that is contained within it; much remains inarticulate and undeveloped. But what has been neglected cannot be made up for in a later epoch; the forms of presentation are too closely bound up with the contents of any particular time. Webern's instrumentation must not, then, be regarded as a completion; what it makes us aware of, in fact, is that the idea of a truly satisfactory instrumental presentation of the ricercar is located in the no-man's-land between what was not yet possible in Bach's time and what is no longer possible in our own.

Schreker and modernism: on the dramaturgy of *Der ferne Klang*

Schreker wrote *Der ferne Klang* between 1901 and 1910, in the decade which – as most historians agree – saw the beginnings of New Music, established by a generation of composers to which Schreker belonged. But Schreker's music remained excluded from the concept of New Music as it evolved in the 1920s. It seems almost as if the very nomenclature of the historical periods – the habit of distinguishing 'New Music' from 'Late Romanticism' – was one of the factors that stood in the way of a Schreker revival, a taking up of the broken thread, after 1945. (Although the terminology with which criticism helps to smooth the way for historiography, even if it is sometimes led astray, may be unimportant with regard to the history of composition itself, it is crucial for the reception history of a work.) Schoenberg wrote in the *Musikblätter des Anbruch* of 1928[1] that he and Schreker shared the same fate, that of being suddenly consigned to the past as 'Romantics' when they had only recently been abused as 'musical enfants terribles' [*Neutöner*] and 'musicians of the future'; but it was Schreker, not Schoenberg, to whom the label of 'Romantic' or 'late Romantic' stuck. No one needed to take any notice of him, therefore, when the time came to do justice to the New Music.

But while Schreker is hardly a part of the New Music, there is no doubt whatever that he is a representative of what Hermann Bahr called 'the modernist movement'. Its beginnings were established later in music than in literature, and were marked by the appearance around 1890 of works such as Mahler's First Symphony and Strauss's *Don Juan*. When it ended, however, is a matter of dispute; and the controversy about words – since words make reception history, even if they do not make the history of composition – should by no means be dismissed as being of no import-

ance. The expression 'late Romantic', which did so much harm to the
reception of Schreker's music, must be abandoned, at any rate as the all-
embracing name of an epoch. The period was in fact characterised by
contradictions and conflicts: in the eyes of their contemporaries Strauss
and Mahler represented musical modernism, while Pfitzner declared his
opposition to it (and even Kaiser Wilhelm said it 'would not do'). It is
absurd to couple these three composers together as 'late Romantics',
simply in order to impose a semblance of inner unity onto the period in a
manner which derives from the propositions and methodologies of
Geistesgeschichte. Furthermore, 'late Romanticism' is a term with a
pejorative ring, reminiscent of 'décadence'; it was used by followers of
Neoclassicism and New Objectivity who, in striving to dissociate themselves from the immediate past, tried to bring the phenomenon into disrepute as an extension of the 'dreadful nineteenth century'.[2] Certainly it
is almost impossible to disentangle the confused web of apologetic and
polemical motives which hide behind the changing nomenclature; and as
for trying to neutralise the interests which lie behind 'cognitive interests'
by calling them by name, there is no end to it. Even the term 'New Music'
is by no means simply descriptive. The concept embodied by the term
pushes the emancipation of the dissonance into the foreground. The
emancipation of the dissonance is unquestionably a fact of profound historical significance, and in that sense the term can be said to indicate that
a break between epochs has occurred. More importantly, however, it performs the apologetic function of rescuing Schoenberg's early atonality for
the 'twentieth century', because it allows the modernist movement –
which, it can be claimed from viewpoints other than that of the emancipation of the dissonance, lasted right up to the period around 1920 – to
be subdivided into various parts whose differences became stylised into
contrasts. The result of all this was that finally everything that was not
New Music in the emphatic sense saw itself thrust back into the
'nineteenth century' as a form of late Romanticism. But for Schoenberg to
be saved for a New Music beyond modernism there had to be a sacrifice;
and this was Schreker. Not that the concept of New Music as it was conceived in the 1920s was completely unjustified; but it expressed only part
of the truth, and it is useful, when presenting a view of New Music that
unites Schoenberg with 'Les Six', to look into a concept of musical
modernism that does historiographical justice to the feeling that an inner
affinity existed between Schoenberg and Schreker, an affinity which is
expressed in the catchword 'Secession'.[3]

Paul Bekker went further than anyone else as an apologist for Schreker.
He praised him as the only modernist composer who, in a similar way to

Wagner, though without being stylistically dependent on him, conceived dramas 'out of the spirit of music', instead of providing music for literary texts, dramatising ideas or supplying musical illustration for a piece of cheap theatrical sensationalism.[4] On the other hand, Bekker did not fail to realise that in some scenes *Der ferne Klang* came close to the form of naturalism that was represented in fin-de-siècle musical drama by Charpentier's *Louise*.[5] Around 1900, when Schreker began to compose *Der ferne Klang*, operatic naturalism could still be considered modernist; and the contradiction between naturalism and the Wagnerian axiom that Bekker applied to Schreker, namely that musical dramas were 'musical deeds made visible'[6] – the contradiction, that is, between crass everyday naturalism and musical metaphysics – is not perhaps the worst point of departure if one is trying to understand what connection exists between Schreker's work, which was strongly orientated towards the traditions of the operatic genre, and those tendencies which seem to be bundled together under the concept of modernism.

The poetics of an opera composer are his dramaturgy. One should not therefore be deterred by literary sensitivity from taking Schreker seriously as a dramatist – as a librettist working 'out of the spirit of music' – without being obliged on that account to describe him as a 'poet-composer'. In any case the idea of relating the dramatic conception of *Der ferne Klang* to the non-classical dramaturgy of the late nineteenth century is not so misguided as it must appear to an observer who regards Schreker as nothing more than a literary dilettante and eclectic. If Adorno thought it was enough to expose a stage direction of *Der ferne Klang* taken out of context as a 'literary monstrosity'[7] for Schreker to be dismissed as a librettist, a victim of the deadly quotation technique, he failed to realise that in opera it is not the verbal detail that counts, however dreadful it may be, but only the scenario: the configuration of affects that impel the characters in the action and of the situations in which they become entangled.

The naturalism that barred *Der ferne Klang* from being performed in the court theatres must be understood aesthetically as a violation of the classical rules of style. It was not the depiction of brutality and drunkenness in itself that was considered offensive, but the fact that, instead of being distanced by means of comedy and opera-buffa stylisation, they appeared as motives in a tragic plot which came uncomfortably close to the audience. Schreker, as he wrote in his 1930 article 'Wie entsteht eine Oper?' ('How Is an Opera Created?'), was 'quickly resolved to make a break with all Wagner imitation' by 'putting on the stage simple, everyday bourgeois people, sometimes speaking vulgar slang – an adventurous undertaking'.[8] It would be going too far to speak of social criticism. For the vulgarity, which Schreker contrasted with the sublime, was motivated first and foremost by aesthetic or even aestheticist considerations, and thus belonged precisely in the context of those diverging tendencies which made up the contradictory image of the modernist movement around 1900.

Naturalism in opera, no less than in the novel, was a two-sided phenomenon. When the Goncourt brothers in the foreword to *Germinie Lacerteux* (1864), the first manifesto of naturalism, proclaimed the right of the 'lower classes' to be taken seriously in literature, one can hardly fail to recognise that the unusual, provocative choice of material – the novel tells the story of a sexually enslaved servant girl – was motivated by the search for new aesthetic stimuli. And the fact that in Zola's *Germinal* the pathos of social criticism predominates and leads to the attempt to find reasons for the events in social causes rather than in 'universal human' emotions is no justification for distinguishing between a 'real', socio-critical naturalism and an 'unreal', aestheticist one. It is exactly the double motivation, which allows the artist to vary the emphases, that is characteristic. Literary situations, like social ones, always contain various possibilities for future development and are therefore open to reciprocal influences. And in the configurations they create with one another, the literary protagonists, contemporary critics or later historians can decide to emphasise one or another of these elements, with the result that it is by no means astonishing if both 'formalist' and 'materialist' interpretations are able to find the advocates they need.

Naturalism does not predominate throughout *Der ferne Klang*, as it does in Charpentier's *Louise*. Bekker spoke of a 'tendency towards symbolism' which then gained the upper hand in Schreker's second opera, *Das Spielwerk und die Prinzessin*.[9] But one should be wary of applying the style–historical label of symbolism. Naturalism, however soberly positivist it appeared in theory, was by no means averse to employing blatant, commonplace symbols in literary practice. That the game of skittles in *Der ferne Klang* with which Grete's father sells off his daughter is seen as the allegory of a hopeless fate is a motive that could come from Zola. On the other hand, crudely powerful symbols such as that cited were not exactly characteristic of late nineteenth-century symbolism (the term was coined by Jean Moréas for want of a better one). Yet it is certainly possible to speak of symbolist features in *Der ferne Klang*, albeit for other reasons. The 'Waldzauber' in the closing scene of the first act seduces Grete – in a sudden change from despair to vague, alluring expectations – into abandoning herself to a life that offers the misery of a cocotte's existence as the only alternative to the oppressive restrictions of a small town. As a piece of dramaturgy born out of the spirit of music, the 'Waldzauber' represents more a mythical power similar to that portrayed in Maeterlinck's dramas, where it holds sway over people's lives in an unfathomable and absurd manner, than a poetic symbol for comprehensible emotional processes. The abrupt change – what Bekker perceived as the 'complete mental transformation of the character'[10] – must seem like a flaw in dramatic structure to a critic influenced by the classical theory of drama. But if one accepts the break, without aesthetic or moral distrust, as a sudden change of mood, it is all the more typical of the modernist, non-classical dramaturgy which Schreker made his own in Der ferne Klang – if only to a limited extent, as we shall see below.

It could certainly be maintained that introducing a Maeterlinckian symbolism into the libretto of an opera was simply giving back something that had been borrowed from it in the first place. The notion that the real protagonist is an inexplicable fate which expresses itself in moods is reminiscent, as a dramaturgic idea, of music dramas in which the central motives of the action arise out of the 'mystical depths' of the hidden orchestra. The dialogues in Les aveugles are no longer dialogues but merely scraps of sentences which, distributed arbitrarily among barely distinguishable characters, paraphrase a state of the soul and of the world. They resemble an operatic ensemble in which – as in the closing scene of the second act of Lohengrin – the differences between the characters are suspended in the unity of the musical expression of an oppressive mood.

Thus around 1900 a literary style – symbolism – coincided with the idea of a musical drama conceived 'out of the spirit of music'. (Bekker claimed that Schreker's inheritance from Wagner went beyond epigonal imitation.) Symbolism unexpectedly updated the aesthetic principle that operatic plots should be 'musical deeds made visible', a principle which in the history of opera had always attempted to predominate, and gave it the opportunity to be modernist in a sense reaching beyond music. This by no means implies that modernity is a mere illusion, a deceptive dressing-up of ancient operatic conventions in the stage properties of a literary fashion. It implies rather that the concept of opportunity should be taken seriously by historical theorists: the tendencies that are naturally effective in opera do not always converge with what is fashionable in literature at a particular time. But when these elements come together – as they actually do in Schreker's Der ferne Klang – the result is a topicality of style which does indeed belong to the aesthetic qualities of a musical work. If musical works refer to extramusical, intellectual concerns of their time instead of remaining caught up within the limits of their genre, this should by no means be despised. For although the spirit of the age, the authority invoked by old-fashioned *Geistesgeschichte* to bolster its cause, cannot really be regarded as an influence that pervades equally all the events and institutions of an epoch, one cannot deny that it exists and that the question of which phenomena partake of it and which do not is not at all an insignificant one.

True, it is hard to speak of a consistent and unified dramaturgical conception where *Der ferne Klang* is concerned; to deny the eclectic features of the work would be a false apology. The dialectic in which Fritz is trapped – the tragic irony that it is the very road he follows in pursuit of the distant sound which takes him further and further away from his goal – derives from the repertoire of classical dramaturgy. The antithesis between art and life, to which Fritz in his guilty innocence becomes a victim, was a theme which appeared in countless variations around 1900, in works ranging from Ibsen's *When We Dead Awaken* to Hofmannsthal's lyric dramas and Thomas Mann's novellas – as a sign that aestheticism had arrived at an unhappy awareness of itself. But the fact that this antithesis does indeed attest to Schreker's participation in the spirit of the age is, however, of only passing significance from a musico-dramatic standpoint, because – in contrast to symbolist dramaturgy, whose affinity with music is clear – it involves a concept about which little or nothing can be said in purely musical terms. Music can indeed bring art and life together, as is the case in *Der ferne Klang*; but it cannot express the contrast out of which the dramatic dialectic develops. In the words of Wagner, the antithesis remains a mere 'literary intention', without 'realising itself for the emotions' by means of music.

The conflict in which Fritz finds himself involved in the second act is also borrowed from the repertoire of traditional dramaturgy as codified by Gustav Freytag: Fritz turns his back on Grete because she has become what he has – unintentionally – made her. And for precisely this reason he loses the path along which he could find himself and his work. (As so often in German bourgeois tragedy, moral bigotry appears as the motive and condition without which the tragic mechanism would come to a standstill;[11] Hebbel's 'Darüber kommt kein Mann hinweg' – 'That is something no man can get past' – is the motto of the whole genre.) Fritz is a *dramatis persona* in the conventional sense: the active agent of the action, whose autonomous decisions trigger off a tragic dialectic which turns out to be a consistent set of causal connections. In the words of Gustav Freytag, the hero is 'the blacksmith hammering out his fortune and misfortune';[12] it is his character, not a fate decreed by the gods, that determines the decisions which trap him in the machinery that destroys him.

But the music in Der ferne Klang raises a protest, so to speak, against the dramaturgy of the bourgeois tragedy and its moral implications. It is the expression of an interior action which virtually contradicts the exterior one. In the second act the decisive situation of the first is repeated: once more Fritz hears the distant sound which he believed he had almost lost, sensing it rather than actually comprehending it; and once more he turns away from Grete, without understanding that she is the very sound he seeks. He expresses a truth about Grete that is realised in Schreker's music, but he does not know what he is saying: 'Ich höre ihn wieder, den Klang der Harfen, doch nicht mehr wie einst, sanft lockend, verheissend, ein Frühlingswind, der die Harfen streicht: ein brausender Sommersturm tost durch die Saiten' ('I hear it again, the sound of harps, but not as before, softly beckoning, promising, a spring wind that stroked the harps; now a raging summer storm roars through the strings'). What in the traditional dramaturgy of the work's outer layer appears as Grete's depravity – as the misery by which Fritz feels repelled, even though it is he who is responsible for it – turns out to be the exact opposite in the musical dramaturgy, in which Schreker so to speak makes Karl Kraus's defence of the prostitute his own: the overwhelming presence of the distant sound. Musically Fritz expresses a feeling of which in the context of the naturalistic structure of the drama he is not allowed to be aware: as a singing dramatis persona he is the expression of that which, as a character involved in the action, he misunderstands.

The repetition of a situation in which a hero fails twice, only to find the redeeming word he is looking for at the third attempt, is a fairy-tale motive. And from the historical point of view this inner affinity to fairy tale, which was already pointed out by Bekker,[13] is no accident. Taking its cue from one particular aspect of Wagner's work (the first and second acts of Siegfried), fairy-tale opera was one of the possibilities explored around 1900 as a solution to the problem of how to escape the oppressive demands of music drama. The fairy tale was an attempt to succeed Wagner by circumvention, and as such was endorsed by Bayreuth.[14] But if the fairy-tale elements in Der ferne Klang are on the one hand a justification for the fact that a drama with naturalistic features is presented as an opera and not as a spoken play, on the other hand it unmistakably devolves on the music to supply motivation for, and explain, events which would scarcely be intelligible without some form of musical legitimation: music and fairy tale support one another. In psychological terms, Grete's abrupt transformation in the third act – seen against the background of the second, in which true love and false love become confused, with the result that the mask appears as a face and the face as a mask – remains virtually incomprehensible. The transfiguration that grows out of the spirit of the music at the words 'Die Bäume rauschen ein wundersam Lied' ('The trees are rustling a wondrous song') is like a fairy tale in the literal sense. But in the age of positivism – which in the dramaturgy of *Der ferne Klang* is reflected as naturalism – a fairy tale where what failed twice succeeds at the third attempt can only be motivated by music.

Bound up with the fairy-tale motive is a metaphysical world view that derives from Wagner's *Tristan*: a metaphysics of music in which the symbols of love and death merge into one another. That Fritz dies because he is worn down by a futility for which he himself is responsible may be accounted a realistic motivation. And his resigned 'Doch nun ist's freilich zu spät' ('But now it is all too late') in the penultimate scene is unmistakably a motive from Ibsen: that the passing of time as such, and not what happens in the course of it, gives rise to a tragic situation which would not be totally explicable on the basis of the events alone is an idea that Schreker took over from the modernist, non-classical dramaturgy of the late nineteenth century.

But the true motivation behind the ending has to be sought beyond the realistic level of the drama. The longing for death which Grete, almost in Tristan's words, bursts out with in the closing duet – ' . . . die sehrende Glut, die der Tod nur kühlt: die Sehnsucht nach Liebe' (' . . . the consuming fire which only death can extinguish: the longing for love') – envelops Fritz. If Grete, like Senta, longs for death, it is Fritz, as with the Flying Dutchman, for whom it is decreed. And it is only in the light of the Wagnerian metaphysics in which love and death are intertwined that the dialectic that drives the action of *Der ferne Klang* to its conclusion can be made comprehensible: the dialectic that for the sake of art Fritz should have made full use of his life and ought to have clung to it, instead of withdrawing from it, and that when he finally recognises his mistake he must die. In the music, the recognition that art and life are one triumphs over the fact that it comes too late. For death, which is the seal of futility on the realistic level, cannot be distinguished from love in the interior action that is expressed by the music – the love which according to the fairy-tale scheme may not be lost three times.

For Schreker, the metaphysics of *Tristan*, alongside the motivations of fairy tale and the symbolism of Maeterlinck, was apparently one of the justifications for wanting to write operas rather than toil over music dramas in the shadow of Wagner. And that a response to *Tristan* which led to a return to opera meant a reduction in quality was something of which Schreker – at a moment in music history when the break with Wagner was as obvious as Wagner's unavoidable, oppressive presence – was presumably barely conscious. Wagner's theory that dramas should be 'musical deeds made visible' was inspired by his experiences in composing *Tristan* and differs fundamentally from the axiom in *Oper und Drama* that music was or should be a means to a dramatic end – and thus from the aesthetic programme on which Wagner based *Der Ring des Nibelungen*. But that the description of drama as a 'musical deed made visible' was not intended as a justification of opera – as distinct from music drama – should go without saying. Nevertheless, the misunderstanding was possible, and if Paul Bekker is to be believed it made history through Schreker. Bekker's defence of Schreker even influenced his interpretation of Wagner; and thus the politics of music influenced the writing of history.[15] What is significant, however, is that Schreker's restoration of opera still clung to a piece of the Wagnerian tradition at the very point at which it sought to escape from music drama. It almost seems as though Schreker was only able to justify to his aesthetic conscience the unfettered musical development which he used to transcend the naturalistic elements in his drama by conjuring up the atmosphere of *Tristan*, in which music expressed a second reality beyond that of the empirical world. In a historical situation where, on the one hand, the spirit of the age pressed towards naturalism and, on the other, music – apart from verismo – was post-Wagnerian music, opera presented itself as an overlapping of a naturalistic level with an emphatically musical one which was legitimised by recasting the *Tristan* aesthetic into a defence of opera – though not without the *Tristan* metaphysics, the intermingling of love and death in the light of a music conceived along Schopenhauerian lines, being imposed on a realistic dramatic action.

Structure and expression
in the music of Scriabin

The decades from Wagner's death to the beginnings of New Music around 1910 are an embarrassment for the historian who only feels at his ease when an epoch has clearly discernible outlines. An age that apostrophised itself as 'modernist' and whose vocabulary revolved around the word 'life' was dismissed polemically as 'Late-' or 'Post-Romantic' by subsequent detractors, as if it had been nothing but an end and a decline. At the same time, the attempt to absolve the atonality of Arnold Schoenberg of the charge that it constituted an abrupt and unexpected break with the past resulted in the discovery that the variety of ideas, forms and techniques that the late nineteenth century had left behind also contained traces of a prehistory of New Music. Mussorgsky, Debussy and the Strauss of *Elektra* became chief witnesses for the case that the New was not quite so new as, in the initial confusion, it had appeared.

It would be evasive, however, to talk of a mere period of transition. That old and new, consequences of the past and premises of the future, mingle in one particular epoch is a commonplace which tells us little. A period is understood only when we have grasped how it saw itself; and indeed in this respect the principles that it produced for the public, whether they took the form of manifestos or self-exegeses, are less decisive than the problems with which it struggled.

Crudely simplified, the difficulty facing a composer around 1900 can be summed up in the formula that the connection between technique and articulation, between structure and expression, had become precarious – for all art from the avant garde right down to kitsch. It is precisely in kitsch, which represented a constant temptation and threat to the avant garde (whether that of Impressionism or of Jugendstil), that the problem

201

becomes most clearly evident. For the characteristic thing about kitsch is the yawning gap between charm of the material and technical refinement, on the one hand, and emphatic or transfigured expression on the other. What is lacking are means of structural and formal mediation. The vibrato of a Wurlitzer organ is at once nervous stimulant and sublime sentiment: religious worship as a narcotic.

But the relationship between technique and expression is precarious, if not disrupted, even in works of undeniable stature. The break between self-satisfied cantabile and orchestral sophistication in Strauss, or between rhetoric and pedantry in Reger, is impossible to ignore, and the temptation to describe it as kitsch is sometimes irresistible – as if there were no difference between Salome's blasphemies and 'The Maiden's Prayer'.

Generalisations, however, are of limited value. It is only by examining the individual case that the substance and scope of a problem can be clarified. And so I shall try to demonstrate the dialectic of structure and expression in early twentieth-century music by analysing two works by Alexander Scriabin, his Seventh and Ninth Sonatas.

Scriabin was born in 1872, two years before Schoenberg. At roughly the same time as Schoenberg, around 1910, he broke with the 300-year-old tradition of tonality. His late works, from Op. 58 onwards, among them the Seventh Sonata, Op. 64, and the Ninth Sonata, Op. 68, are documents of New Music.

That his musical language grew out of the tradition of programme music is as unmistakable as its preoccupation, bordering on the obsessive, with matters of construction. Scriabin designated a whole series of works *poèmes* or tone poems: *Poème divin*, *Poème satanique*, *Poème du feu*, *Poème de l'extase*. However, he regarded the programme as a secondary concern; in a letter of 1907 he wrote: 'I would not wish to have the text printed in the score. Conductors who want to perform the *Poème de l'extase* can always be told that there are commentaries on it. But it would be better if they began by having a good look at the music pure and simple.'

Scriabin's music is defined first and foremost by its harmony: by the structure of the chords and by the relationships between them. Sound [*Klang*] is the central category. But the concentration on harmony made Scriabin sensitive to effects of sound that were worn out. His late works, from Op. 58 onwards, excluded the common triad and simple forms of the seventh chord, as well as the fifth-relationship between chords. In music of the seventeenth to nineteenth centuries the fifth-relationship constituted the fundamental principle of chord connection; in fact the cadence, the very model of tonal harmony, was based on it. The removal of the fifth-relationship thus put at risk the connection between the chords, which however was something Scriabin did not wish to do without, since his compositional technique was governed by harmonic, and not by melodic or polyphonic, considerations.

Scriabin sought a way out of the dilemma, a substitute for the tonal cadence, in a method which has been described as the 'chord centre technique' [*Technik des Klangzentrums*, literally 'technique of the sound centre']. Six or seven notes form a complex from which it is possible to derive different chords by varying the choice of notes. The connection between the chords, therefore, has its basis in the fact that they have a common source in the chord centre.

The traditional cadence was functional. It resulted from the interaction between chords which were distinguished from, and yet at the same time related to, each other through functions such as tonic, dominant and subdominant. In Scriabin's chord centre technique, by contrast, the chords act like parts of a whole, not like roles in an ensemble. The relationships are complementary, not dialectical.

The basic form of the chord centre – which, however, Scriabin modified in certain works – is a chord made up of two augmented, one diminished and two perfect fourths, for example, c–f sharp–b flat–e^1–a^1–d^2. The transfiguration of the altered fourth-chord into a 'mystic chord' is a theosophical addition to the musical reality, an embellishment to which a listener who has not been initiated into Scriabin's 'Mystery' may be as indifferent as he may be to Scriabin's own attitude towards the programmes that underlie many of his works.

But even the physical justification for the chord that Scriabin attempted is so inadequate that it itself requires an explanation. The notes c^2–d^2–e^2–f^2 sharp–a^2–b^2 flat, which make up the 'mystic chord', correspond to the eighth to the eleventh notes of the harmonic series on C, plus the thirteenth and fourteenth notes. Scriabin was apparently convinced that the fact that the chord could be derived from the harmonic series in this way was enough to guarantee that it was comprehensible and made musical sense: what was given by nature could not be false in art. But although his belief in science was characteristic of the period around 1900, the argument on which Scriabin based his conjectures was extremely flawed. The first twenty intervals comprising the harmonic series range from the octave to the quarter-tone and include the musically useful alongside the useless. The harmonic series justifies everything and therefore nothing.

The origin of the chord centre must be sought not in nature but in the history of harmony. The fourth-chord is nothing but a dominant-ninth chord with flattened fifth (C–E–G flat–B flat–D) and a major sixth above the root (A) added as 'non-harmonic' note; this sixth derives from the 'Chopin chord' c–b flat–e^1–a^1. The chord is Scriabin's concise formula for harmonic 'modernism' and results from his sensitivity to hackneyed sonorities such as the diminished seventh, which the chord centre excludes.

That the altered fourth-chord is a historically-derived construct, and not an acoustical phenomenon taken directly from nature, is of crucial significance for its expressive content, for the relation between expression and technique in Scriabin's music. Musical expression relies on differences from the established pattern and from the familiar and conventional. The diminished seventh – a byword for musical thoughtlessness in the nineteenth century – was still expressive in the eighteenth century, when it was new. But in order to be perceived as expressive, a deviation presupposes an awareness of or feeling for the norm from which it departs. For the altered fourth-chord to be felt as expressive, therefore, it should not be forgotten that it derives from the dominant-ninth chord. The fact that it still carries the traces of its origins determines its expressive character.

At the same time, the chord is to be regarded as a sonority in its own right; unlike the traditional dominant-ninth chord it is not resolved but stands by itself. The question of whether Scriabin's chord centre is 'still' an altered dominant-ninth chord, and thus a tonal chord, or whether it is 'already' an atonal construct misses the point of the chord, which exists precisely in the limbo between 'still' and 'already'. The chord is tonal insofar as the root, the major third and the minor seventh make up a dominant-seventh chord and preserve the tendency to subordinate the other notes to them as altered and added notes. On the other hand, it is atonal insofar as its tonal consequence, the resolution onto the tonic, is excluded.

The chord centre forms the substance of the musical texture; from it the melodic motifs, in the form of broken chords, are derived. However, the categories of chord and motif are hardly adequate to a description of what is happening, though they could not be replaced by others.

In traditional compositional technique, to which these concepts refer, harmony is the foundation which supports the melodic motifs. To use the language of Gestalt psychology, chord and motif are like ground and figure, clearly distinguished from one another. But in Scriabin, on the other hand, the chords also perform the function of motifs, if a 'motif' is a structure whose repetition and variation, expansion and contraction, provide the basis for the development of a movement. Chord and motif appear as two sides of the same coin. 'Melody', wrote Scriabin, 'is harmony dissolved, and harmony is melody gathered together.'

The Seventh Sonata, Op. 64, consists of a single movement, extending to 343 bars. The basic form of the chord centre is modified by the major ninth being altered to a minor ninth. The chord appears in the form c–f sharp–b flat–e^1–a^1–d^2 flat. At the beginning, the notes C–F sharp–e provide the bass foundation, the notes b flat–d^1 flat–a^1 a middle layer and the notes a^1–d^2 flat–e^2 the melodic motif (Ex. 1). The fact that Scriabin

Ex. 1

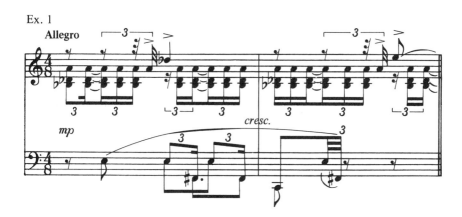

notates the melodic motif as a^1–d^2 flat–e^2 instead of a^1–c^2 sharp–e^2 must not be dismissed as a mere caprice of orthography. As a ninth, the note d^2 flat is to be connected with the C which is the root of the chord centre, without however completely obscuring the triviality of the A major triad that is stated in melodic form above it. Scriabin uses the banal, though he modifies it. In bars 3–4 the chord centre is transposed down a major third from C to A flat; and in bars 5–7 the thematic complex of bars 1–3 is moved up from C and A flat to D and B flat.

This brief analysis of the opening suffices to indicate the difficulties Scriabin was bound to encounter in writing a sonata movement lasting hundreds of bars. Bars 1–3 and 5–7 relate to each other not as antecedent and consequent of a period – a relationship of antithesis – but as model and sequence. The procedure of transposing a phrase to other degrees of the scale is, together with the technique of breaking off fragments, the only method of musical development that Scriabin, working under the constraints of the chord centre technique, has at his disposal. But in traditional sonata form, sequence is a technique of elaboration. The difference between period construction and sequence, between closed and open structure, is one of the characteristic distinctions between exposition and elaboration in a sonata movement.

Scriabin had to dispense with this structural distinction between the sections; and it was not the only feature of sonata form he abandoned. Since the chord centre is constantly being transposed, it is impossible to contrast subordinate theme with principal theme by means of some characteristic transposition which would be analogous to the tonal contrast found in tonally-based sonata form. Scriabin seems to have felt that the lack of modulation from principal to subordinate theme was a formal deficiency, for he sought to replace tonal harmonic development with a mechanical rule for regulating the transpositions of the chord centre. Distances between the roots are arranged according to the principle that a major third down alternates with a tritone up. The principal theme is based on the scale degrees C–A flat–D–B flat–E–C; the transition, which is characterised by a fanfare motif, on the scale degrees F sharp and D. The root of the subordinate theme is G sharp.

The sectional organisation of sonata form – exposition, elaboration, recapitulation and second elaboration or coda – was taken over by Scriabin from tradition dutifully and uncritically, even though the tonal foundations of the scheme were neutralised by the method of the chord centre. The formal difference between exposition or recapitulation on the one hand and elaboration on the other has shrunk almost to insignificance. In exposition and recapitulation the individual sections – principal theme, transition, subordinate theme, closing group – form clearly separate units, both in the way they contrast with each other and in terms of motivic content; in the elaboration, however, principal and subordinate themes are juxtaposed directly and combined to form a complex which is transposed wholesale to other degrees of the scale.

But even though the technical premisses of the form have become tenuous, Scriabin adheres rigidly to the conventional contrast of character between the themes, to the antithesis between dramatic and lyrical attitudes (Ex. 2). The contrast in character between the themes, however, is just a mask, the worthless residue of a sonata form whose technical premisses have fallen apart. Although technique and expression are clearly connected on the small scale – in the structure of the chord centre – there is an enormous gap between them in the overall form.

In addition to sonatas Scriabin wrote lyric piano pieces, and the ninth, penultimate sonata shows that the contradictions that exist between sonata form and the chord centre technique tend to be resolved through a return to the tradition of the lyric piano piece.

Ex. 2

bar 1

bar 29

Here Scriabin eschews the thematic aspect of sonata form, which in the Seventh Sonata had frozen into a mask. The motifs become extremely short, a feature which had been suggested by the chord centre technique. The first cell consists of four notes, B–G–B flat–C sharp. At the beginning they are presented in two-note chords and developed in sequence (Ex. 3).

Ex. 3

Moderato quasi andante
legendaire

pp

The note C sharp is the root of a chord centre whose structure is the same as that in the Seventh Sonata [that is, C sharp–G–B–F–B flat–D]. A contrasting motif, headed 'mystérieusement', presents five notes of the chord centre over the root A (Ex. 4). To the same degree that the motifs have contracted, the sonata form becomes problematical. True, Scriabin adheres rigidly to the pattern of the exposition: the transition is distinguished as a subsidiary part of the form by the way in which it dissolves

Ex. 4

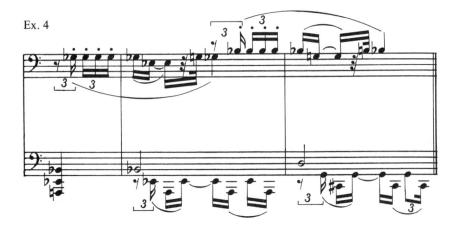

melodic outlines in trills and fleeting figurations; the subordinate theme maintains the lyrical attitude prescribed by tradition; and, as in the Seventh Sonata, the elaboration begins by compressing together in a short space of time motifs which in the exposition had been spun out at length and by mixing up the constituent parts of both principal and subordinate themes.

Halfway through the work, however, Scriabin changes the formal principle. The tradition he draws upon in the second half is that of the lyric piano piece, and in particular that of the virtuoso type developed by Chopin and (especially) Liszt. The inner contradiction which seems to be inherent in the linking of the concepts 'lyric' and 'virtuoso' is a feature of the genre itself. This type is characterised by a transition from lyricism to drama or brilliance. And Scriabin reverts to the structure of the virtuoso-lyric piano piece in his attempt to find a way out of the dilemma caused by his discovery that the method of applying sequential treatment to the smallest motifs cannot be reconciled with the claims of sonata form. To put it crudely, the problem is how to go on composing in the middle of the work when sequence technique is just as exhausted as the procedure of developing motifs separately in the exposition and then mixing them up in the elaboration.

The second half of the work is a crescendo in which the tendency of the virtuoso-lyric piano piece towards drama and brilliance breaks through. A rhythmically concise motif, which contains three notes of the chord centre (five if the left-hand part is included), forms the driving force in the second part of the elaboration (Ex. 5). The recapitulation, instead of acting as a return to the opening, is sucked into the crescendo. The principal

Ex. 5

theme evaporates in brilliant figuration; and the subordinate theme, following Liszt's example, culminates in an orgy of self-indulgent pathos.

It is no coincidence that we are reminded of Liszt. In the Ninth Sonata, just as in the Seventh, Scriabin rescues his form by wearing a mask.

Plea for a Romantic category: the concept of the work of art in the newest music

In the language with which the musical avant garde contemplates itself the phrase 'work of art' has become a spectre in the discourse; it seems hollow and stale. Composers can hardly bear to have the forms which they produce apostrophised as works of art. The fact that they are irritated by the phrase seems to be an integral part of the whole situation; the music which, for reasons of terminological embarrassment, is called post-serial refuses to accept the aesthetic categories of the nineteenth century, which considered the concept of art and of the work to be of central importance. A piece of aleatoric music is neither a work nor a closed form; nor does the concept of art describe accurately the sense or the function at which it is aiming.

That the concept of the work of art, the fundamental category of aesthetics, can age may be a disconcerting insight or a challenge for those who cling to the eternal verities. Yet one should be aware that the concept of art in the emphatic sense it has acquired in the aesthetics that have established themselves as the philosophy of art is hardly more than two centuries old. To question the motives and reasons for the tendency to relinquish the concept of art and of the work thus involves an examination of nineteenth-century aesthetics, aesthetics, that is, which seem dead and buried, but which one should not dismiss scornfully. It is to them, after all, that music owes the reputation which it has in the general awareness, and from which even the attempts to demolish it derive their claim to significance. The idea of an art religion, the nineteenth-century tendency to raise art to dizzy heights, is the precondition for the blasphemies of musical dadaism.

I

The mistrust of the work category is motivated by a number of different factors, and to distinguish between them may be of some use if it can be done without pedantry. The most noticeable one is the idea of work in progress. The composer conceives of a musical shape, which appears to the listener as a complete self-contained work with a clearly defined beginning and end, as being part of an evolutionary process which has always surpassed that which has been achieved at any given moment, and in which the goal, inasmuch as there still is a goal, is of virtually no importance compared with the manner in which it is pursued.

On the one hand the idea of work in progress implies a keen historical awareness, not in the form of memory of and affection for what is past, but in the form of a tendency to view one's own present historically, from an inner distance in which it shrinks to a transitional point between past and future. History does not appear as the mere genetic condition for musical works, but as their substance. The idea of the isolated, closed work which juts up out of history to outlive the age in which it was created fades in the face of the experience of a historical movement which passes through the works, eating them up, as it were, and leaving them behind as empty shells.

On the other hand the idea of work in progress betrays a tendency for art to approximate to the scientific law of development according to which a result is of importance less for its own sake than for the significance it has as a precondition for further steps. In short, the solution of old problems is of interest primarily on account of the new, as yet unsolved ones which it gives rise to. Music history appears to be a history of problems, the model for which is scientific progress. And if the development of serial music – a development in which the contradictions of one work were solved in the next, only to lead to new contradictions – makes it seem appropriate and indeed necessary to portray it as a history of problems, it also seems as though thinking of music history as a history of problems was not without influence on the development of serial music.

Ever since its earliest, tentative formulation in the sixteenth century, the concept of a musical work has been linked with the idea of survival or even of timelessness. That a work does not end with the moment of its creation, but survives for decades or centuries without ageing, is seen as a guarantee of aesthetic quality, even as the only safe one, though one cannot deny that sometimes a trivial work, which is not a work in the real sense, displays more tenacity in staying alive than an important one.

(Perhaps, as Rudolf Stephan once remarked, the ability to die is part of the dignity of musical works.)

In the past few decades composers – particularly those who have ventured furthest into unknown terrain – have become suspicious of the criterion of survival. They do not feel that they are part of any tradition, and thus reject the idea of forming a tradition themselves. Although they have every reason to hope that a future audience will accord them what the present-day audience withholds, they insist unflinchingly on their intention of writing only for their own time and leaving the future to its own new music. Music as they understand it expresses the meaning or the absurdity of the historical moment to which it owes its being, and forfeits its substance as the present recedes into the past. Rapid ageing is not felt to be a defect or a sign of failure, but is taken as a matter of course, as something that is self-evident. It almost seems as if this disinclination to entrust oneself to the future is the mirror image of a weary attitude to history which has been noted repeatedly in the last few decades. A heightened historical awareness which considers that participating in history as a process is more important than producing works that jut up out of history runs the danger of being inverted into an ahistorical aware-ness which restricts itself to the concerns of the present and shuts itself off both to the future and to the past.

The erosion of the work concept is to no small degree the result of the tendency to emphasise the importance of music-making, that is, the importance of the activity as such and not of the object at which it is aimed. The decisive factor is not considered to be the repeatable work which is preserved in writing, but the unique act of making music, which resists being pinned down. What a composer commits to paper is not so much a text as a graphic means of causing music to be produced. An ideology of directness and spontaneity is spreading among composers who are tired of the discipline of serial thought, and it leads one to suspect that it is nothing more than a mask concealing a relapse into a second primitivism.

One should not, for example, accuse the destruction of the work con-cept of violating the nature of music, but rather accuse it of the reverse, of relinquishing a category which, while not being founded in the nature of music itself, has been of fundamental importance for music as an art. In music the work concept, a recent and endangered category, is undeniably precarious. It includes the idea of a shape, the element of concreteness, whereas music, at least in its original sense, is less an object which can be subjected to scrutiny than a process into which the listener is drawn. Herder still made a distinction between arts 'that supply works' and arts 'whose effect depends on energy', considering music to be one of the 'energetic' arts, for in essence it was an activity (*energeia*) and not a work (*ergon*).

Yet it would be wrong to be rigorous in denying music the chance to become an aesthetic object. The history of music, at least in Europe, has been a history of progressive objectification. To be sure, its concrete character shows itself less in direct than in indirect form, that is, not while the music is being played but only when the listener, at the end of a movement or section of a movement, turns back to what has just passed and recalls it as a self-contained whole. To the extent that music is form it attains its essential character, to put it paradoxically, precisely at the moment when it is past. Retained in the mind, it recedes to a position removed from the listener which it did not occupy when directly present as a process. It becomes an object. And at a distance it constitutes itself as a clear, plastic form. Concreteness, retrospection and form are independent correlatives, each of the three factors being a precondition or support for the others. Conversely, music that tends towards the evanescent, towards 'moment form', is to all intents and purposes not concrete. The objectification of music is as it were revoked. Music falls back to the stage at which it was merely a process. And the work character of the music is annulled together with its concreteness. The emphasis on the activity as such instead of on the object at which it is aimed, the transformation of musical texts into drawings which do not represent music but which are supposed to induce it to happen, and the shrinking of form to the musical moment are different aspects of the same thing: the abandonment of the work concept, which in its precipitate fall has dragged down musical form with it.

But nothing could be further from the truth than to make a sweeping assertion that forms which have been termed open forms are incapable of aesthetic objectification. It is precisely those pieces in which the sections are interchangeable, being abruptly set off against each other by sudden general pauses or contrasts on the one hand and appearing to circle around themselves in a non-developmental manner on the other, that are particularly perceived as objects. It is not an accident that one is prompted to make comparisons with painting and sculpture.

In passing, a word on how to understand the general pauses. Listeners whose feeling for musical form has evolved by experiencing developmental forms sense them to be meaningless interruptions and holes in the musical tissue. Yet the seemingly primitive character of the caesuras, interruptions or sudden changes is not a defect betraying an inability to mediate between contrasting sections, but a sign of an unusual way of experiencing musical time, the beginnings of which can be observed as far back as the early nineteenth century in parts of Schubert's instrumental works. To clarify the point, one can begin with the contrast to developmental form, the prototype of which is the kind of sonata form established by Beethoven. In this the passing of time cannot be felt as such precisely because it is under the composer's control; being an aspect of musical development, it is subsumed in the progress of events. The music is, as it were, in control of time instead of being subject to it. It is a different matter in the case of forms whose sections seem to circle around themselves on the one hand and stand next to each other, either paratactically or in unconnected fashion, on the other. The individual self-contained section, instead of developing what has happened in a previous phase or preparing for a subsequent one, appears to be the pure present, an expanded moment in time. But time becomes apparent when it is interrupted by a pause or when there is a sudden contrast, and indeed time as such, sundered, as it were, from the process of which it was a part, as opposed to time in a developmental form. The dividing caesura and the seemingly empty general pause make the listener, who had sensed a musical section as a single moment in time, quite suddenly aware that 'time has passed'. That is the only function of the seemingly functionless pauses.

II

The concept of art in the emphatic sense, which for some composers has become an embarrassment or a burden which they seek to discard together with that of the work, is hardly two centuries old. Although he took over the *Sturm und Drang* concept of genius, Kant still spoke of art as of an embodiment of rules. The concept of art first acquired metaphysical dignity in the Romantic era.

When Robert Schumann wrote that the aesthetics of one art were also those of the others, the only difference being the material they employed, he was aiming at an idea of art common to poetry, painting and music, of which a form had to partake in order to be a work of art. And the factor that distinguishes a musical work of art from tonal mechanics he called 'the poetic'. Music was supposed to turn into a tone poem, to rise above the realm of the trivial, of tonal mechanics, by means of its spirituality and soulfulness. That the word 'poetry' designated the idea of art itself, on the one hand, and a particular genre, the art of writing poetry, on the other, could only lead to confusion. Its equivocal nature wrongly suggested that all art was essentially poetry; and thus the tendency to define in poetic terms that which turns a piece of music into a work of art often had disastrous consequences in nineteenth-century aesthetics.

In Romantic theory the material that distinguishes one art from another is a piece of low-level empirical knowledge, beyond the accidental and restricting qualities of which art seeks to progress. That the material must necessarily be consumed by the form was a *topos* which no one doubted. And Schumann, in terms which were hardly different from those applied to material, spoke of compositional technique not without an undertone of contempt when he referred to it as mechanical. Even Schumann, however, was aware that intentions become amateurish for want of sufficient technique, particularly when they are aimed at the highest goal. Yet he treated technique as a secondary, subservient aspect which, however unavoidable it may be, should not obtrude itself upon us in an independent manner.

If Schumann only considered musical material to be justified when it was subsumed in poetry, then nowadays it has emancipated itself to acquire a meaning of its own. Form becomes a means of unfolding material instead of material being subsumed in the form. And in the extreme instance, in the case of Cage, the material appears as the very nature of music, which is to be liberated from the tyranny of the forms imposed upon it by the human spirit.

The functions of the concepts on which Schumann's aesthetics were based have been turned upside down. The poetic quality which Schumann equated with the idea of art has become an attribute of kitsch, having sunk to the realm of the trivial; and it was precisely between this and the music which he styled poetic that Schumann sought to make a distinction. Conversely the mechanical, which, as the hallmark of triviality, formed the antithesis to poetic quality in Schumann's aesthetics, has been accorded aesthetic value in the twentieth century as long as it came to the fore independently. There is also talk of the mechanical nature of serial practices in analyses or commentaries of an apologetic character. And the artificial aspect, the making and production of art, is, following the example of Valéry's poetics, openly displayed with the same zeal with which it was concealed in the Romantic epoch.

The predilection for a musical language of engineering, which engineers themselves view more with suspicion than with sympathy, is the reverse of the tendency to throw off an artistic concept whose emphasis has become unbearable. Those who do not wish to be suspected of nursing a penchant for kitsch talk about music in an aggressively self-satisfied, matter-of-fact manner and leave the theological metaphor, the concept of creation, to composers of operetta.

But the conclusion that a piece of music is nothing more than one commodity among others, a musical artefact in a world of technical artefacts of which it becomes a part, seems to be invalid, however enticing it may be for certain composers. Reversing the division of music into works of art and useful commodities is not dependent on the good intentions of composers who feel dejected by the isolation of the avant garde.

The category *Gebrauchsmusik*, together with its complementary antithesis, the emphatic concept of art derived from the Romantic era, arose as a result of the disappearance of a more comprehensive category. A Bach invention is not a musical commodity, nor an étude, nor a work of art in the emphatic sense, but something else: an example of a musical function which preceded the schism and for which there exists no unambiguous definition. Those who speak in anachronistic terms of seventeenth- or eighteenth-century *Gebrauchsmusik* distort the truth and covertly attempt to obtain for modern *Gebrauchsmusik*, the result of the schism, the appearance of what was in truth peculiar to music before the schism: the unity of utility value and art character.

Attempts at mediation, of which there has been no lack in the history of New Music, sink to the level of arts and crafts, a category of which one has come to speak slightingly as a matter of course, even though its original utopian message is not in doubt. Inherent in the concept of arts and crafts is the idea that it should be possible to close the gap between art and commodity. But the decline of the phrase in everyday parlance is characteristic of the depreciation of the object that it signifies. It would indeed be tempting to investigate the reasons for this failure. Yet it must suffice to point out that the existence of lower music, the pressure from below, is already enough to force advanced music, which is clearly in part spurred on by the fear of banality, to remain art in the emphatic sense.

III

The Romantic concept of art encompassed the rejection of dogmatism, of the constraints of aesthetic rules. The domination of the norm was opposed by the sovereignty of the subject, though without – and this distinguishes the Romantic era from *Sturm und Drang* – lapsing into blind veneration of original genius and degrading the work of art to the status of a mere by-product of a subjectivity seeking to express itself. The idea of the self-contained work now advanced to the centre of the theory of art, that centre which in rationalism had been occupied by the concept of the rule and in *Sturm und Drang* by that of the genius. One fails to do justice to the Romantic theory of art if one fails to recognise that by emphasising the work concept it warded off both dogmatism and subjectivism.

But the point at which the concept of the work disintegrates is also the one at which the diverging tendencies which it had held together, namely, the tendency to dogmatism and the opposing tendency to subjectivism, re-emerge independently.

There can of course be no talk of a simple return to what is past, even if only with respect to fundamental aesthetic categories. The rules and constraints of serial music relate to the dogmatism of the eighteenth century in the same way as does a developing science to an orthodox creed which accedes to change only with reluctance. Composition becomes work in progress which is never completed, but rather – as Stockhausen would say – resembles a succession of inventions and discoveries in which a result is important less for its own sake than for the consequences that it bears within it. In addition the concept of the rule, around which eighteenth-century dogmatism revolved, was rejected as outmoded and replaced by a more modern one, that of the method. Yet both categories have this in common, that they emphasise the aesthetic form of the result less than the legitimacy of how it came about.

As an aesthetic authority the concept of the rule has been replaced by that of logicality, a concept which includes the idea that every aesthetic element must have a compositional–technical correlative. To demonstrate the logicality of a form is the aim of a method which conceives of itself as immanent criticism, though the demands of immanence cannot, strictly speaking, be met: the relinquishing of general concepts to which they lead would force the critic to silence. Of course all that is meant is that it is possible, without appealing to preconceived norms, to distinguish in aesthetic and compositional–technical terms between what is right and what is wrong. But the attempt, if it is not to be wholly futile, must necessarily assume that a piece of music forms a self-contained whole, the parts of which relate meaningfully to each other and to the overall form. What cannot be tested against a rule is only accessible to a well-founded judgment if it can be defined as a function in a context. The concept of logicality is the correlative to that of the self-contained work, the central category of the Romantic theory of art.

IV

The interpretation of the tendencies, methods and results which have been characteristic of the avant garde of the last decade and a half has on the whole been left to the composers themselves, without a clear distinction being made between reflection, which forms part of the work of composition, and a commentary to a completed work. Irrespective of whether or not there are difficulties attached to the reception of the new, there is a difference in principle between the point of view of a composer, for whom a work is primarily a thing of becoming, and that of the listener, who bases his judgment on the result, a difference which is admittedly mitigated by recompositional listening on the one hand and an alienation of the composer from his own work on the other, but which can never be entirely overcome. By their very nature there is a difference between self-exegesis and commentary by others, between theory as a vehicle of composition and as interpretation of the result. But the fact that the concept of the work of art is under a cloud in that it seems faded and the worse for wear is to no small degree founded in the lack of understanding of the difference between the two points of view.

That the work of the composer ends where that of the listener begins – with the completed work – is the tangible and banal exterior of the psychological fact that composers not infrequently tend to assign more significance to the process of creation, to the genesis of a work, than to the result, and sometimes in fact so emphatically as to make it seem that the objectification of the compositional process in a structure that outlives it signifies an alienation of art from its true being. The composer conceives of the work, which presents itself to the listener as an unbroken facade, as of a process which is in reality never-ending. And sometimes he is reluctant to come to an end because this also implies renunciation. Some of the possibilities that began to appear as the work progressed remain unrealised. They are sacrificed to the closed nature of the work, which almost always has attached to it an element of violence.

Thus, if for the composer the work is less a clearly defined object than an embodiment of possibilities, realised and not realised, then the listener who analyses the work must assume in turn that it is finished in two senses of the word: that it is both complete and perfect. Analysis is an attempt, which never quite succeeds, to understand and demonstrate that all parts of the work relate in a meaningful way to each other and to the whole, and that each one is subsumed in the function it performs. The triumph of analysis consists in demonstrating that a work – at least, a successful work – cannot be other than it is. Where a composer sees possibilities, both realised and suppressed, the analyst is trying to discover necessity. He speaks of chance or of what is not essential only with reluctance.

Choosing the composer's point of view or that of the listener determines whether the category of the work of art still performs a function or whether it shrinks to insignificance. The most superficial analysis suffices to make it clear that the motives on which the mistrust of the art and work concepts is based are closely connected with the tendency to regard music as a process and not as a structure. The disintegration of closed forms into open ones and the emphasis placed on music-making, on the activity as such instead of the object at which it is aimed, the indifference to the disappearance or survival of musical structures, and the devaluation of the result into a mere by-product of the development of methods: all the facts that lead to the creation of the work concept can only be understood from the point of view of the composer. For the listener it is exactly the opposite: the creative process and the genesis of a work are subsumed in the result. He conceives of music as a structure which is capable of surviving. And an open, variable form seems to him to be a closed and established one because he is unable to relate the version that he is hearing at this moment to other alternatives which the performer could have chosen but did not choose. To do justice to a work of art, which the composer declines to do, is a matter for the listener.

A plea for the category of the work of art may be suspected of being regressive in character. Yet none of the motives which lead to the disintegration of the concept of art need be rejected. To perceive their one-sidedness does not imply that they have to be discarded. The idea that we are attempting to resurrect an element of Romanticism which is dead and buried misses the point. We have merely attempted to show that the category of the work of art, though it is undeniably of Romantic origin, continues to perform a function. Around it are grouped the concepts which help to articulate the listener's point of view, in complementary antithesis to that of the composer.

On the decline of the concept of
the musical work

The concept of the musical work, that is, the idea of the autonomous, self-contained work, was not a subject of aesthetic debate in the era of aesthetics, the nineteenth century. This was not because it was considered to be of no importance, but because it was so self-evident that no one became aware of the problems involved. The fact that for some decades now, especially since the appearance of Adorno's *Philosophie der neuen Musik*, it has attracted attention, not only of a speculative kind, but also for reasons connected with compositional experience, seems to show that it has become a questionable concept.

In music the concept of a work arose at a relatively late stage in history, and, in contrast to the concept of the work in the visual arts, has always been a precarious one. For music is directly and primarily experienced as a process or a performance, and not as a form which confronts the listener. It forces itself upon one instead of being observed from a safe distance. It is therefore hardly a coincidence that it was only in the sixteenth century that the concept of a work was taken over from the poetics and theory of art by the aesthetics of music – and even then only hesitatingly and sporadically – and that it did not establish itself in the general consciousness of the educated before the eighteenth century. Popular music in fact was never even thought of in terms of works. Where artificial music was concerned, the concept of a musical process being a clear, as it were, architectonic form (Schlegel's architecture metaphor expresses one of the most profound breaks in the history of musical hearing) – a concept, in other words, which forms one of the preconditions for understanding a musical shape as a work – always remained a postulate that was only partially and insufficiently realised.

So while the concept of a musical work was self-evident in the nineteenth century according to the letter of the aesthetic law, it was of restricted validity and always in peril from the context of actual musical behaviour. Anyone who nowadays opposes the domination of the concept of the work, which he feels to be constricting, or who speaks of the decline of the concept of the work, is not so much turning against a firmly established tradition as helping to destroy a precarious idea, the truth of which was, admittedly, not called into question in the nineteenth century but whose claims were nonetheless not fulfilled. The polemics against the concept of the musical work are directed against a dominant and yet powerless idea.

II

The concept of the autonomous musical work is closely bound up with the institution of the bourgeois concert which crystallised in the eighteenth century. One may describe the connection without having to decide whether the institution was the result of the idea or whether the idea was the result of the institution. The idea that music, even music without a text, can be listened to for its own sake instead of accompanying an action or gracing a ceremonial event is not at all self-evident; indeed it is remarkable. The institution of the concert is as artificial as the works which it serves or which serve it. And the aesthetic justification for autonomous instrumental music was still precarious early in the nineteenth century – at the time Beethoven was writing his symphonies, which were not mentioned in Hegel's aesthetics. The interpretation of instrumental music as 'tonal speech' – as vocal music without a text – and the quest for 'suppressed programmes' are attempts at justification sustained by the assumption that music should express or represent a concrete content if it claims to be heard for its own sake.

Concert music should not be confused with the social music-making which is hardly less typical of bourgeois culture – even in the sixteenth century – and which in any case hovers between autonomy and functionality. Whether music is primarily a function of social life or whether social life is a function of music remains a problem which cannot be resolved in this context. Listeners who do not join in are, it is true, sometimes admitted, but their presence is not a precondition, as it is at concerts. At any rate the real listeners are the players themselves, and this tells us from an aesthetic angle that social music is perceived as it were from the inside and not from the outside, as structure and not as form. But formal hearing, perception from the outside, is constitutive for music which presents itself as a work.

The fact that social music presupposes a different kind of listening from concert music is the reason for far-reaching compositional and technical differences between the genres. As a musical image of a conversation, social music – to make use of rough categories – tends towards a polyphony in which the voices combine and interact on an equal footing. (Comparing chamber music with a conversation did not originate with Goethe, but was a *topos* which went back to the sixteenth century.) It would hardly be an exaggeration to state of polyphonic writing that it is most clearly heard from one's own part when it blends into a context of other voices. The categories of listening from outside – firm formal design, clear grouping and close thematic–motivic interlinking of the sections – are of minor importance in social music such as the madrigal or the ricercar. In the case of concert music, however, it is polyphony that is out of place; in the eighteenth century it was considered to be a sign of a learned musical style which was unsuited to a concert audience. Rather, the decisive factor is on the one hand the 'architectonic' aspect of form, the clarity achieved by the repetition of sections, and on the other hand the 'logical' aspect, the development of themes and motifs whose distribution over a whole movement imparts an inner coherence to the musical process.

Thus the aesthetic raison d'être of concert music is (and the comparison with social music-making was intended to show nothing but this) musical form in the sense in which the concept was understood and compositionally realised in the eighteenth and nineteenth centuries. And if nowadays, together with the category of the work, the institution of the concert seems to be in peril – as yet more in the mind than in reality – then the concept of musical form is also directly affected. Anyone who finds concerts unbearable – that is, anyone who cannot tolerate the state of being forced to listen without being allowed to participate – and who wishes to participate instead of being a mere recipient, is forced to jettison formal hearing (or listening over large stretches, which presupposes aesthetic distance) and to concentrate on musical moments in time which may or may not stimulate actions; in other words, to listen from one moment to the next. The development of large-scale form, which formed a fundamental trait of eighteenth- and nineteenth-century compositional history, is as it were taken back and repealed. The consequence of a decline in the institution of the concert would be the reduction of musical form to moment form, as Stockhausen called it: to a concatenation of moments which exhaust themselves in themselves.

III

While the concept of a musical work may be suspected of being an out-moded and eroded category, a fragment of the past in the present, the aesthetic expectations which are bound up with the category of improvis-ation, the opposite of the work concept, are excessive and utopian. Improvisation has become a slogan which has attracted vague and diver-gent hopes, a catchword which seems to hit the mark as long as one does not think about its meaning but which dissolves into insubstantiality as soon as one begins to try to pin it down.

Aesthetic reflection can assume that improvisation, as opposed to com-position, is characterised by the constraints of the momentary. In a com-position worthy of the name, the single musical moment is part of a coherent pattern which determines its character, and to which it owes a significance it would not have if it were taken on its own as an isolated moment. To say that it is merely a potpourri, a succession of musical stimuli, the arrangement of which produces no distinct form but which relies on the principle of lively contrasting effects, is the worst imaginable criticism of a composition in the epoch of formal aesthetics. In improvis-ation, on the other hand, the emphasis falls on the individual musical moment without the disregard for the aesthetic postulate of the primacy of the whole constituting a flaw. The detail does not so much refer to the musical context – the earlier one from which it came and the later one towards which it strives – as attempt to do justice to the situations that form the basis of improvisation and unmeasurable fluctuations to which they are subject. Thus psychological criteria are sometimes more valid than aesthetic ones, which derive from thinking about compositions and how they are perceived.

Whereas in a composition the parts of the process are supposed to be retained in outline in the mind so that they can coalesce into the image of a musical form – into an image in which non-synchronicity turns into paradoxical synchronicity and succession into simultaneity – in an improvisation only the here and now, the direct impression, is of decisive importance, and non-retrospective perception which is absorbed in the momentary would not be out of place, though it would signify a reduc-tion. Composition tends towards objectivity; improvisation is mere execution. The goal of formal hearing, that is, the hearing of compositions in an appropriate manner, is the solidification of music, which is primarily a process, into an object which keeps the listener at a distance, not unlike a sacred object. Improvisation on the other hand attempts to reduce the distance to the listener, or even abolish it. Instead of confronting the music, the listener is supposed to be drawn into the musical process.

The firmly rooted habit of seeing the lack of notation in improvisation as a sign of freedom is the reason for deceptive expectations which pervade the theory of aleatoric music and of musical graphics just as much as they pervade the aesthetics of jazz; the expectation that improvisation should be able to advance to make discoveries which remain closed to the slow work of composing constricted by reflection. Improvisation appears to be the vehicle of innovation in music. The idea that composing is tied to norms and conventions that improvisation is able to disregard is, however, outmoded on the one hand, for emancipation from rules has become a negative rule in composition; and, on the other hand, it is a misnomer inasmuch as improvisation is actually dependent on formulas and patterns. In order not to grind to a halt it has to have at its disposal a supply of polished *topoi* from which it can select whatever seems appropriate at any particular moment. The fact that what is not notated is unpredictable, and that on the other hand infringements of the rules of composition, which are unavoidable when improvising, can be turned into effects, in no way guarantees musical innovation, which should not be confused with the unexpected, the surprise of the moment. To produce something substantially new is more likely in the patient effort of composing than in the swift moves of improvisation. And that music has a history, and not merely a tradition, is due to the notation by means of which it developed from improvisation into composition.

Improvisation is tied to the moment to which it attempts to do justice. Thus, either the musical context disintegrates into moments which stand juxtaposed as isolated stimuli, or the details are borne by a scaffolding which is so firmly established that even an excessive amount of improvisation cannot conceal it. The one is true of extreme pieces of aleatoric music, in which incoherence is not an accidental defect, but an aesthetic intent; the other of jazz, the harmonic–metrical schemes of which form a firm and banal basis for melodic–rhythmic fragmentation. But the more imperceptible the discernible coherence becomes, the smaller is the chance of producing something new, for newness is less a quality of the momentary than a quality of the context in which it occurs.

IV

The mistrust of the work concept in music is, as those who share it are convinced, a sign of great sensitivity to fossilisation and inflexibility. There is even talk of reification and alienation, where people are not afraid of high-sounding words. Yet it sometimes seems as if the categories that come from dialectics are unexpectedly transformed into mere catchphrases, thus themselves being subject to the same kind of petrification that they single out in order to avoid.

It is undeniable that there are cases where music may be interpreted as being the results of reification: one thinks of Adorno's research into the fetish character of music. Yet it is also difficult, though unavoidable, to determine the point at which, to use the language of Hegel, renunciation or realisation becomes objectification, and at which objectification becomes reification or alienation.

A musical idea which does not realise or detach itself, that is, a surplus intention which does not attain phenomenality, is of no interest to aesthetics. It is futile, a private concern of self-contained 'inwardness' [Innerlichkeit].* Musical realisation can, however, as we have seen, exhaust itself in mere performance, in music as an activity, without the musical process being objectified as a clear form, the parts of which relate to each other and to the whole. Perception adheres to the details on the one hand, and on the other feels itself borne along by the musical train of events to which it entrusts itself unthinkingly.

It is only through an objectification which proceeds beyond a realisation as mere process and execution that music acquires work character. But the objectification without which an art that leads to works is unthinkable may not without further ado be understood as, and suspected of being, reification or alienation. Far rather, important interpretations of musical works have been praised because they recompose a work, as it were, and do justice to it as a work precisely because they seem to do away with the petrification into a text which is there from the very beginning.

It is not that music is protected against reification on account of its intangible nature, which Kant termed 'transitory'. That a state of affairs, the origins of which have been forgotten, establishes itself as self-evident; that rules, which arose out of certain unrepeatable historical situations, coalesce to become norms with comprehensive claims; that ordinances, which were made by human beings and which are thus changeable, mas-

---

* See the chapter entitled 'Dialectics of "Sounding Inwardness"' in Dahlhaus's *Esthetics of Music*, trans. William W. Austin (Cambridge, 1982), pp. 46ff.

querade as natural events or natural laws – in other words, typical alienation phenomena, the basic form of which is the veneration as a god of the
self-contained fetish – these were doubtless of no little importance in the
history of music, in that they retarded progress and thus need to be criticised in a way which will reduce what is seemingly natural to the historical
preconditions to which it owes its origin and its limited validity. Yet alienation cannot be avoided simply by suspecting the objectification, the
work character of music, of being alienation. If criticism is not to be
wholly futile it must be aware of the difference between objectification
and reification, of a difference, the criterion of which is whether the
historical reasons for the existence and justification of a work, of a
compositional–technical norm or of an aesthetic postulate are still
operative or whether they are not.

V

The reverse of the idea that improvisation is the way to arrive at music as
it really is, undistorted by convention, and that composition is petrified
and sterile, is suspicion of and contempt for musical notation and the text
character it imparts to music. Yet text character is not the same as the
written form as such. A text is not music by virtue of the fact that it is
notated, but only when its creation presupposes notation, and indeed a
kind of notation which represents the structure of the work instead of
merely prescribing how the music is to be performed. Text character and
work character are closely connected.

The untold number of attempts that have accumulated in the last
decade to add to or reform musical notation are ambiguous as regards
their general tendency. Roughly speaking, they are aimed either at greater
notational precision, or at a dissolution of the text character which has
gradually evolved since the twelfth century.

So-called graphic notation, the principle of which resembles that of
sixteenth- and seventeenth-century tablatures, prescribes the performer's
actions instead of delineating the musical structure. It is scarcely possible
to acquire a musical idea of the work from numbers which serve as
shorthand for the fingering on a lute: they merely indicate how it is to
be performed. Thus graphic notation coincides with the view that music
is primarily a process and execution, whereas staff notation, the antithesis
of graphic notation, is the notational form associated with the work
concept.

The work and text character of music, which already seems endangered
by the tendency to use graphic notation, is dispensed with entirely when

it comes to musical graphics. A graphic score is more of a challenge than notation; it is not the image of a composition, but rather a stimulus to improvisation. The consolidation which the notational representation of music, the objectification in the shape of a text, is felt to be, is supposed to be dissolved by the fact that there is no longer an object–sign relationship between the music and the graphic correlative, but merely an associative one.

By relinquishing communication by means of representational notation one seeks to attain musical immediacy. Notation is rejected as if the written form, the text character of music, were a shell which had to be broken in order to get at what is the essential point. Yet it is doubtful whether the immediacy of which originality and newness are expected is not itself a phantom. The initial associations to which a piece of musical graphics gives rise are almost always banal, for spontaneous reactions adhere to what is familiar and part of the usual routine instead of bringing forth something that is new. Detours, reflection and experiments are far more likely to lead to originality. But the medium of musical reflection is notation. Thus it is not only a vehicle of convention, from which the enthusiasts of improvisation seek to liberate themselves, but it can also in fact be a means of avoiding the kind of triviality that is brought about by spontaneity.

VI

Ever since Adorno's *Philosophie der neuen Musik* the denial or destruction of work character has been bound up with an emphasis on musical material, without however the concept of material, which in Adorno's work is a Marxist variant of the concept of musical language, having remained unchanged. The decline of forms – and work character is linked to forms – which the paradoxical term 'moment form' at once brings to our attention and conceals, appears to be the reverse of the emancipation of material.

The contraction of all-embracing musical form to moment form does not necessarily mean that the connection between the parts, the 'moment forms', is severed and that form dissolves into a mere juxtaposition of unrelated moments. It can also consist in a shift of emphasis from the context to the detail. The individual event is no longer a function of that whole which is to be perceived as form, but it is context that serves to highlight the detail, which becomes the centre of one's attention. Even the negation of musical coherence as practised by Cage is dependent on that which is negated. For the fact that a listener attempts to link and relate musical details – and they are already 'musical' by virtue of the situation itself – is the usual norm of acoustical perception in a concert (as opposed to everyday life). Thus lack of coherence is not so much something that can be taken for granted as a goal which can only be reached by disturbing and destroying coherence. Formal disintegration is a procedure which requires continual renewal. It is not a given state of affairs *per se*.

But the significance of form declines to the same extent as that of the material increases. And here form and material have to be thought of as relative categories. The motif is the form of the tones and noises, the phrase the form of the motifs, and the whole movement the form of the phrases, with the result that from the disintegration of the overall form there results, as in a potpourri, a lack of connection between the phrases; from the dissolution of the phrase a juxtaposition of unrelated motifs; and from the destruction of the motif the isolation of tonal details. The fragmentation of form in the 'sound composition' [*Klangkomposition*] of the last decade and a half is the consequence of a growing complexity of the material. The expansion of tonal resources – some composers are insatiable in their pursuit of unusual acoustical phenomena – consists primarily in an expansion of the role played by noises or sound mixtures. But, seeing that noises form only the rudimentary beginnings of scales and systems, they help to constitute musical forms and structures to a lesser extent than do notes. The simplest of formal categories (extreme contrast, transition, repetition, variation) can be attained by means of noises, but not the more complicated and richer relationships (complementary contrast, development, elaboration), which can only be achieved by using notes. And therefore it seems as if the differentiation of the material by noises signifies a loss of formal, functional differentiation – unless a combination of tones and noises can be found in which the noises participate functionally in musical structures without on the other hand having to curtail the wealth of acoustical material. At present material and formal differentiation are moving in opposite directions. And isolated material stimuli which lack the support of forms and structures are rapidly expended. Nothing in music seems as outmoded as yesterday's surprise sound effect.

VII

The tendency towards the disintegration of structure into a concatenation of isolated stimuli is a feature which the music of the avant garde shares with its antithesis, trivial music, with the result that it seems as if attempts to mediate between the different positions have a basis in fact instead of merely having airy-fairy ideological roots. The concept of a work, which never became an accepted feature of trivial music, except as a mask and a false claim, is now also being suspended at the other end of the spectrum, in music which rejects being art.

The latest attempt to mediate, which sees pop music as being a musical analogy to pop art, differs from earlier attempts at reconciliation – here one should recall the jazz adaptations in the period of New Objectivity in the 1920s or the ennobling of popular dances in nineteenth-century salon music – in that it has critical intentions which are undeniable even if they remain ambiguous. Pop music as practised by the Mothers of Invention, for example, is music about music; and their technique is that of the alienating quotation or of montage. Trivial music is not so much the area it belongs to as the object it represents; it is its musical subject-matter, as it were. Thus musical subculture becomes its own subject-matter.

The method of the alienating quotation – one means of alienation, for example, being the confrontation of beat and electronic music – is intended to be polemical, and in two ways at that. On the one hand trivial music is held at a distance: the listener is supposed to see it in all its aggressive superficiality instead of accepting it uncritically. (By means of alienation, according to Brecht, what is seemingly self-evident becomes unusual, and what is unusual becomes changeable.) On the other hand, by quoting trivial matter in the first place and (in extreme cases) by being nothing but quotation of trivial music, pop music is directed against the esoteric quality of the musical avant garde and of art in general. It is an anti-art. The object of the quotation technique is just as much an aspect of the polemics as the procedure itself.

Yet the double negation runs the danger of turning into affirmation. The means of alienation are not immune to being assimilated and expended as additional stimuli. Then they no longer perform the function of creating distance, but are themselves subject to the entertainment value of trivial music against which they were directed. And again, if avant-garde techniques predominate in a piece, the element of triviality may be felt to be an interesting admixture instead of signifying a protest against the esoteric and art character. Reciprocal polemics become reciprocal plundering.

In order to escape false assimilation as a mere stimulus, the means of alienation, without forfeiting their function, would have to have a compositional–technical basis instead of merely being the result of psychological calculation. The beat quotation in the electronic context would have to be justified by the constructive concept of the music, and, equally, the electronic factor in a piece of beat music would have to be connected with compositional consequences drawn from the use of beat. The aesthetic compositional–technical postulate, however suggestive it may be, is doomed to failure. For the feature which avant-garde 'sound composition' and trivial music have in common and which forms the starting-point for attempts to mediate between them, is just the opposite of construction and compositional consequence: namely, the dissolving of form and structure in order to emphasise the musical moment and the momentary tonal event. Thus the neutralising of the critical possibilities implicit in the affinity between avant-garde and trivial music is already prefigured in the musical preconditions of the affinity itself.

VIII

A judgment about music which either does not attain work character or denies it, must, in order to be plausible, rely in the main on criteria of social psychology rather than on those of aesthetics.

To make an aesthetic judgment is to make a distinction between art and non-art, and involves an attempt to provide reasons for one's decision. Both the poeticising paraphrases of music which predominated in nineteenth-century compositional criticism, and also the technical and formal analysis which is supposed, in the twentieth century, to replace the outmoded habit of paraphrasing, perform the function of justifying or making plausible the decision that a piece of music is or is not art. Romantic criticism as represented by Schumann started out from the difference between 'poetic' and 'prosaic' music, that is, between art and non-art; and from the idea that it was a feature of 'poetic' music that it inspired the sensitive critic to paraphrase, whereas the 'prosaic' left him cold. Schumann himself confessed that he had nothing to say about trivialities. And in the twentieth century a similar conviction that the bad cannot be criticised informs the method of music analysis whose aim is value judgment. What is banal cannot be analysed, the criteria of analysis, as Hans Mersmann put it, having 'nothing to hold on to'. Again the applicability of the critical method seems to be a sign of the art character of the works criticised. Aesthetic judgment, then, proves to be a historically circumscribed form of evaluation which is based on the work concept and on the sharp distinction between art and non-art. In recent years, however, a tendency has been linked with the suspension of the work concept to replace aesthetics, which were suspected of having erred into metaphysical regions, by research into reception which conceives itself to be an empirical, socio-psychological discipline. Yet while it may be undeniable that research into reception can do justice to music which lies beyond the work concept, its claim to be 'unconditionally' empirical is questionable.

Research into reception which assembles and counts opinions about musical works, and which may even seek to uncover motivations, leaves it open whether the musical shape that it presents to those taking part in the experiment is to be construed as a mere stimulus structure or as an aesthetic object, a work. To say that it is intended to be an aesthetic object would mean that a listener who is incapable of constituting an aesthetic object in his mind would not come into question for the purposes of the experiment. The investigation would be predetermined by traditional aesthetic criteria. At the same time, falling back on the mere stimulus structure, towards which reception research tends without openly saying so, is just as much devoid of 'neutrality'. Rather, the dissolution of musical form into a group of isolated stimuli, which are juxtaposed like splashes of colour, is a feature of avant-garde 'sound composition' on the one hand and of trivial music or trivialising listening on the other. A theory which falls back on the stimulus structure so as not to get lost in the labyrinths of aesthetics is thus – just as much as the aesthetics with which it takes issue – an expression of definite, historically and socially delimited tendencies and not 'unconditional' reception research.

IX

Ever since the time of the Renaissance, when it was first formulated, the idea of the musical work, of *poeisis* as opposed to mere *praxis*, has been indissolubly linked with the idea that a work can survive the death of its creator. And aesthetic judgment – to say whether a musical shape is or is not art – always encompasses, be it explicitly or tacitly, a prediction about the effect it will have in the future. That the art character of a work proves itself through survival, through jutting up out of the time of its creation – that rubbish vanishes quickly – and that the rightness of the prediction shows the quality of an aesthetic judgment is one of the characteristic convictions of the nineteenth and early twentieth centuries.

Equally the dissolution of the work concept, the falling back from *poeisis* to the immediacy of mere *praxis*, is bound up with the tendency to emphasise the here and now: the musical moment as the expression of an unrepeatable situation. Music that is of any value at all is considered to be what the respective present understands about itself and nothing else. Once it has performed the function for which it was destined, it may be, and in fact is supposed to be, forgotten, instead of being handed down as a petrified shape and an empty shell. The sum total of tradition, the corpus of works of the past which loom into the present, appears to be a hindrance, which, if one had the power to do so, one would sweep away in order to make room for the musically new. And yet one concedes to the future its own new music instead of forcing upon it the relics of the present.

The rejection of the criterion of survival, whose anthropological substance was the hope of surviving one's own death, is thus one of the signs of that growing lack of interest in history which is a contemporary malaise. This state of affairs, however, cannot be countered meaningfully by reproaches, but solely by means of analysis.

The decline of historical consciousness is just as ambiguous and self-contradictory as historical consciousness itself, the dialectics of which may be expressed by stating that the sympathy for the past and the understanding which emanates therefrom entail at the same time a distancing. To fulfil the postulate that an earlier epoch should be understood on the basis of its own assumptions instead of being judged from the vantage of the present is on the one hand impossible without an empathetic affinity with what is strange and distant, without the antiquarian trait of history. But on the other hand the historian understands the past precisely on account of its difference and strangeness, its distance from the present. That the differences are greater than expected is one of the historian's basic experiences.

And not only the dead, but also the living past, the mass of old and ancient traditional works in one's own present, become distant when looked at with historical consciousness. To traditionalism, which sees the traditional norms, works and institutions as self-evident, natural and therefore as sacrosanct, historicism, which sees them as historical and thus as changeable, is a critical authority. It is no accident that historical awareness arose at the time of the Enlightenment, and not only in the Romantic era. Historical consciousness is itself, even if linked to Romanticism, a piece of enlightenment. And the rejection of historicism signifies a contraction of thought, not an emancipation.

X

One of the consequences of the decline of musical form into isolated moments which stand next to each other as tonal events without being structurally connected is a tendency towards programme music which is becoming more and more apparent without being openly stated and called by name. At the same time, programme music is supposed to fulfil the hybrid claim that music is, to parody a Hegelian formula, 'its time in the form of notes' – a claim which represents the reverse of the renunciation of the survival of musical works, of significance beyond the present. But the concept of programme music must not be too tightly defined if the chance of historical insight is not to be sacrificed to the pedantry of a system of aesthetics. Stockhausen's *Hymnen* or instrumental group improvisations upon linguistic texts are doubtless far removed from the programme music of the nineteenth century, but hardly further than Liszt's 'conceptual works of art' were from the naively descriptive music of the eighteenth. That one concedes that the category of programme music is far-reaching and comprehensive means that historical links and similarities between compositional problems of different eras become recognisable which would remain hidden if one surrendered the unity of the concept.

But the programmatic element with which the post-serial avant garde, hardly different in this respect from the nineteenth-century New German progressive party, hopes to impart to music a philosophical–literary or socio-political significance, by means of which it reaches beyond the narrow and constricting confines of mere music, is not seldom the reverse of formal instability. It performs a compromise function. The extramusically-based connection covers up the cracks in the musical text or even redefines them as expressive or descriptive representational and communicative means. The decline of musical structure into moments which are self-sufficient as tonal events instead of constituting form, is no longer justified in aesthetic, compositional–technical terms by the paradoxical phrase 'moment form', or even accorded the status of historical necessity. Rather, it appears as a defect which the programme is designed to overcome. The fact that one seeks to cover up or compensate for the shortcomings of musical form presupposes that one senses them as such.

Thus the tendency to make use of a programme implies, even if only unconsciously or in a covert manner, the admission of a weakness which is attached to the recourse to the momentary – a recourse which represents the ultimate consequence of the decline of the work concept in music.

The musical work of art
as a subject of sociology

I

There is no agreement about what the sociology of music is or what it could be. No one doubts the scholarly usefulness of research into the social conditions that give rise to musical works or the subsequent history of the latter, into the functions that music performs, or into the institutions that sustain it. But the claim of music sociology to be able to decode the 'real' musical reality in social terms – and without this claim it would be a harmless subsidiary discipline about which it would hardly be worth arguing – is neither obvious nor indisputable. Viewed as a musical reality which is to be analysed sociologically and 'caused to speak', the musical work of art appears in competing scholarly systems as 'objective' or 'objectified' spirit,[1] or as the individual 'experience of music',[2] or as the situation in which a musical shape is transmitted to the listeners through a player.[3]

The decision in favour of a certain method is closely bound up with what is seen to be the primary subject-matter of the sociology of music: the definition implies a judgment or prejudice about what music 'really' is. It is possible to speak of 'objective spirit' in the most uninhibited way by using the language of Hegel, which can then be translated into Marx's terminology in order to decode the state of society. The historical step from Hegel to Marx is as it were methodologically repeated. But while the dialectical Hegelian–Marxist interpretation as worked out by Adorno is based on the emphatic concept of the musical work of art, the empiricist one starts out from the listener, whose reactions are considered to be material which is capable of being processed statistically in a meaningful

234

manner. Finally there is situational analysis, for which there are only postulates and sparse beginnings, except in ethnology, at the present time. It takes its starting-point in the experiences and methods of anthropology. Thus it is possible, roughly speaking, to distinguish between three methods – the dialectical, the empirical and the anthropological – which are based on differing concepts of music.

It must however become apparent to a historian of music that the change in the definition of the subject-matter of music sociology is connected with the area selected: the decision to deal with different historical and social evolutionary stages and manifestations of music (without, it seems, music sociologists being sufficiently aware of the attendant dependencies and their consequences). The competing theories can – and this moderates the contrast – be related to different situations (there is however no dearth of overlapping).

The anthropological maxim that musical reality consists of nothing other than the situation of making and listening to music (or participating in it) may be true of non-European music and of European music of the Middle Ages and of the early modern age. But it fails in the case of artificial music of the last two, or, in certain genres, the last four centuries. (The interpretation of the work of art as 'objective spirit' denotes a problem which does not disappear just because one rejects the idealist solution.) On the other hand, the emphatic concept of art, which is presupposed by the dialectical method worked out by Adorno, rests on the historical process whereby the musical work and text become independent to form an 'opus perfectum et absolutum' – an emancipation, the beginnings of which do indeed reach back to the sixteenth century, but which first became accepted as a fundamental aesthetic fact in the general consciousness of the educated around 1800. (To this day the concept of a work remains foreign to *Gebrauchsmusik*, and the jargon phrase 'opus music' betrays a feeling of being different on the part of those excluded from artificial music.) The empirical method, finally, which treats the musical object as a mere stimulus structure and which, without an analysis of the work, simply takes account of listener responses, which are regarded as being equal in principle and thus countable, is evidently most nearly suited to the modern mass consumption of light music which was unknown to previous centuries.[4]

Thus the fact that the object of music sociology is variously defined rests on the interaction of three factors: the conception of what music 'really' is; a methodological decision; and a primary choice of subject-matter. But the conclusion that *Gebrauchsmusik* should be analysed using the anthropological method, artificial music using the dialectical

(Hegelian–Marxist) method, and that of the culture industry using the empiricist method is so eclectic that it is hardly tenable for the philosophical conscience. The unconcerned coexistence of the different approaches seems an uneasy truce to which it is difficult to lend credence; and thus it is not merely a delight in polemics that motivates the ensuing argument.

II

The postulate fundamental for the dialectical method, namely, that the single musical works as individual, unrepeatable shapes – and not merely the genres and forms that they represent[5] – should be decoded socially, is based on the firm belief that the sociological method will be able to retrace a step which formal music analysis felt compelled to take decades ago: the step from a generalising or exemplifying procedure to an individualising one. The older method of 'explaining' musical works as examples of formal patterns and genre norms became outmoded and suspect, at the latest at the beginning of this century, as a result of the work of August Halm and Heinrich Schenker. In analyses worthy of the name the individual shape no longer appears as the representative of a pattern; rather, it is the pattern that serves as a means with which to arrive at a description of the individuality of the work. The 'real' musical reality is sought in the individual entity, not in the genre. (The generalising procedure, which in retrospect seems curiously 'inartistic', was in the nineteenth century rooted on the one hand in the belief in the substantiality of musical forms and genres,[6] and on the other in the aesthetic doctrine which stated that form could and even should be schematic, because the 'content' – which was considered to be the individualising aspect – was what mattered.)

An individualising presentation of the kind that is the goal of recent formal analysis has hardly ever been achieved in the attempts at sociological interpretation which have proliferated in recent years. In a monotonous manner the same unchanging categories – division of labour, alienation and materialisation, conspicuous consumption and the intellectual legitimation of material power – are illustrated by an ever-changing series of examples. Musical works of art whose aesthetic quality no one calls into question are treated as if they belonged to the products of the culture industry, for the generalising sociological analysis makes them seem to be interchangeable examples of a type. If one Bach fugue is a tonal reflection of the principle of manufacture, then so is another. The individuality of the entities, which constitutes their very essence, is not within the reach of social decoding, at least at present.

It is not that the procedure of investigating musical works as documentary proof of general social tendencies is nonsense in principle. It is simply that the claim that the 'real' musical reality of works of art can be understood in this way is totally unjustified. To treat works of art as documents is quite legitimate (and unavoidable when one is writing history). Yet it should happen in the knowledge that one is missing the point of the mode of existence which is their inherent goal.

Of course, a disciple of the present-day doctrine which states that it is not the aesthetic raison d'être but merely 'social relevance' that matters would retort that the basic aesthetic assumption of individualising formal analysis, the category of the autonomous self-contained work, is a conceptual phantom. And though it may seem tedious to recapitulate the argument concerning aesthetic autonomy, work concept and art character, it is nevertheless unavoidable if the debate concerning the possibilities and difficulties inherent in a sociological analysis of musical works is not to be impaired by omitting mention of the decisive differences in what is assumed and what is implied.

The polemics directed against the concept of aesthetic autonomy – polemics the vehemence of which is not seldom inversely related to the cogency of the arguments employed – have become confused, on account of the fact that the difference between a historical fact which one has to accept as such and a methodological principle on which opinions are divided has been neglected or even deliberately blurred. Those who have not been struck by the partial blindness of many a dogmatist cannot deny the fact that the principle of autonomy became the rule in artificial music around 1800, and even earlier in certain musical genres. That is to say, music was or was supposed to be listened to for its own sake instead of accompanying or embellishing an extramusical event. And this as an aesthetic object whose inner logic – in a remote analogy to that of a poetic or philosophic text[7] – could be comprehended by means of a kind of attentive listening not altogether dissimilar to attentive conceptual thought.

The 'intrinsic method of interpretation' [*werkimmanente Interpretation*], which conceives of a piece of music as being a self-contained functional context, is independent in principle of the fact that around 1800 – and not before 1800 – the autonomy concept became the dominating aesthetic idea of the age. Regardless of the fact that the autonomy concept is a Classical–Romantic category, that is, one which, though historically influential, is historically limited, one can on the one hand apply the method of 'internal' formal analysis to fifteenth-century masses and motets which are far removed from autonomy aesthetics, and on the other reject it and sense its limitations in the case of nineteenth-century artificial music – on the basis of the conviction that the isolated work torn out of its social context is not musical reality but a meagre abstraction.

The scholarly uses and drawbacks of the maxim that it is not a musical work 'per se', but the social context of which it is a part – a context which is to be elucidated sociologically and socio-psychologically – that should really be the object of the analysis will be shown by the results, which for the time being have failed to materialise. Yet for a historian it seems pertinent to object that it would (at the very least) be expedient to start out from the assumptions of the epoch, the musical heritage of which one is investigating. True, there is no hard and fast, epistemological norm which would force one to adopt nineteenth-century modes of thought when attempting to elucidate the music of the period between the French Revolution and the First World War; but it is probable that it is of scholarly use to understand an era 'from the inside'. One can clearly arrive at more cogent and complex results in the case of works by Beethoven, Brahms or Schoenberg, which are intended as a musical form of conceptual development, and which for this reason justify the claim to be heard for their own sake, by means of an 'internal' formal analysis than by adhering, on account of one's dislike for 'intrinsic interpretation', to the ideology–critical thesis that the education that one had to have at one's disposal in order to follow musical logic was a privilege which served to legitimise intellectually what was material domination. It is true that music that performs a ritual function can be properly described only as part of a process which reaches out beyond it. To restrict oneself to the musical facts would be narrow-minded. However, a description of concert life, a statistical breakdown of listener responses and a sociological analysis of documents relating to the history of the work's influence will probably not shed much light on Beethoven's *Eroica*, at least not of a specific kind. No one – with the exception of scattered adherents of a rigorous aesthetic Platonism – denies that the autonomy of musical works is merely 'relative'. Autonomous music also performs social and socio-psychological functions, and the autonomy principle itself can be interpreted sociologically. Yet it seems as if it would be of greater scholarly use to proceed from the aesthetics of autonomy as the basis for musical analyses than to permit oneself to be misled by the 'relativity' of autonomy.

The 'intrinsic method' of interpretation is sometimes subject to the misunderstanding that it proceeds ahistorically – as an interpretation 'sub specie aeternitatis'. Yet the claim that it rejects having recourse to biographical and socio-historical facts on principle in order not to be disturbed in its discovery or construction of internal structures is a crude exaggeration. All analyses of musical works, including strictly 'intrinsic' ones, must have a sound historical basis – at the very least a negative one – in the sense that historical experience helps to avoid interpretative errors. The 'intrinsic' method is characterised less by the repertoire of resources it can muster than by the kind of knowledge being sought. To take into account 'external' facts in order to understand a text more precisely is not looked down upon to the extent that the uninformed among the detractors of the method imagine. But the goal of an interpretation is the presentation of the artistic character of the works, a presentation in which the 'external' context as such is effaced and subsumed in the 'internal' functional context of the music. Yet it seems as if both the supporters of the doctrine which says that only a sociological decoding of musical works makes their 'meaning' clear, and the adherents of the theory that says that the social functioning of music, of which the work forms merely a subordinate part, is the 'real' musical reality, are interested primarily in elucidating social processes, into which the music merges; or in social structures which it 'causes to speak in a non-conceptual manner'. The anthropological method revokes the crystallisation of the process 'music' into the object 'music', and the sociological method the dichotomy between work of art and document. (Sociological decoding of the work of art as a document is supposed to reveal its 'essence', which according to this view does not consist in its art character. The crucial factor is not what makes art what it is, but that of which it speaks.)

III

The idea that one has to interpret a piece of music sociologically in order to grasp its 'real' reality was developed primarily in polemical exchanges with the principle of aesthetic autonomy. As a result, any attempt to pin down or provide a sketch of the degree to which the contrary convictions are of use as the basis for analyses involuntarily assumes the form of a critique of the criticism.

1. One of the patterns of thought that derives from the legacy of the nineteenth century is the distinction between 'aesthetic being' or 'aesthetic value' on the one hand and 'historical growth' or 'historical genesis' on the other.[8] This dichotomy implies that, while a musical work is indeed the product of historical preconditions, it is abstracted from history as an object of aesthetic contemplation. The state of enraptured listening acquires, as it were, metaphysical dignity. And the aim of an aesthetic compositional–technical analysis consists of nothing more than

to pin down and conceptualise the phenomena and contexts which become apparent when one immerses oneself in a musical form, the while forgetting both the self and the world.

Yet the category of 'aesthetic being' is an empty, deceptive phrase both for the empiricist and for the Marxist. To speak of an identity of musical works which survives and maintains itself, an identity which asserts itself in spite of or regardless of socially based changes in reception is considered to be bad metaphysics. Yet the identity – which should not be confused with immutability – can be simply determined on the one hand, without the help of metaphysics, as 'intention';[9] and on the other hand it gains support from the fact that in an unbroken context of tradition the unchanged factors almost always predominate over the variable ones. (Whether a Machaut motet is still 'itself' after six hundred years may be doubted; but the identity of a Beethoven symphony is sufficiently well established.)

2. Methodological criticism of the autonomy principle is sometimes the surface of political and moral polemics against the state of aesthetic contemplation. Nothing is to be tolerated which 'turns its back on the world' and which withdraws itself from 'the demands of the day'. The moral zeal on which this criticism is based says nothing for or against its epistemological validity, though it explains the pathos of the polemics. Aesthetic contemplation, which is only seldom totally successful, is distorted in the eyes of its detractors as a kind of aestheticism which informs one's whole being. To put it crudely, the political and moral zeal is directed against an opponent who hardly exists.

3. The sharp distinction between art and non-art is suspected of being ideological. The Classical–Romantic concept of art is accused of being nothing but part of the ideological trappings of the ruling class, an idea in the service of a certain interest. 'Enjoying art' seems either wholly or 'in the final analysis' to be conspicuous consumption. And the category of taste, which is informed by the spirit of the ancien régime, turns out to be the expression and tool of a social tendency, inasmuch as its primary function consists in demarcating and warding off what is beneath it, to the aesthetic exclusion of those who do not 'belong' socially.

That aesthetic awareness is not infrequently shot through with feelings of prestige will probably not be called into question. But the kind of reductionism that betrays itself in the words 'nothing but', that is, the claim that a sociological reduction can demonstrate the untenable nature of aesthetics, is unjustified. A half truth is loudly proclaiming to be the whole truth. And that social factors are 'in the final analysis' the ones on which all else is based does not mean that one should in each and every case rank the social aspect higher than the aesthetic one. Besides, the drabness of the sociological claims, which one can repeat, but which one can hardly expand upon and develop in analyses of individual works, stands in disconcerting and shameful contrast to the formal wealth that is uncovered by aesthetic contemplation.

4. The claim that the idea of aesthetic autonomy merely deceives us about the social reality in which nothing exists that does not perform a function, is too crude on the one hand, and too platitudinous on the other, to permit meaningful discussion. (The – changing – social significance that a piece of music acquires is supposed to pass as its essence, without bothering to enquire about the claim that emanates from the object itself.) But Marxists who are not impervious to art actually tend to quote Friedrich Engels,[10] speaking of a 'relative autonomy' of art and of 'interaction' between the base and the superstructure, and citing the primacy of the economic sphere only 'in the final analysis'. But the argument about whether or not the economic sphere always and exclusively represents the 'final court of appeal' is, from a scholarly point of view, altogether of secondary importance, however gripping it may seem from an ideological one. For one can describe and analyse the connections, the mediations and the fundamental relationships that exist between the various constituent parts of a social whole without ever being forced to decide for or against the idea of the fundamental – and not merely casual – priority of the economic sphere. (The casual hegemony of the economic sphere in the eighteenth and nineteenth centuries, for example, is a fact; the fundamental one, however, is an axiom.) Karel Kosík attempted to resolve the problem that at times it is the economic sphere and at other times politics or even religion that seems to predominate in structuring society, by making a terminological distinction between the 'economic factor', the influence of which may vary, and the 'economic structure', which is of primary and basic importance in all kinds of society.[11] Yet the concept of economic structure is so abstract, vague and all-embracing that the claim that the 'economic structure' always and in principle forms the foundation and the 'final court of appeal' can hardly be distinguished from the platitude that the human beings who act together and against each other themselves make the world in which they live.[12] (If human activity, characterised as 'work', is wholly subsumed under the concept of the 'economic sphere', then the theory which states that the economic sphere

has the first and final word is meaningless, even though it cannot be refuted.)

5. The conviction that a musical work is a function or a dependent variable of the social context from which it derives or into which it was placed implies in methodological terms that the process of becoming an aesthetically autonomous (or pseudo-autonomous) form signifies an unreal abstraction and distortion. Nineteenth-century autonomy aesthetics should not be taken without further ado to be an underlying assumption for formal analyses of works from the Classical–Romantic era, but should be subjected to ideology–critical reduction and destruction; they should not be taken as a guiding principle, but as an object of scholarly investigation. Yet the concept of 'relative autonomy', which is after all a Marxist category, states not only that autonomy is limited and non-existent in the final analysis, but also that – in spite of its relative nature – it is possible to speak meaningfully of aesthetic autonomy. And it even seems as if, viewed realistically, it is less a theoretical than a practical problem of scholarship, a problem whose basic features remind one of the perennial difficulty of hermeneutics, which was only ever capable of being solved from case to case and never in principle: that is, the difficulty of how to determine 'appropriately' the context of a particular place in the text. That the single event has to be understood in the context to which it belongs is a postulate that is as abstract as it is self-evident. But, taking a single, unique case, how large is the context that is required to understand a sentence 'sufficiently'? Does it include the paragraph, the chapter, the book, the whole literature of the age, the latter's social structure, or the world as a whole? The decision is supposed to be 'appropriate'. Yet 'appropriateness' is a vague category which functions only within the confines of a traditional cultural context. One can indeed base the stipulating of a context on experience and on arguments, but one cannot give reasons for one's choice that are logically compelling. ('Cognitive interests' – and the desire to explain every musical fact in socio-economic terms is without doubt a 'cognitive interest' – are irrefutable.) Yet it should really be self-evident that it is 'inappropriate' to expect to find economic preconditions, implications and dependencies in every analysis of a piece of music, for in the case of artificial music they have very little to do with the aesthetic, compositional–technical facts that impress themselves upon us as the primary musical reality. History – even music history – is written less on the basis of axioms than on the basis of innate 'feelings'.

IV

Adorno's sociology of music, whose explicit aim is to become aware of 'a social content in the autonomous shape of the forms in terms of their aesthetic content',[13] can be understood as an attempt to overcome a contradiction which seems almost incapable of being bridged: the contrast between an aesthetic compositional–technical analysis, which proceeds by individualising, and a sociological interpretation which tends to view musical works as documents and examples of general social tendencies and structures that always remain the same, albeit in the most varied forms. The postulate that the social content of music has to be pursued 'right into the smallest technical cells'[14] says nothing less than that it is possible 'to cause to speak' socially the whole wealth of musical connections that a formal analysis is capable of uncovering. The work of art is supposed to become the subject of a sociological analysis, without harming or neglecting its individuality and its art character. Adorno wanted to prove analytically the idea that music is 'part of society through and through' without lapsing into a non-artistic language and giving up the insights of traditional aesthetics. And one can hardly deny that categories such as 'breakthrough' and 'the progress of the world', on which Adorno's dialectical interpretation of Mahlerian symphonic movements is based,[15] are real concepts which convey a meaning. In determining the aesthetic content, they are based on detailed formal analyses on the one hand and, without doing violence to the matter in hand, they enable a sociological decoding to be carried out on the other.

At the same time Adorno not infrequently displays a penchant for aphoristic allusions to socio-musical parallels and analogies, allusions which are by no means intended to be taken playfully, but the logical status of which is difficult to perceive or even questionable. When he compares serial technique, in the sense of total integration, with the social over-predominance of 'bureaucracy',[16] or when he conceives of the musical dialectics which, in sonata form, mediate between harmony (the general) and thematicism (the particular) as a reflection of the conflict between society as a whole and a 'particular interest',[17] then he provokes the impatient objection that these are merely verbal analogies which have no basis in fact but owe their origin and a semblance of plausibility to a generously ambivalent use of words like 'integration', 'subject and object' or 'general and particular'. And an assertion like the one that the musical dialectic between the rationality of compositional technique and the irrationality of expression represents a reflection and consequence of the social conflict between the rationality of the technical means and the irrationality of the 'indigenous' ends, which are at cross purposes,[18] is simply impossible to understand. For even the most daring of psycho-analytical theories would find it hard to establish a link between the irrationality of the emotions and that of economic liberalism.

Yet the blind spots are not simply an accidental defect. Rather, the con-trast between the methods – between the formal–analytically indi-vidualising and the sociologically generalising procedure – returns as a flaw in the individual analyses, though Adorno was able at times, by dint of great effort, to reconcile the opposing views by force. And the verbal analogies perform the function of hiding a gap which the arguments could not close.

Sometimes the individualisation of a social interpretation is simply borrowed: the sociological analysis appears as a kind of parasite of the formal one. It does indeed form a consequence of the aesthetic, compositional–technical presentation, but does not in fact follow on from the latter's individualising features, adhering rather to the general features of the history of form or material which seem capable of being decoded sociologically with much less trouble. It is not the description of a certain, unrepeatable assertion as a whole but a few remarks about forms or material tendencies in general contained therein that provide the starting-point for sociological deliberations, for translations from the lan-guage of music theory into that of sociology. Thus, for example, a detailed analysis of motivic technique in the first of Schoenberg's Five Orchestral Pieces, Op. 16, culminates in the observation that 'the growth in com-plexity, as if according to the fundamental tenets of the contemporary sociology of Herbert Spencer' goes together 'with growing integration as its correlative'.[19] It remains unclear whether the digression into the sociological realm (which, moreover, could be replaced, without sacrific-ing the pertinent point, by a digression into the realm of biology, though this would not have been to Adorno's liking) is meant to be merely an illustration of the connection between complexity and integration, or an allusion, even if only a passing one, to a sociological exegesis of Schoen-berg's motivic technique. But in any case the 'correlation' to which the sociological commentary refers is not peculiar to Op. 16. Rather, it is a feature common to all of Schoenberg's works since the time of the transition from tonality to atonality.

V

A music–sociological analysis which proceeds from the isolated self-contained work in order to decode its formal features as 'sedimented content' and 'cause it to speak socially' may be suspected of being a semi-speculative undertaking, the results of which do indeed on occasion appear suggestive but are rarely capable of being demonstrated conclusively. The 'anthropological' method, however, which sees a musical utterance as a function – as a dependent variable – of a social context, has set as its goal the description or reconstruction of a piece of the present or the past strictly empirically: just as it 'really' was. The epistemological and practical scholarly difficulties which one encounters when attempting to justify on the one hand and to discharge on the other the postulate of an empirical sociological interpretation of musical works are, however, not insignificant.

1. The context as a function of which a musical shape is to be understood is variable. Thus the suspension of the isolating procedure of 'intrinsic' analysis is aimed – or so it seems – at historicising the method. Not only the genesis and influence of a piece of music but also its substance is to be considered as being historical. But every method of writing history is based on a decision about what 'belongs to history' and what does not. The idea that in addition to the works themselves their reception is history in an emphatic sense is not at all self-evident. The decision is dependent on a 'cognitive interest' – a feeling for what is of 'essential importance' and what is not. Yet it is uncertain whether the 'cognitive interest' which underlies the anthropological–sociological method – the description of music as a dependent variable of a situation – is in fact aimed at the reconstruction of past musical reality, or whether it exhausts itself in the ideology–critical intention of merely showing the present involvement of music in social functional contexts. One evidently feels more driven to history by the force of logic than attracted to it by inclination.

2. The method is not infrequently musico-politically motivated. The idea that what matters is not the works 'per se', but the social context in which they perform a function, serves the musical conservatism of certain socialists as a defence against the annoying reproach that they have 'lagged behind' compositional development. One suspects the avant garde of the others of being without a social function in order to defend one's own non-avant garde, by praising its 'functional' character, against the charge of being 'superfluous' which the kind of music history based primarily on compositional categories and on the concept of the new might level against it. (It is, or should be, self-evident that, although the musico-political motivation helps to explain the topical and vehement quality of the methodological debate, it says nothing about whether the

competing procedures are incontrovertible or flawed from the epistemological point of view.)

3. The point of the 'anthropological'–sociological approach – provided one draws the logical consequences from the concept's premisses – should really be the attempt to 'integrate' music history into 'general' history. For the idea that music – taken as a whole and not merely incidentally – is the function of a variable social context forces one to conclude that a social structure and its modifications, that is, a 'general' history which is construed primarily as a social history, forms the context and referential system within which a musical shape or process should be interpreted if it is to be comprehended in its 'real' reality. Yet it is impossible to predict how the epistemological programme which says that music analysis must be 'historicised', music history 'integrated' and 'general' history 'sociologised' could be realised and put to concrete scholarly use.

4. If the striving for the larger totality is endangered by a penchant for empty programmes, then detailed analysis is endangered by a lack of documents. The difficulties which stand in the way of reconstructing the social context of individual works of the past – that is, of not restricting oneself to a sociology of musical genres[20] – are well-nigh insurmountable. (As the genres in the nineteenth century formed the substance of the individual works to a lesser extent than in the sixteenth and seventeenth centuries, an interpretation of the genres will not suffice to do justice to musical reality in the age of aesthetic autonomy.) Only in rare instances, such as the St Matthew Passion, the Ninth Symphony, *Der Freischütz* or *Der Ring des Nibelungen*, are the sources sufficiently comprehensive to enable one to give an account of the reception history which is not wholly platitudinous. (Any attempt to write the history of the influence of Beethoven's Op. 59 would probably be futile.) In addition, the literary and pictorial evidence of the reception of musical works – and it is all that we have – is not direct, but consists in the refracted reflections of a past musical situation which are influenced by the traditions of literature and painting. The idea that, in describing the musical past, one could replace the characterising of 'objective' works by the description and analysis of complex 'processes' in which the notes on the page, the interpretation and the reception interact, may seem attractive on account of the promise it contains of 'getting close to reality'. Yet it proves to be a utopian vision in the main. Only a shadow of past musical reality, whose relics and petrified shapes the works seem to be, can be reconstructed.

VI

The scepticism which is provoked both by the idea of sociologically 'decoding' individual, autonomous works and by the postulate that a musical shape has to be construed and analysed in principle as one of the factors in a social 'process' or 'structure' is based less on epistemology than on practical scholarship. There is no reason whatsoever to doubt that some of those analyses in which musical forms are to be interpreted as 'sedimented contents' or past musical 'situations' reconstructed in their 'totality' may be successful and may make their point. Yet the sociological blueprints, despite the emphatic tone with which they recommend themselves to our attention, are too vague and rudimentary at present to be a satisfactory replacement for the method of 'intrinsic' analysis and for a method of writing history which seems to mediate between the history of form and material on the one hand and on orientation towards the art character of the works on the other.

Nonetheless, it can hardly be denied that traditional music history is forced to grapple with a problem which seems well-nigh impossible to solve: the problem of how to write a history of 'art' (that is, of the works themselves, and not merely of the material and the forms) which is nonetheless a 'history' of art (and not a museum catalogue). And it may very well be that musicology is one of those disciplines in which 'fundamental' problems are not solved, but instead gradually become obsolete, only to be replaced by others equally incapable of being solved.

Form

TRANSLATED BY STEPHEN HINTON

I

The urge to define, grasp and contain appears to be as ineradicable as the opposing urge to dissolve and break out. Definitions have a calming as well as a restricting effect; one seeks support from them while at the same time regarding them with suspicion.

What is musical form, if it is meaningful to speak both of sonata form and of statistical form? I fear the answer is: nothing but a word on the one hand, and, on the other, a confused mass of facts, whereby it is not at all certain whether they can be subsumed under a single concept.

The expression 'form' is as respectable as it is ambiguous, and is therefore serviceable as a catchword. Catchwords are defined less by their content than by their function. And it is noticeable that in literature form tends to be a critical catchword, yet in music an affirmative one. Anyone who declares support for literary formalism may entertain the hope of being counted among the avant garde; an apologist of musical form, however, provokes the suspicion that he is trying to lay down norms for compositional practice. If literary formalism represents the critical antithesis of attempts to assert the primacy of content, then the aesthetics of musical content are dead and buried. Formalism is the aesthetic morality that is taken for granted; yet as soon as clearly defined forms, rather than form in general, are discussed, formalism is suspected of wanting to incarcerate music in schematic patterns.

The critical function that formalism performs in literature has fallen in music to the concern with material. Yet matter and form are correlative concepts; the one is empty without the other. The concept of material as

248

propounded by Adorno means preformed material. It is only formally defined matter or materially defined form – *materia secunda* or *forma secunda* (to use the language of scholasticism) – that has a real existence. One can, for example, view a drawn line from four different angles: as traces of lead, as an ornament, as a sine curve or as the image of a snake. But it is impossible to apprehend the line as pure matter beyond all forms of contemplation (and even viewing it as traces of lead is a form of contemplation).

Pure matter is a mystical category. Grasping it may be a goal that one may approach by means of, to use the language of mysticism, 'deformation' and 'de-becoming', yet without reaching it. Mysticism and art, however, are mutually exclusive. Mystical 'deformation' – the attempt to break out of the forms of contemplation felt to be a prison – is completely at odds with the intention of making form perceivable. And however inappropriate it might be to judge using aesthetic criteria mystical tendencies that take their cue from acoustical facts or productions, it is nonetheless crucial to emphasise that music as art is incompatible with mysticism.

II

Form, according to Aristotle, is relative. In contrast to individual notes, the motif represents a form, as does the period in relation to the motifs and the movement in relation to the periods. And the conditions of formal concision are different on each level. A theory of form that neglects as indifferent or accidental the scale on which a formal component is effective is fancifully misguided.

Thus the statement, for example, that form is large-scale rhythm is a metaphor that should not be taken literally; it is of no use as a principle of a theory of form. The concept of rhythmic correspondence does not extend beyond the scope of the period. An antecedent and a consequent can just – and by no means always – be perceived as analogous to a weak and a strong beat, as rhythmically corresponding parts; correspondence between longer sections has to be justified thematically. The false assumption that form is a large-scale rhythm has the consequence that sections comprising hundreds of bars are seen as corresponding parts, though thematic connections are either lacking or only vaguely implied. The mere exactness or similarity of the continuation is supposed to be sufficient to justify a connection that corresponds to the relation of antecedent and consequent. The model of the period is blindly applied to stretches that are too long to be discernible as periods.

If it is sometimes difficult in the case of earlier music to avoid mistakes about the scale on which a formal principle is effective, then the possibilities for confusion have, in recent years, become boundless. Let it suffice to demonstrate this with a single example: that of statistical formation.

The procedure of describing a section or a group by the vertical or horizontal density of events is not unambiguous. In principle, all polyphonic music can be viewed from the point of view of density, and it is not clear where statistics are meaningful and where they are not. On the other hand, statistical concepts would be the most meagre of all imaginable categories if vertical and horizontal density were to represent nothing more than the remainder of differentiation after the levelling-out of harmonic and rhythmic details. One would have to enquire, then, after the conditions under which statistical definitions could become effective without there having to be a loss of concision as far as detail is concerned. And one of the conditions would appear to be clarity in distinguishing between differences of scale.

Statistical categories are the more general ones and thus relate to fairly long stretches. If, however, the horizontal density of notes is to be, on the one hand, perceivable as a group feature and, on the other, compatible with the concision of rhythmic details, then there must be no doubt as to the approximate length of sections that are supposed to count as groups; an extreme change of scale in the course of a piece would make for confusion. What is a detail and what is a group must be as unmistakable as the difference in earlier music between motif and period. The clarity of statistical formation and the stability of formal scale are mutually supportive. The comprehensibility of a group resides in the forcefulness of statistical formation; as does, conversely, the perceptibility of statistical formation in expectations of the length of groups.

On the other hand, it is not futile to remind oneself how in earlier music the individual characteristics (the melodic, rhythmic and harmonic details) and the more general statistical features (average pitch level, vertical density and dynamic level) were distinguished from each other. The pitch level was less a melodic than a timbral, instrumental aspect; the harmonic–tonal function of a chord was dependent on the vertical density, that is, the number of notes; and a *sforzato* that performed a rhythmic function, such as accentuating a syncopation, was possible at different dynamic levels. The principle behind the distinction is clear. The details are independent of the statistically ascertainable features, since they are defined by categories other than merely high and low or loud and soft: melody by the character of intervals, harmony by tonal functions, and dynamics by rhythmic functions.

The premises of earlier music – tonal harmony and metrical rhythm – cannot be restored. That, however, the special conditions of distinguishing detail from statistical formation are inoperative does not mean that the principle is dead and buried. The idea of basing individual characteristics on categories that extend beyond features to which statistical formation adheres retains its significance, even if the means with which it was realised are spent and have to be replaced by others.

III

If one is going to nominate a feature common to recent compositional tendencies, even the superficially divergent ones, then one would have to speak of a fear of things becoming fixed, the mistrust of consolidation. It is significant that the difference between consolidation and objectification – a difference that is decisive, however small it may seem – is seldom mentioned, if it is mentioned at all. The dialectic at work in the categories is reduced to an indiscriminate mistrust of everything fixed and complete. What is real or realised is felt to be – to put it bluntly – a betrayal of what is possible.

The objection is levelled against the clearly defined musical work. The expression 'work' is beginning to sound empty. The emphasis is supposed to be placed on the creation of music, not on the result; musical listening, it is argued, is the reconstruction of the process of composition, not the apprehension of a given artefact. 'The work of art', wrote Paul Klee, 'is first and foremost genesis. It is never experienced as a product.'

The concepts of form coined by Stockhausen – 'pointillist form', 'group form' and 'statistical form' – also refer primarily to the creation, not the existence, of music. Stockhausen makes a distinction between form and formation; and the expression 'pointillist form' is an abbreviation for 'pointillist form-genesis'.

No one would wish to contradict the requirement that musical form has to be grasped in performance as the process of interaction between the individual components of a work. And in view of the popular misconception that musical forms are patterns filled out with varying content, the polemical assertion that it is the genesis that is decisive, not the final product, is entirely justified.

However, the antithesis of genesis and product, as formulated by Paul Klee, becomes precarious as soon as it falls into the hands of epigones and no longer functions as criticism but as dogmatism. The mistrust of patterns and the endeavour to draw formal categories into the performance of music and understand them in that context turns into a tendency to disparage form as an artefact and a result, and ultimately to reject it as superfluous and as an impediment. Anyone who emphasises the performance of music and neglects the interaction between formation and form, genesis and result is moving towards the abolition of formal categories.

One would not include Stockhausen among those who despise form; yet the concepts 'pointillist' and 'statistical', though they were introduced as formal categories, do not refer to form but to compositional technique. They describe the structure of individual sections, not how they cohere. A complex of notes can be defined as 'pointillist' or 'statistical'; to say as much of a relationship between two sections would be meaningless. The concepts 'pointillist' and 'statistical' say little or nothing about form, the relation of parts to one another and to the whole.

To object that the difference between compositional technique and form has been transcended and rendered inoperative in the newest music, and to say that anyone who insists upon the difference is applying an obsolete standard, would be futile. Decrees are not enough to eliminate and render ineffective the difference between structure and function, between the composition and the coherence of parts. The difference remains, whether or not one is inclined to talk about it. However, vocabularies that contain the word 'form', although they may describe nothing more than compositional technique, are misleading with regard to the fact that the problem of form, or of musical coherence, which they have seemingly solved, has not even been posed.

IV

The concept of parameter is a fetish to which theory clings all the more stubbornly, the more clearly experience reveals the dubious nature of its usefulness. One might accept that an expression for the physical correlative of a sound quality is applied to the sound quality itself, if the correlation were complete; but it is not. Timbre is a sound quality, not a parameter, since it does not fulfil the condition of being variable independently of the other parameters.

It is not certain whether the other sound qualities signified by the expression parameter are suitable as the starting-point for the development of formal categories. The concept of parameter is tangential to the accustomed categories; and, although tradition may be a weak authority, it is by no means futile to remind oneself of the difference.

The difference is concealed by efforts to bring the categories melody, rhythm and dynamics into line with the idea that music is made up of parameters. Melody is supposed to be definable as an arrangement of pitches, rhythm as one of note values, dynamics as the gradation of degrees of loudness. However, the reduction of the traditional categories to sound qualities is arbitrary. For melody implies rhythm, and rhythm implies aspects of dynamics. Whereas a parameter is a simple sound quality strictly separated from the other parameters, melody and rhythm are complex matters or forms of perception that merge into one another.

What is simple, the individual parameter, is abstract; a sound quality, separated from the other ones, has no real existence. Only what is complex is concrete, the note as the embodiment of its features. And the analysis of serial music, if it is facts of perception that are to be described, must itself form concepts that describe what is concrete. The term 'pointillist' is characteristic, defining notes as individuals, not as relative positions in three or four rows.

Even when the parameters are individually and separately subject to the serial principle, a group of notes is nonetheless perceived as something that results from the interaction of sound qualities. This fact makes it seem reasonable to investigate the relations between parameters. It scarcely needs to be mentioned that parameters are qualities that fit only reluctantly into a common scheme that is the same for all of them; the primitive kind of parallelism that attempted to subject dynamics or articulation to the same conditions as pitch is a thing of the past. Boulez has observed: 'One should no longer have any illusions about our perceptional ability to trace different acoustical phenomena such as pitch and duration back to common patterns.' However, bearing in mind the unequal behaviour of the parameters is only an initial and basic precondition for an analysis of the relationships among sound qualities. In traditional music, a description of interactions is a retrospective procedure, an attempt to explain complexes that present themselves to our immediate perception as complete and undissected. Thus, in the idea of rhythm, for example, relations between the duration and dynamics are included which one seldom has to (nor needs to) become conscious of to listen in an adequate manner. It is precisely one of the functions of the traditional categories to make the compound appear as an undivided unity. Categories are forms of contemplation, and they regulate perception. And the concept of rhythm, which combines duration with aspects of dynamic gradation, represents the exact equivalent of a way of listening.

It is probably impossible to restore unaltered the complex categories which relate several parameters. Analytical thinking, the correlative to composition with separate parameters, cannot be revoked. Thus it is all the more necessary to become aware of the interaction of the sound qualities. They can neither be ignored, nor are they, as in tradition, self-evidencies implicit in the categories of musical listening which do not require explication. There is no alternative but, in an analytical context, to solve problems concerning the interaction of parameters which in earlier music were solved without being thought of as problems.

Schoenberg wrote in 1926: 'Real thought, the musical idea, the immutable, is determined by the relationship between the pitches and the division of time. Everything else, on the other hand – dynamics, tempo, timbre – and what results from them – character, clarity, effect etc. – is really only a means of presentation serving to make the idea comprehensible, and can be changed.' To dismiss the distinction Schoenberg makes as being the expression of an outmoded state of compositional technique would be blind presumption, for it could very well be that the hierarchy of sound qualities of which Schoenberg speaks, the priority of pitch and duration, is a fact which one has to take into account and not a mere assumption which one can ignore. The most obvious differences are those between pitch and timbre. Whereas in the case of pitches the relative quality – the interval character – is of decisive, and the absolute quality of minor, significance, the opposite is true in the case of timbre, which is perceived primarily as an absolute quality.

Relationships between tone colours – degrees of similarity and difference – can only be defined in vague terms; and the idea of transposing the relationship between two tone colours would border on the fictitious. Duration and dynamics occupy the middleground between pitch and timbre, from the point of view of concision and transposability of relationships. Duration is nearer to pitch, dynamics nearer to timbre. Thus it is not an empty assertion to say that sound qualities form a hierarchy.

It is not difficult to sketch some of the consequences for a theory of form that emerge as a result. Degrees of loudness and timbres, however much they may be graded, are restricted to elementary, rudimentary formal connections. They are either similar or different and antithetical, and nothing else. Other categories appear not to be accessible to subordinate, peripheral sound qualities. It is scarcely conceivable that something could be composed which concisely and unambiguously performed the function of a continuation or a complement merely by making use of timbres or degrees of loudness. Yet no one is safe from mistaking the limits of his imagination for those of reality, least of all the theoretician.

V

Banal matters, and they in particular, are also sometimes forgotten or ignored. The spread of an analytical technique which Boulez has aptly called 'book-keeping' compels one to recall the fact that formal categories are not reducible to features that are present in the score and, conversely, that it is not sufficient to register characteristics of a composition in order to arrive at formal concepts by summarising and generalisation. 'Inductive method' is not infrequently a synonym for thoughtlessness.

Thus, for instance, the features on which the division of a period into an antecedent and a consequent is based are not always the same. The harmonic outline can be decisive, but so can the melodic connection or the rhythmic correspondence of the halves; and components that in one case are constitutive diminish in importance or are omitted altogether in another. It is not possible, then, to reduce the concept of the period to fixed characteristics that recur in each and every case. And, conversely, it is improbable or even impossible that the method of registering features would ever have led one to formulate a concept such as that of the period.

Formal concepts are regulative concepts. They mark points of view from which notes or groups or notes are supposed to be brought together and related. They are not derivable from the mere accumulation of perceptual data. If anything, it is the other way round: perception depends on formal categories. In Schoenberg's Piano Piece Op. 11, No. 1, for example, it is not immaterial whether bars 9–11, a variant of bars 1–3, are understood as the conclusion of the first, or as the beginning of a second period. There are interactions between the division (the form) and the melodic connections (the content). On the one hand, the motivic connections establish one of the prerequisites of the formal functions; on the other, the motivic connections that are emphasised depend on the formal function. If the modified return of the main thematic idea in bars 9–11 is understood as the beginning of a second period, then the alterations of the melody come under the concept of variation. They appear as the augmentation and inversion of intervals: the minor third b^1–g^1 sharp and the minor second g^1 sharp–g^1 are expanded in bars 9–10 to a major third f^1 sharp–d^1 and a major second d^1–c^1; and the falling semitone f^1–e^1 is inverted in bar 11 to become a rising semitone a–b flat. If, on the other hand, one views bars 9–11 as the conclusion of a tripartite period, the features that make the third phrase appear as a complement and consequence of the first two, bars 1–8, come to the fore. The rising semitone is then less a mere variant of the descending one than a complementary 'answer'; and the sequence f^1 sharp–d^1–c^1 in bars 9–10 is understood not only as an extension of b^1–g^1 sharp–g^1 but also as a transposition of e^1–c^1–b flat, the beginning of the second phrase. The motivic connections are a prerequisite as well as a function – a dependent variable – of the formal categories that determine musical listening.

The expression 'period' describes a pattern, a model; more precisely, since the eighteenth century it has been so closely associated with a particular pattern that it has been unusable in any other context. But because the model is incompatible with the conditions of contemporary composition does not mean that the general concept it represents is a thing of the past. The category of complementation on which the period pattern is based is not tied to any particular version of it. It is still relevant independently of the preconditions of compositional technique.

Yet in a strict sense one can only speak of a formal category in music when it is neither so general as the category of complementation nor when it has the task of disguising metaphorically the description of one particulara case. A use of metaphor which plunders the arsenal of scientific terminology is merely the reverse of 'book-keeping'.

What one ought to be looking for are categories that a listener must have at his disposal in order to understand the relationship between two sections as being one of complementation; regulative categories, which mark points of view from which individual features fit together as meaningful constructs. A theory of form remains unfounded if it cannot find support in intermediate categories which mediate between blind facts and empty universals, categories which neither hover in the rarified air of abstraction nor amount to no more than pigeonholing the registering of features. The category 'period' may be taken to be paradigmatic. Whether the concept 'group' can perform a similar function, or whether a group is defined by nothing more than the fact that a sound quality or compositional feature is sustained during a section, appears to be an open question.

VI

The attempt to develop concepts of form that go beyond definitions of compositional technique is impeded by the idea that dodecaphony is incompatible with categories such as theme and development, transition and countersubject. The claim that Schoenberg's method of forcibly combining twelve-note composition and developmental form is in itself contradictory, and the results inconsistent, has become a *topos* it is not necessary to talk about because it is supposed to be self-evident. It would appear, however, that the arguments on which the objections to Schoenberg are founded are themselves based on a misunderstanding, namely, on the confusion of abstract relationships and concrete forms.

A theme is a melodic shape, a real structure. But the sequence of pitches – and thus also the row which regulates it – is a dependent component which has no real existence without rhythm and dynamics. It is only together with an arrangement of durations and a gradation of degrees of dynamics that a sequence of pitches becomes a musical phenomenon.

However, if a sequence of pitches is already an abstraction, then a row is one to an even greater degree. It consists of nothing but the relationship linking basic set, inversion, retrograde and retrograde inversion. The name 'basic set' is misleading, for the initial shape in which a row appears is no more important than later ones. The name suggests that we should treat basic set and row as equivalents, thereby confusing the means of representation with what is being represented. The basic set is just one form of the row among others. What can be notated is a particular interval, a major third, for instance. The concept of a row, however, refers to the abstract factor which is common to the major third, the minor sixth and the major tenth, both upwards and downwards – to a feature for which there is neither a name nor a sign.

The meaning of the serial principle is distorted by talking about exposition and derivations of the row. A row relates to the individual form by means of which it is represented, as the formula $n/n + 1$ does to the ratios $1:2$, $2:3$, $3:4$ etc. And it is just as nonsensical to describe particular forms of a row as derivations of a basic set as it is to maintain that the ratios $2:3$ and $3:4$ are derivations of $1:2$. A row is nothing but an embodiment of relationships.

If one thinks of the row as an abstraction, then the assertion that dodecaphony and developmental form are incompatible becomes questionable. Categories such as theme and continuation, complement and continuation, complement and contrast, transition and subordinate theme are not affected by the serial principle; dodecaphony neither suggests nor justifies them, neither precludes them nor divests them of meaning. Form is independent of the serial principle in the same way as the syntax of a language is independent of phonological rules. One can change the one system without tampering with the other; in the case of categories such as conditional or final clause it is irrelevant whether the pitch at which the syllable is spoken registers a difference in the meaning of the words or not. Categories of musical form refer to things that are real, to melodic–rhythmic forms, not to abstract components. Nor does the generalisation of the serial principle to cover all parameters affect the difference between syntax and phonology. It is not the arrangement of rows but the musical forms resulting from the interaction of pitch sequence, rhythm and dynamics that comprise the substance of form. The serial principle is neutral; it does not establish form, but it does not preclude it either.

Schoenberg understood form as coherence. He only partly realised his intention to write a theory of musical coherence. One suspects that a repeat attempt under conditions that make it still more difficult would similarly remain a fragment. Yet difficulties constitute a provocation, or at least they should do.

CONCLUDING REMARKS

I

To expect a discussion about musical form to produce definitions and prescriptions would be naive. It is by no means certain what form in music is, and any attempt to formulate rules would provoke nothing but derision. Even the premiss on which the discussion was based, the assertion that the newest music had encountered difficulties that one would have to understand as formal problems, did not pass unchallenged. Some composers seem convinced that form is something self-evident which does not need talking about. Nothing that appears, they argue, is without form; in order to be perceivable a thing or a process must present itself in a form. Thus they conclude that it is absurd to speak of formlessness.

Yet the universal concept of form that embraces everything in existence is not a topic of music theory. That is not what was meant, and was only used to deny the existence of the problem at hand. Even debris has a form; but it is not the object of discussion between architects.

On the other hand, nothing would be more erroneous than to assert that it is only compositional practice that has lost its bearings. Theory is in no less of a predicament. The concept of form itself – and not just the creation of forms – has become a problem.

This concept of form derives from nineteenth-century formal theory, and the traces of its origins are still in evidence. A historical digression is thus unavoidable. Anyone who wishes to get away from the past, instead of merely denying its existence, must first become aware of it.

The concept of form that was developed on the basis of the model of the song, the rondo and the sonata, rests on two principles which have become doubtful in the twentieth century, yet which were so much taken for granted in the nineteenth century that they did not need to be explicitly described and were thus not recognised as problems. The first premiss was the distinction between content and form. It was not intended as a division; no one denied that content and form constituted a whole. Yet one regarded the indivisibility on the lines of the unity of soul and body. The form was considered to be the shell surrounding the content, and the theory of form a parallel to anatomy; the soul was consigned to aesthetics, the theology of art religion.

One can only do justice to the theory of form if one recognises that it was thought of as a complement to aesthetics. Musical poetics, a coherent and unified theory of the creation of musical forms, did not exist; it was divided into aesthetics and theory of form.

The double meaning of the concept of the theme is a typical example. Whereas in formal terms a theme was considered to be a complex of motifs, in aesthetic terms it was seen as the expression of content. The elaboration of a theme was thought of as the development of the motifs on the one hand and as an explication of the contents on the other. A theme was a character, as it were, who had to be taken through changing situations in order to show the stuff he was made of.

The second principle of the theory of form was the idea that a musical form belonged primarily to a genre and was only secondarily an individual. No one denied that an individual is not only an example of a genre, but also a person. Yet the soul was the concern of aesthetics. In the theory of form the features common to musical works counted as essential, whereas the distinguishing ones were regarded as being inessential. The theory of form was a description of genres. True, the theory of form repeated the universal debate; whether a genre was an idea *ante rem*, an essence *in re* or an abstraction *post rem* remained uncertain. That, however, concepts of form were concepts of genre appeared to be beyond dispute. Whatever did not belong to a genre counted as 'formless'; musical malformations were analogous to the monsters of zoology.

Both principles – the distinction between content and form as well as the explanation of forms as genres – have been abandoned in the twentieth century, and it would be anachronistic to adhere to them. Traditional theory of form and its correlative, the aesthetics of content, are dead and buried. Yet the decline has left behind problems that cannot be solved by not talking about them.

First, a theory of the new and newest music would have to attempt to develop musical poetics which are not split into theory of form and aesthetics. And secondly, it would have to establish the possibility of appraising musical forms without invoking concepts of genre. As long as one understood forms in terms of genre it was not difficult to justify the assertion that a work was formless; the criticism may have been narrow-minded, but it was not unfounded. If, however, a work is an individual without genre, then the judgment seems to be based on nothing. Nonetheless, no one doubts that one can distinguish between successful and unsuccessful forms; and the difference that exists must also be explainable.

II

The erosion of the concept of form upheld by the theory of form led to the concept of structure acquiring a significance which one can describe, without exaggeration, as a hyperfunction. 'Structure' has become an in-word. Moreover, in-words sometimes serve no other purpose than to conceal difficulties; they are ideology, false consciousness, in verbal form.

The concept of structure occupies a position midway between categories that are clearly distinguished in traditional music theory: between 'form' and 'compositional technique'. And the mediating character, which permits a *quid pro quo*, leads one to draw false conclusions. Protected by the ambiguity of the concept, the error thrives that it is sufficient to solve difficulties in compositional technique in order at the same time to solve formal ones. The problem concealed by using the term 'structure' as an in-word is the problem of form. No one denies that it would be unnatural to keep form and structure firmly apart. That, however, it is impossible to break something down into pieces does not mean that a distinction is nonsensical. And it is perhaps not unfruitful, by analysing verbal usage, to call to mind some of the differences between form and structure.

First, the term 'structure' suggests details, connections in a small space; the word 'form', on the other hand, the outline of the whole, relations over wide stretches. Form is a relative concept; a motif is the form of its notes, a theme the form of the motifs. Yet the level to which the concept of form primarily refers is that of the whole movement.

Secondly, the expression 'structure' can be related to abstract components, to pitches or durational values separated from the remaining sound qualities. It is reasonable to speak of the structure of a series of pitches, though a series of pitches without duration or dynamics has no real, perceivable existence, for it is a mere abstraction. What is meant by the term 'form', on the other hand, is a concrete musical shape in which pitch, duration, dynamics and timbre interact. One automatically hesitates to ascribe a form to an abstract sequence of pitches; a row is a structure, but not a form.

Thirdly, structure tends to be a technical concept, which suggests the genesis of a work, the process of production, whereas form is an aesthetic category which refers to the result, the audible shape. A structure need not be perceivable; the method need not be apparent from the result. The idea of an inaudible musical form would be a contradiction in terms. Structure is the aspect of the work directed at the composer, form that which is directed at the listener.

If one accepts this analysis of the use of the word as adequate, then the fact that the term 'structure' has become an in-word in the last fifteen years appears symptomatic. The emphasis placed on the term is characteristic of the thing it signifies: a compositional structure that seeks to attain self-awareness in the concept of structure.

First, attention was focused primarily on details, not on the form of the whole. Secondly, a network of connections was created from the abstract components of music, the parameters of pitch, duration, dynamics and timbre, but often the concrete melodic–rhythmic forms, the result of the interaction between individual sound qualities, were left to chance, though they alone are the object of musical perception. Thirdly, there was a tendency to neglect the result in favour of the process of creation; caught up in the problems of method, one treated the product almost with contempt, as if it were a by-product of composition and not its goal.

In contrast, it transpired in the discussion about form that it was the point of the congress to draw attention to the concept of form as a counter-principle to that of structure. If we are talking about form, then we should – generally speaking – remember the trivial fact that it is nonsensical to sacrifice the outline of the whole to the structure of the details, the concrete musical shape to the preparation of abstract components, and the result to the method.

III

Next to structure, 'open form' appeared to be the central point around which the discussion revolved. Yet in order to be able to talk about the matter one must analyse the word and distinguish between several meanings of the expression 'open form'. For the arguments brought forward either for or against 'open form' sometimes pertained to matters that, apart from the name, had little or nothing in common.

By 'open forms' one understood, first, pieces in which individual sections are fixed and unalterable, yet where the sequence of the sections is variable and left to the performer. The variability is, however, aesthetically fictitious. For the listener it does not exist; he does not relate the version he is hearing to other possible ones the performer could have chosen, but did not choose. What is a variable form on paper is fixed in performance; and, insofar as form is a category that refers to the perceivable result and not to the method, 'open form' is not 'open'.

In the case of a second method, described by Earle Brown, the composer limits himself to providing materials the arrangement of which is variable. Not only the arrangement of the sections is alterable but also the structure of details. One can, without the expression being meant polemically, speak of a 'building-block principle'. If the preformed materials were motifs, then the variable interweaving would be comparable with traditional motivic work, with the difference that the work is not the job of the composer but of the performer. The method appears to be based on the intention to restore the game quality of music. What is supposed to be decisive is not the complete work as a law and an obligation to which performer and listener submit, but the activity of music-making. The ultimate consequence would be the assertion that the evolution from musical activity to producing works, from *praxis* to *poiesis*, has been misguided. Yet it is difficult to accept this view.

According to a third version, the concept of 'open form' means that the division or articulation of a musical shape is a matter for the listener. Mauricio Kagel characterised structure as a passive aspect and articulation as an active one; and he appeared to be thinking of the activity of the listener who is supposed to impose order upon a structure presented to him. However, the procedure has certain drawbacks.

On the one hand, a lack of concise rhythmic articulation provokes a relapse into primitive forms of reaction on the part of the listener. Rhythmic structures that are not clearly articulated are related to a regular beat pattern and perceived as incoherent syncopations.

On the other hand, musical form, coherence on a large scale, is endangered or even negated by the ambiguity of articulation. A single section may be articulated in different ways, all of which are meaningful. Yet it is improbable, even if not impossible, that a large number of sections will form a coherent whole if the articulation of the individual sections, on which the connection between the sections depends, is left to the listener.

If form is clearly articulated, then an error on the part of the listener will be corrected by the continuation. Anyone who mistakes a consequent clause for an antecedent one will be made aware of his error by the break in musical syntax which becomes apparent in the transition to the next section. If he clings to the misunderstanding, then the form disintegrates – the music becomes incomprehensible. If, however, all possible articulations are equally correct, then the form, which is not present in the object, can also not be established by the subject. The formal imagination of the listener is not enough when it comes to larger contexts. If form is to be heard it must also be composed.

IV

The tendency towards 'open form' is a protest against the fixed patterns of which the theory of form is accused. The embodiment of what composers take particular exception to is the A–B–A formula, ternary form, which a century ago was considered to be the origin and foundation of all musical forms. Yet it seems on the one hand that an injustice is being done to the fixed patterns, and that, on the other hand, there is a renewed tendency towards the abstract (which was criticised in the case of the theory of form) in compositional procedures, albeit in a new guise.

Abstract patterns are not the goal but rather the starting-point of music analysis. They perform a heuristic, not a normative function. In its immediate, abstract form, a formula such as A–B–B–A says little or nothing about the music which one is attempting to describe. In order to become significant it has to be interpreted. Only the individual case will reveal whether the opening sections A–B belong together, and whether the closing sections B–A are to be understood as the inversion of A–B, or whether the return of A constitutes the formal framework into which section B and its repetition are inserted. The pattern is not a representation of the form but an instrument towards its understanding; one can only pass judgment on tools on the basis of the use one makes of them. *Musique informelle* strives away from the abstractness of the pattern, from form as formula, yet it falls victim to a second abstractness which is just as empty as the first. The symptom of extreme *musique informelle* is the heterogeneous nature of the details from which a musical shape is constructed. Disconnected matter stands side by side in sharp contrast. Yet the more heterogeneous two events are, the more abstract is the connection that exists between them. The interval of a fifth and the noise of a machine are linked by nothing except the common feature of being acoustical data. The designation 'acoustical data' is the most abstract definition in music one can imagine.

It would appear to be the goal of *musique informelle* to draw undivided attention to the isolated detail, to the individual musical moment. What is acoustically given is supposed to appear in the pure present, without links to the past or the future. However, the possibility of severing completely the connection between individual musical moments is doubtful. The connection is not eliminated, but simply becomes ever more tenuous and abstract.

In contrast, musical form consists in a balance between detail and con-text, between the heterogeneous and the homogeneous. If the juxta-position of fifth and machine noise is an example of heterogeneity, then the metrical framework of the eight-bar period appears as the paradigm of homogeneity: beats, bars and groups of bars are subjected to the same law of alternation between strong and weak.

Anyone who speaks of balance arouses suspicion of having classicist inclinations. But the point of a discussion about form is less to defend cer-tain positions than to reach agreement about concepts. One does not need to want form – and form is balance. Yet if it is not form one wants, then it is not form that one should talk about.

Composition and improvisation

The tendency to break up ossified structures, to violate or disavow the norm, to cast off the burden of tradition and to make the seemingly self-evident seem questionable and mutable, is one of the fundamental traits of the recent past. There is hardly a sphere of activity in which it is not present, in either an irritating or a liberating manner. In music the disagreement and the delight in destruction are directed against the traditional concept of composition, the finished work, the letter of which is laid down, and the spirit of which was declared immutable by idealist aesthetics. The firmly rooted idea that music in its highest forms is a text with art character is dismissed as being outmoded, as being a relic of a dead past. And inasmuch as these polemics are a sign of a fundamental change in musical consciousness and not merely a transient fashion, the disintegration of the composition and work concepts would signify nothing less than giving up the central category of European music of the last five hundred years. In place of composition the fundamental concept would be that of improvisation, which constitutes the essence of early European music and of non-European music.

The tendency towards improvisation is motivated in a number of different ways: first, by the development of compositional technique in the post-serial music of the last decade and a half; secondly, by an affinity to jazz, which, it is true, has existed for decades but which in the past produced nothing except a superficial, contradictory hotchpotch of heterogeneous musical materials; and finally by the hope that musical improvisation is the expression of, and a means of achieving, an emancipation of consciousness and of feeling. At the same time the dadaist, anti-art trait, which is part of both the disagreement and the polemics against the category of the musical work, should not be overlooked.

Philosophising chroniclers of New Music sometimes cling to the idea that the trend towards improvisation which emerged from the development of compositional technique after 1950 was a historical necessity. This idea is undoubtedly an exaggeration, since in general the concept of necessity is extremely questionable as a historical category; music history does not come about at the behest of a world spirit, which pursues its nefarious aims behind composers' backs, nor is the evolution of composition subject to the same strict logic or compulsive force as that of an exact science.

Be that as it may, the fact that around 1958 chance, under the name of aleatoric technique, was elevated into one of the basic principles of music was a reaction to inner contradictions in serial music. Serial technique had run up against a dilemma, a disparity between the parts and the whole. If the details of a musical text were serially determined as regards pitch, duration, dynamics and tone colour, and the serial mechanics left to their own devices, the overall form was a matter of chance. Conversely, when the features of the overall form, the duration of the parts, the ordering of the tempi and the variation in the density of the textures were determined on the basis of serial planning, then it was impossible to work out the details in serial form to their logical conclusion. The idea of a music which grows solely from a single principle, and in which the whole and the details are determined serially, proved to be a utopian dream. Either the overall form or the details departed from the principle of serialism and were thus, according to serial criteria, left to chance.

This partial element of chance contradicted the serial principle, which aimed at determination. In order to counter it one had the choice between falling back on the past and forging ahead. Either one could go back to traditional compositional techniques, and consign what was chance according to serial criteria and what was not embraced by the serial principle to free organisation by the composer; or one drew exactly the opposite conclusion and declared that what was chance according to serial criteria should simply be chance, and should be left to the discretion of the performer, that is to say, to improvisation.

In aleatoric music the elements of composition and improvisation, of what is firmly established and what is variable, are intertwined. To put it crudely, either the sections or the materials are firmly established, and the ordering of what is given is variable; or the composer merely sketches an outline which has to be filled in by the performer.

From the dilemma of serial music and from the impossibility of determining both the form of the whole and all the details using a single row, there resulted the possibility – but not the necessity – of a transition to aleatoric technique, to partial improvisation. To speak of a constraint to which composers were subject, of an inescapable alternative between aleatoric technique on the one hand and bad, because anachronistic, music lacking substance on the other, is out of the question. The fact that the possibility of aleatoric technique was put into practice without hesitation is typical, however. It seems as if around 1958 people were tired of serial discipline and musical rationality. Serial technique seems with regard to certain of its features to be the ultimate consequence of the tradition of counterpoint and thematic–motivic work, in other words, of the tradition of the strict, contrapuntal style. Compared to this the movement towards aleatoric technique and chance, towards arbitrariness and improvisation, seems like an attempt to break the shackles. An emancipatory element, the urge towards an unfettered musical state, has been unmistakably a part of the New Music from the beginning, ever since Schoenberg's emancipation of the dissonance around 1910, though it was repeatedly suppressed by disciplining tendencies, to which both dodecaphony and the serial method belong. Rigorous musical rationality and a latent dadaism, an urge to destroy the traditional European concept of art and composing, are perpetually interlocked in the evolution of New Music, hardly less in the case of Schoenberg than in that of Stravinsky. And thus it is not surprising that the extreme tension of a constructive rationalism in serial music was followed by a sudden change to the opposite extreme.

Whether the expectations which attached to improvisation and aleatoric technique, expectations which revolved around emphatic ideas of spontaneity, newness and revolutionary content, were real or imaginary is difficult to decide at present. It is true of music, as of politics, that the present conceals itself to the same extent as it presses itself on our attention. The significance of what is happening at the moment may be grasped directly in an emotional way, but the forging of concepts which are not to be mere slogans in party strife presupposes distance. It is difficult to speak of the present without becoming incoherent.

The difficulty can, however, be obviated somewhat by taking the roundabout path via history and drawing comparisons with earlier stages of evolution in order to arrive at clearly delineated concepts. It is not that the past is an authority on which to base a judgment about the present or a valid prediction. Arguments based on analogies with history are almost always questionable; history is not a collection of examples from which a rule may be deduced. Looking back at what happened in the past is useful, however, if it highlights differences in addition to partial conformity or similarity. Perhaps it may even help us to see possibilities which are concealed in the new. Yet historical reflection is hampered by the fact that the concept of improvisation is almost as difficult to pin down as is the musical practice which it designates. For the features which it encompasses do not totally agree. Nothing is certain except the trivial fact that the basic trait which distinguishes improvisation from composition is lack of notation. Yet the statement that improvisation lacks notation is not reversible. Music lacking notation is by no means always or even in the main improvisatory in character. Songs and instrumental pieces which are handed down virtually unchanged for decades or even centuries without ever having been written down do not belong to the realm of improvisation, despite the fact that they are not handed down in written form. They lack a feature which we instinctively associate with the idea of improvisation: spontaneity and uniqueness, the fact that they are tied to a non-recurring situation. Improvisations which are repeated are for this reason alone no longer improvisations.

At the same time it would be bad Romanticism to insist on unbroken spontaneity and immediacy. Analysed soberly, improvisation almost always relies to a large extent on formulas, tricks of the trade and models. The prudent method of sketching in mentally the starting-point, the materials, the outline or the articulating joints of a musical improvisation is probably more the rule than the exception. The improviser must be able to fall back at a moment's notice on a repertoire of clichés, on a store of prefabricated parts, which he may indeed modify or combine differently, but which he does not invent on the spur of the moment if he does not wish to get into difficulties or grind to a halt. The idea that he can commit himself entirely to the vagaries of chance is a fiction, even if, as in the case of the illusion of immediacy imparted by the theatre, it is an aesthetically legitimate fiction. The appearance of spontaneity belongs to the musico-scenic role played by the improviser. It is appearance and not reality that is aesthetically decisive. To speak of deception would entail being rigorous in a non-artistic manner; it would be an infringement of aesthetics by moral categories.

Thus improvisation, under the cloak of aesthetic immediacy, is based in part on formulas, habits and rules. Yet if the degree of regulation or the dependence on models is so great that free play shrinks to a residue, it no longer makes sense to speak of improvisation. Early mediaeval polyphony, which was not written down, except for pedagogical reasons, but in which rules governed and prescribed everything the performer did, can hardly be regarded as being a form of musical improvisation. Nor does it form a mere transition or intermediate stage, but appears rather to be a third form, next to composition and improvisation, for which no name has been found. (The terminological deficiency was doubtless a hindrance to reflection about this matter.)

While certain essential features of improvisation emanate from a dialectic of commonplace formulas and spontaneity, it seems as if improvisation is subject to an aesthetic principle which one could call the economy principle. Sophistication on the one hand is bought at the expense of primitivism on the other. Whereas composition tends to balance the various aspects of compositional technique – according to an aesthetic compositional–technical postulate advanced by Arnold Schoenberg, melody, rhythm and harmony have to be equally developed – the close proximity of what is undeveloped and of what is differentiated is characteristic of improvisation. Compared with composition, improvisation is one-sided. It almost always concentrates on a single, isolated feature of the music, be it rhythm, harmony or tone colour. And the primary feature, the real object of the improvisation, stands out from its surroundings on account of its novelty, its differentiation or its surprise effects, whereas everything else, being a mere foil, remains conventional and formalised.

In the fantasias of the eighteenth century, which are nothing but improvisations written down, it is harmony that departs from the norm and that transgresses the rules of regulated voice leading by means of abrupt chord changes or peremptory dissonances which seem like rents in the musical tissue. Melody on the other hand is not developed.

In jazz – if we disregard the attempts to overcome these constraints in the case of free jazz – the metrical scheme and the harmonic basis form the background for improvisation. The firmer and more self-evident the support that improvisation finds in the stereotypes, the never-changing beat and the simple, conventional harmony of the popular hit, the more richly it is evidently able to unfold. What is undeveloped forms the counterpart of the sophisticated. Going by compositional criteria one would be forced to speak of inner contradictions in the voice leading, of arbitrariness and of a lack of balance. The improvised dissonances appear as scattered additions to the pre-given harmonic scheme, as isolated splashes of sound, instead of being integrated into a context which one might call a developing relationship between voices, or counterpoint. What looks like a simple defect when seen from a compositional angle is, however, quite legitimate aesthetically when viewed in terms of the economy principle of improvisation. The harmonic scheme is of the greatest simplicity, and a contrapuntal conjunction of the voices is not even attempted, so that another feature of the music, the momentary tonal stimulus, can come to the fore with even greater effect.

Improvisation tends to become a potpourri of isolated stimuli, a succession of momentary effects. Either the overall form and basic design is crudely schematic and externally prescribed, or it is of no consequence and left to chance. A form which is both differentiated and unschematic, and which is nonetheless clear and comprehensible – the aim of compositions with artificial ambitions – can hardly be attained by means of improvisation.

In jazz it is the popular hit model which, as a basis of improvisation, guarantees the formal coherence and binds the individual parts together in a way improvisation on its own would hardly be able to do. One could speak of a principle of compensating simplicity. The improvisation itself is relieved from reflecting about the form. And it is significant that the initiated do not judge jazz improvisation in formal terms according to the manner in which the details join to make a consistently developing whole, but exclusively in stylistic terms, from the perspective of the homogeneous or heterogeneous nature of the musical means.

While in jazz improvisation the form is subject to a rigid scheme and externally delineated by the model of the popular hit, in aleatoric music it results from the interaction of composition and improvisation. Aleatoric technique is based either on a predetermined overall composed form or on prefabricated details. The historically earlier and aesthetically more legitimate procedure to which the term aleatory was originally restricted is the method whereby the outlines of the whole are fixed compositionally and only the details, which are to fill in the framework, remain variable and the domain of improvisation. The principle appears to be the consequence of the experience that more complex forms evidently result only from composition, whereas improvisation concentrates on detail, that is to say, adheres to the musical moment, and in order to balance this out either remains tied to simple schemes of grouping or, going to the opposite extreme, tends towards formal disintegration, towards a musical pattern which is less a clear-cut shape than a process into which the listener is drawn, and the end of which seems to be not a conclusion but a termination or an interruption.

By contrast, the inversion of the primary aleatoric method, the procedure of working out the details by means of composition and leaving open the conjoining of the individual sections to form a whole, is aesthetically questionable. For the strong point of improvisational practice, the compelling presentation of momentary effects, remains unused, and its weakness, the inability to form more complex, unschematic and yet intelligible forms, comes to the fore. The result is almost always a simple concatenation of sections which, on the one hand, are abruptly separated from one another by general pauses, and which, on the other, either stand unconnected side by side or relate to each other only by means of the simplest of contrasts, such as high and low register, *piano* and *forte*, dense and thin textures.

Yet the recourse to improvisational techniques, which has become the dominant fashion of the avant garde ever since the decline of serial technique, cannot be understood only in terms of the history of composition. Of no lesser importance is the development of performance practice and the relationship between composition and performance.

On the one hand the role of performance decreased because music was written down with ever-increasing exactness. The history of composition appears to be a process of rationalisation and integration stretching over centuries, in the course of which more and more aspects of music – first pitch and duration, and then tempo, dynamics and tone colour – were committed to paper, that is to say, something that had been the sole concern of the performer became an aspect of composition. Yet on the other hand performance, though it seems to be condemned to a secondary and dependent existence on account of the development of compositional technique and of notation, has not only maintained its place in concert practice but has actually enlarged it. In the general musical consciousness the emphasis is being placed more and more on the execution of a work, less and less on the work itself.

The divergence of composition and concert practice corresponds to a curious two-way split in aesthetic convictions. Indeed the indecision about whether composition and interpretation, what is notated and what is not notated, constitutes the essence or substance of music reaches right into the consciousness of the individual listener. On the one hand one conceives of a composition, in analogy to a poem, as a text, the meaning of which is conveyed through interpretation. The text does not appear as the model for or the cause of the interpretation, but the interpretation appears as the presentation of the text. Yet on the other hand it is generally believed that the most important aspect of music cannot be written down, that it resists notation. The performer does not infer it from the text, but rather over and above it by means of intuitive communication with the composer – insofar as he does not wholly add it himself to that which is notated.

The development of composition, as a process of rationalisation and integration, tends towards the abolition of the performer, which was postulated by Stravinsky and realised in electronic music. It is the ultimate consequence of the conviction that for those able to read them the decisive factor is contained in the written notes themselves. But the contrary tendency, which culminates in aleatoric music and the improvisational practices based on it, is full of mistrust towards what is written down. Notation seems to be an alienating of music from its true nature, which is merely execution. And composition, which is felt to be petrification, is contrasted with improvisation, of which one has hopes of freedom, without being aware of the dialectics of spontaneity and commonplace formulas. It is also not noticed that the avant garde shares with the concert practice which it abhors a decisive feature: the emphasis on execution rather than on the work itself.

To expect enthusiastically that musical innovation can be brought about through improvisation in a way which is barred to composition is probably an illusion. It is based on a thought model which is as questionable as it is entrenched: on the idea that innovation results from the transgression of norms and that composition is tied to rules which improvisation can disregard.

Yet, in the first place, transgressions of norms are only a sign of newness when they are based on a concept and when they form a coherent pattern, instead of being accidental and isolated.

Secondly, what is new in music can be both emancipatory and restrictive in character. Around 1910, in free atonality, it consisted in the abolition of norms, whereas around 1950, in serial music, it consisted in the ever stricter formulation of rules.

Thirdly, for at least one and a half centuries the obligation to produce something new has been the law to which the development of composition, and not only improvisation, has been subject. In the same measure to which musical works from the past have to maintain themselves in the concert and opera repertoire, works written at a later date, in order to seem different and to demonstrate their aesthetic right to exist, have to be new not only chronologically but also as regards their quality. The continual change in compositional technique appears to be the reverse of the historicism which prevails in the concert hall.

Fourthly, it is a matter of debate whether newness can be more easily attained by the ready use of improvisation than through the patient effort of composing. The trust in immediacy and the distrust of reflection is partly a Romantic prejudice.

One could, turning the accepted view upside down, even claim that newness is primarily a principle of composition, whereas improvisation, which can hardly exist without a stock of formulas and models, tends towards traditionalism. At any rate it needs a support: ready melodic turns, an underlying bass, a harmonic scheme which it paraphrases or a theme which is to be developed. If a support is lacking, it runs the danger of degenerating into an amorphous racket.

Improvisation rarely leads to the creation of form and structure. The inherent possibilities with which it can influence the development of music lie above all in the differentiation of details. But the external formal support which it requires can also consist of composed structures instead of the primitive models on which it is always thrown back when seeking to emphasise the difference between itself and composition, and its independence of the latter. Improvisation which attempts to escape both amorphousness and formal schematicism – the concatenation of unrelated sections in certain aleatoric pieces is just as much a sign of formal primitivism as is the reliance of jazz on the popular hit model – is thus dependent on the interaction with composition. Musical cogency is not to be expected from a disintegration of composition into improvisation, but from a compromise between the two.

A rejection of material thinking?

I

The catchphrase 'material fetishism' is almost as old as the endeavours against which it is directed. Whatever the word 'material' has been taken to mean – whether it was the history 'sedimented' in the notes, as Adorno would have it, the 'tendency' of which was carried to its logical conclusion by the serial music of the 1950s, or the noise material whose suitability for music or even anti-music was explored in the 1960s – the pejorative word was always at hand to express the misgivings of those who had lagged behind what was currently considered to be the state of the art or those who had already moved on beyond it. Not that it was always easy to distinguish between the one and the other, for it could happen that the seemingly regressive had unexpectedly turned out to anticipate an aspect of the future.

If we take the concept of fetishism seriously, instead of misusing it thoughtlessly as a term of abuse, it means – at least in Marx, from whose terminology it has wandered into the common parlance of composers – that people worship an idol of their own making. The individual submits to a force whose objectivity is an illusion and whose substance in fact stems from the individual himself.

Thus the authority in whose name we voice the protest against material fetishism is the composer's subjectivity, which refuses to accept a law laid down by nature or history, a law which states what may or may not be done in music. The unreasonableness of being subject to a 'diktat' of the material – understood as the outcome of a long history of composition and reception which is contained in the notes and noises or their interrelationship – is felt to be unbearable.

274

The protest of the individual against a process which we can interpret either as a necessary objectification or as an ominous alienation – and here we should really stop playing with diametrically opposed interpretations, and instead think about criteria with which we might be able to determine the precise point at which objectification becomes alienation – is so old and worn as a subject of philosophical debate that, unless there is an immediate reason, it is not worth resorting to the battery of arguments with which the debate has been conducted for almost two centuries. We should only call upon philosophy if it proves impossible to proceed without its help. But it does in fact seem as though we would most nearly do justice to those endeavours, the representatives of which feel themselves misunderstood when labels such as 'New Simplicity' or even 'New Tonality' are applied, if we understand them as attempts to reinstate subjectivity as the decisive factor of a 'context of meaning'* in sound. (It is precisely by realising this subjectivity in musical terms that the composer hopes to rescue it from the dangers of its *social* context.) To discuss the rejection of material thinking and the implications in the concept of material which are considered to be restrictive is thus at one and the same time to debate the chances and difficulties of unabashed subjective expression. Anyone who prefers not to talk about the subject, be it for reasons of shyness, suspicion or despair, must remain silent about what is happening in music at the present time.

II

Looking back at the 1950s, it might even be necessary to ask if the interpretation of serial music as the fulfilment of a kind of non-subjective, objective historical 'tendency of the material' was in fact quite as convincing as it seemed at the time, not only to the commentators but also to the protagonists of compositional history. And the step back does not constitute a superfluous detour in the line of argument which we are seeking to sustain.

The contention that there exists a contradiction in Schoenberg's twelve-note works between advanced pitch structure and traditional, outmoded rhythm, a contradiction which was resolved only by serial music, is inaccurate, because both the twelve-note structure and the non-serial rhythms serve the same purpose: namely, to recreate 'large-scale' autonomous instrumental forms within an atonal context. In Schoenberg's musical thinking it is not the analogy between the parameters but

---

* See above, p. 160. [Trans.]

their functional complementation that represents the principle control-ling the relationship between pitch structure and durational structure. Dodecaphony in the 1920s thus stands in a different problem context than it does three decades later, and it is the envisaged compositional goal that determines those questions which are posed and those which are not.

If the contradiction which serial music resolved only arose together with the resolution – it did not exist in Schoenberg's oeuvre – then it seems apposite to replace the interpretation of New Music as the realisation of 'tendencies of the material' with another view, a view which Ernst Krenek suggested as early as 1927 when speaking of the 'freedom to posit axioms' which was at a composer's disposal. According to Krenek, music as an art is based primarily on axioms which are posited neither by nature nor by history but by composers, whose aesthetic intentions decide what is to be regarded as meaningful in a compositional–technical sense.

In order to illustrate the concept of the axiom it may suffice to remind ourselves of the fact that, while the range of 'transitional degrees' in natural sonorities is prescribed to human perception, the choice between the different possibilities of developing musical facts from the acoustical preconditions is a matter for composers. Whether the intervals are divided into two or, as in the fourteenth century, three classes, and whether com-positional technique respects the range of transitional degrees or, as in the case of the fourth over the bass in strict counterpoint, prohibits it, depends solely on the composers' aims. It is left to them to select the axioms of compositional technique that correspond to their aesthetic ideas.

The 'freedom to posit axioms' proclaimed by Krenek thus means nothing less than that it is the individual composer, and not any objective constraint applied by nature or the history of music, who has the final word. If we adopt Krenek's premiss, serial music appears to be not a logical and inexorable consequence of an unresolved and disquieting problem proceeding from Schoenbergian dodecaphony, but an axiom which was posited by the composers of the 1950s of their own accord – composers whose questions were difficult to reduce to a common denominator with those posed by Schoenberg three decades earlier.

Where a diktat of the material seemed to point the way that composers had to go – if they did not wish to run the danger of producing irrel-evancies – a subjectivity was in fact at work which did not disappear by hiding behind the facade of 'historical necessity'. The aesthetic legitimacy of a work like *Gruppen* is based not on the logical manner with which his-torically inevitable conclusions were drawn but on the fact that the aesthetic plausibility of the result made people reconstruct the historical preconditions in such a way as to make it seem that they led up to the result.

The rejection of material thinking which was expressed by the catch-phrase 'material fetishism', without the opposite authority being at first clearly discernible – a rejection which in the course of the 1970s became the ruling paradigm – does not mean that objectivity was exchanged for subjectivity. It means that a latent subjectivity was replaced by a manifest one. History taken in the extremely questionable singular has, to put it crudely, come to be seen as a myth. As an authority presiding over the activities of the individual it has lost the hold on people's minds which was established for it in the nineteenth century by Hegel and Marx. Of course no one denies that there are historical connections, 'histories' in the plural; but we think we now know that 'history' (in the singular) does not exist. 'History' is just as little a historiographical term as 'nature' is a scientific one.

III

If we look back at the 1950s, therefore, Adorno's concept of material, which in the *Philosophie der neuen Musik* takes the place of the objective spirit guiding the course of history, turns out to be a problematical premiss, because it suppresses or represses the element of subjective choice emphasised by Krenek. On the other hand, the present dominant tendency to unabashed, frank subjectivity, which rejects objectively compelling tendencies, contains a theme which John Cage introduced into musical thinking and feeling. To the same degree that composers refused to obey a diktat of history, they were tempted to pursue a contorted idea of musical 'nature', in other words, once more to confuse the aesthetic paradigms of nature and history, even though the new concept of nature had little or nothing in common with the old one, which was last propagated by Hindemith. The difference we are discussing is most easily illustrated by the concepts material and matter, for Adorno's concept of material is a historical category, whereas Cage's idea of matter is a natural one.

Form and matter are on the one hand relative concepts in Aristotelian-shaped European thought. The brick is the form of a piece of clay; the house the form of the bricks; the settlement the form of the houses. On the other hand – and this second feature is crucial – form and matter are correlatively related. The one does not exist without the other, and matter *per se* – even though the word 'matter' suggests something palpable – is just as much an empty abstraction as form *per se*. But it is precisely the idea of attaining an acoustical manifestation of 'prime matter', of a tonal *materia prima*, that constitutes the central point around which revolve those musical or anti-musical happenings that John Cage designs with his untiring inventor's mind. The means with which Cage nonetheless attempts to allow what is actually an empty abstraction to become perceivable, even if only for a fleeting moment, are those of a persistent negation and destruction of all those formal factors which in Cage's opinion block our approach to the 'real nature' of sound. It should be evident that the only way in which 'prime matter' can be attained, if at all, is a mystical one. And mysticism in a quite sober and precise sense, and not in a vague one, is also what in the final analysis lies at the root of Cage's delight in destruction. Most of the destroyers in the history of politics and of ideas were not infrequently passionate mystics.

Yet the tendencies that Cage pursues are deeply contradictory and therefore open to misunderstanding and over-simplification (without which, however, the widespread influence which Cage has had would hardly be thinkable). The fact that the sounds and noises which Cage presents or allows to happen were prised out of their original pragmatic context, so that they do not, as in everyday life, function as signs and symptoms for events in the outside world but form an acoustical 'world of their own', means of course that Cage's anti-art has at least the element of 'aesthetic abstraction' in common with the art at whose destruction it is aiming. Acoustical events are, to use the catchphrases, 'depragmatised' and thus 'aestheticised'. At the same time – and this is a dadaist trait – the external pragmatic context is not meant to be exchanged for an internal aesthetic one; rather, the principle of the context itself – of the acoustical meaning – is the object of an aggressive stance which in the last resort is directed towards the mystical experience of 'pure matter'. But because the generation of an internal acoustical context, which would guarantee an art character, at least of a rudimentary kind, is prevented by what may be termed the obsessive cunning of unreason, the tonal events can after all signify transitions to everyday life – in other words, aesthetic isolation and abstraction is overcome – but admittedly to a kind of everyday life which is not a pragmatic world guided by ends but a challenging and pointless one which holds ideas of meaning and of aims at a distance. What Cage is aiming at is, to quote Kant, non-conceptual and disinterested experience.

IV

To claim that the sound and noise compositions of the 1960s were wholly based on Cage's intention to immerse himself in the nature of sound would, however, be a gross exaggeration. The combination of destruction and mysticism, which is difficult to attain and to maintain, was replaced in the case of the majority of composers who fell victim to Cage's ideas with a rather harmless quest for pure discovery and montage of unknown or (at least in an aesthetic context) unusual and striking sounds and noises. In view of the over-simplification which resulted, it is not surprising that sound and noise composition – which in addition suffered aesthetically because it was dissected by musical pedagogues – soon exhausted itself. This, it is true, has for decades been the menetekel of almost all those movements in art which were initially characterised by their radicalism. (The rediscovery of Jugendstil, which has already lasted longer than the original event, is a notable exception.)

But the tendency that was initially given the misleading and deceptive title 'New Tonality' can at least be hypothetically and tentatively deduced and made comprehensible by referring to the problematical nature of post-serial music. Sound and noise composition shared with serial music, whose antithesis it was, an important and, as may be seen in retrospect, fundamental premiss: namely, the presupposition that the distinction between central and peripheral sound qualities, which in European music had belonged for centuries to the firmly rooted, unchallenged self-evidencies, had to be dislodged if musical progress was to be at all possible. Intensity and tone colour were no longer to be subservient, simply enhancing and colouring the pitch and durational structure, but were to be treated as independent and equal parameters. One can claim without exaggerating that in sound and noise composition it was precisely these sound qualities, which had in the past been treated as peripheral, in which composers tried to make discoveries and exploit resources.

Subsequently, in the 1970s, the post-serial exploration of what had been peripheral in traditional music – a periphery which had suddenly become the centre of attention – led to a restoration of expressiveness which was emphatically directed against primary structural thinking. This is not as surprising as it may seem at first sight. For there is unmistakably a close affinity between the secondary sound qualities, which advanced to become primary ones, and the expressive element of music, since the primary parameters, which were now relegated to a secondary role, had always been thought of as structural and treated as such. In traditional music, pitch and duration were characterised by the fact that the difference between essence and appearance could be structurally determined: the harmonic and metrical function of a chord, that is, its musical meaning as opposed to its purely acoustical facticity, is a structural factor. On the other hand, in the case of intensity and tone colour, there is a 'second layer' next to the acoustical one, less structurally than expressively or colouristically determined. The structural rigour of serial music, which was altogether plausible when it came to pitch and duration, thus became, in the case of intensity and tone colour, a kind of arbitrary act which wanted to impose structure in a precise and rigorous manner where the parameters themselves were hardly conducive to such treatment. So while the turnabout seems at first to be an abrupt break in continuity, it is not at all impossible to understand that the newest music should cling to the restoration of the expressive element, even though it seems that it has long ago jettisoned the idea of the structural equality of the parameters without explicitly stating that this was so. The expressive factors of sound and noise composition are emphasised and taken to their logical conclusion in the light of a subjectivity which once more professes to be what it is. What was the subject of 'research' in the 1960s, as if the material were self-sufficient, was used a decade later as a means with which to serve expressive ends. But the musical structure, to a certain extent the backbone of form, is once again being entrusted to the primacy of pitch and duration. And while there can be little talk of a 'New Tonality' if we are being serious about concepts and unwilling to misuse them as mere labels, it is unmistakable that there is a general tendency, very differentiated in the ways in which it is expressed, to restore the difference between essence and appearance, between musical function and acoustical fact, in the primary structural parameters.

V

Coupled with the rejection of material thinking in the last few years there has been a growing indifference to theoretical concerns. Coming after the addiction to theory in the 1950s and 1960s – the unhealthy growth of self-exegesis hiding behind the mask of a general theory – this may perhaps be understandable; but as a setback, which, like all setbacks, tends towards exaggeration, it can lead to fatal consequences. The attempt by younger composers to avoid by means of pretended naivety an evolutionary trend which Jürgen Habermas has called 'the law of ongoing reflection', is in the final analysis futile, even if it seems initially attractive at a time when people in general are weary of reflection. And if we do not wish to err into the culs-de-sac into which blinkered *praxis* must almost inexorably lead, we can probably do nothing except recapitulate the claims theory has been making for decades and test their validity once more in the changed circumstances of the present.

The principle of 'work in progress', which was one of the dominant ideas of the decades between 1950 and 1970, was inseparably linked with theory inasmuch as compositional history was construed – not only by the commentators but by the protagonists themselves – along the lines of the history of science. In the scientific field, problems lead to solutions, which in turn enable new problems to be seen, with the result that solutions are once more required – and so on in a process, the dialectics of which seem in principle to be unending. But if, as was the case in the nineteenth and also the early twentieth century, it is not the isolated, rounded, complete work that constitutes the real object of compositional effort, but the provisional structure which is burdened with unresolved contradictions and is as it were open to the future, then theoretical reflection which mediates intellectually between earlier and later stages of the individual or intersubjective 'work in progress' proves to be inescapable; and indeed reflection in a form which cannot refrain from verbal formulation and publicity, from dissemination amongst the public which is interested in New Music. For as a mere document of an evolutionary stage a musical work which no longer wishes to be a work in the emphatic sense can only be made comprehensible, at performances in which it is presented to the audience as if it were self-contained, by means of an explanatory commentary which describes the context of the 'work in progress'. The work as an aesthetically present fragment of a non-present evolutionary chain requires theoretical reflection – and that means published reflection – if it is to be understood in the manner in which it is intended.

That every stage of composition, even the most primitive, includes reflection, however rudimentary in character, hardly needs to be restated in an age which has long ago given up the nineteenth-century belief in inspiration – except for sects, which do not stop being sects by becoming the majority. We must however distinguish between an 'implicit' theory, which always conceives of composing as thinking 'in' music, and an 'explicit' one, which manifests itself as thinking 'about' music. (It is self-evident that 'theory' in this context does not mean the fundamentals of composition, which has usurped the term in music education.) What we are talking about is not musical thinking in an absolute sense, or what Schoenberg called 'musical logic', but the extent to which thinking 'about' music performs a useful or even necessary function for thinking 'in' music, which is inherent in all composition, or whether thinking 'about' music is a superfluous addition to autonomous compositional practice, which is the only factor of any importance.

In order not to let the controversy about the advantages and disadvantages of theory for practice (a controversy which has been going on for thousands of years and will probably continue indefinitely) grow to unmanageable proportions, it would probably be most sensible to suppress historical reminiscences, which come to mind involuntarily. Instead we should begin once more with the concept of subjectivity, which has turned out to be the dominant category of the present-day aesthetic debate. And then it is not difficult to make it clear in a few words that a subject which does not work on an object, which does not interact and communicate with other human beings, and which does not have a language that serves to communicate with itself and its environment, is what Hegel called abstract inwardness [*abstrakte Innerlichkeit*] – an 'empty abyss', as Schopenhauer says, for once agreeing with his philosophical opponent. Subjectivity – if I may be permitted the anthropological truism – in fact only comes about in the productive interaction with an object, in the active interaction with other subjects and in the linguistic interaction with an environment which without concepts of structure would be a chaos of sensations – in other words, to use Aristotle's terminology, by means of *poiesis*, *praxis* and *theoria*. But if one concedes that in compositional activity the working on material, the interaction with people whose expectations belong to the premises on which the work is based – no matter whether they are fulfilled or frustrated – and the linguistic information concerning one's own activity and one's own experiences are inextricably interwoven, then it is evident that theory has always been implicit in musical practice. In other words, it is not the alternative between theory and lack of theory that some composers seem to find attractive, but only the fatal choice between consciously designed and sophisticated theory and neglected and primitive theory. Musical thinking is like every other kind of thinking: even if one lays claim to naivety, the choice is not between philosophy and nonphilosophy but between good and bad philosophy.

It is of course legitimate, at a point in history at which the individual musical shape once more presents itself as an isolated, self-contained work and not as a stage of a 'work in progress', to forgo explicit theory and to leave it for the time being at the implicit theory which is there in any case. The need to follow in intellectual terms continually overlapping developments while one is in a concert hall trying to assimilate in aesthetic terms a piece of the individual or intersubjective compositional process which, taken as a whole, is called 'advanced music', has, so it seems, been discarded by composers of the younger generation. Nevertheless it would not be a waste of time to assess the extent to which the attempt, as it were, to encircle thinking 'in' music by a verbalised thinking 'about' music helps or hinders the composition and its proper reception. The Mendelssohnian argument that musical thinking is too complex to be expressed in words is confronted both in the earlier and in the present debate by the antithetical assertion that musical imagination which eschews or attempts to eschew hard and fast verbal definition on principle must end up by becoming diffuse. Although explicit theory may ultimately prove insufficient, it is evidently indispensable as a starting-point. An extreme aversion to reflection, which is afraid of doing harm to thinking 'in' music by using categories which are much too imprecise, in the final analysis allows what it seeks to protect to wither away. The speechless silence which considers itself confirmed and secure in the silent possession of what alone is essential, tends in the end to become intellectual poverty. And although we can hardly wish that the surplus of theory of the serial and post-serial phase will repeat itself in the next few years, there is a danger (and not only in music) emanating from the unconcealed lethargy and the hidden animosity with which a 'conceptual' effort that attempts to express itself verbally as precisely as possible is at present greeted everywhere. A subjectivity which wishes to speak solely in sounds because words are superfluous or even misleading will perhaps at some stage come to the depressing conclusion that it has nothing more to say, even in sounds.

VI

It seems as if with the rejection of material thought and the retreat into the subjective realm there is bound up a restoration of the concept of the work or at least a cessation of the polemics against it. The barrier between material and work which has existed for decades is an involuntary inducement to associate the destruction of one factor with the restoration of another. The problem of the work concept, which arose in the debates of the past, has not been solved, however, and in order to understand what restoration can really mean and what it cannot we have to become aware of the fact that the polemics against the idea of the autonomous, isolated and self-contained object in the 1950s and 1960s derived from heterogeneous and to some extent incompatible motives and arguments. That, once unleashed, serial mechanics, the parameters of which are, it is true, determined by the composer, yet the results of which are largely divorced from the author's intentions and accordingly become accidental, destroy the concept of a work is just as obvious as it is undeniable that rigorous serial structural thinking does not display the least common ground with the tendency to resolve art in everyday life – a tendency which is equally directed against the emphatic work concept. Not infrequently composers said one thing and meant the exact opposite.

The idea of subsuming art in practice so that it becomes a way of life, and indeed a way of life which is fundamentally changed in the sense of being a utopia anticipated by art, is obviously a variant of the Marxist notion that philosophy as abstract thought would become superfluous as soon as it manifested itself in society. What was anticipated in thought – be it philosophical or artistic – is, at the moment when it actually assumes concrete form, condemned to disappear in its abstract form.

The transition from art to everyday life – a transition which was understood as the realisation of utopian substance – through which sound and noise composition in the 1960s, at least in the case of some of its proponents, took a turn towards Marxism, with the result that it seemed as if the material thinking of the composers approached the historical–dialectical materialism sought for reasons of political sympathy, was, however, capable of being interpreted in very different ways, between the aesthetic results of which there was a chasm that could hardly have been deeper. If the realisable utopia was reduced to a distant and almost forlorn hope, as it was by Adorno, whose opponents accused him of resignation, then nothing remained to be done in the midst of the existing sorry state of affairs except to seal off musical works which contained a utopian – and, in Adorno's opinion, a messianic – spark against the fatal surroundings to which they were condemned, with the uncompromising severity of the claim to aesthetic stature. The more catastrophic was the state of the world, the more hermetic was art.

But if it was felt that at least a minute piece of utopia could be realised in the present and that it should not be left to art to save the rudiments of utopian substance for the future, then the transition from art to everyday life became a pressing claim which would brook no procrastination and which had to be fulfilled here and now, even if it consisted of a never-ending series of unsuccessful attempts. The result was (and it would be vain to pretend otherwise) a loosening of the claim of art to what was called 'communication' in an emphatic sense. And the consequences would doubtless have been bewailed by Adorno, were he still alive, as 'deprofessionalisation', as a decay of the metier which could in no way be justified or even excused by the deluded good will with which the artificial standard was sacrificed to a social fiction. The argument that in the midst of an overall situation moving inexorably towards a catastrophe a meaningful transformation of art into life was not possible even in enclaves (which were in any case only make-believe ones) was at any rate at hand, so to speak, to explain what was aesthetically questionable.

On the other hand, the radical thesis that only the overthrow of the whole permits a fundamental change in the individual and in the particular is one of those premises which prevent what they hope will be the consequence. Art remains immured in itself, because a state of affairs in which it would be given the chance to permeate everyday life in a serious manner is difficult to foresee. The debate about the work concept, or more precisely about the relationship between the work as objectified labour and the categories 'communication' and 'interaction', which have become slogans in the polemics against the work concept, is, however, curiously askew, even when both parties base their ideas, or believe they are basing their ideas, on Marxist premises. Adorno was in fact being an orthodox Marxist when he insisted on the primacy of labour which objectifies itself in works. The thought of an interaction between people in which the result seems of secondary and the process of primary importance was quite foreign to him, as it was to Marx.

To be sure, the extreme version of the aesthetic autonomy concept had long ago been given up even by Adorno, who conceived of autonomy as resistance against a depraved society, thus (and his opponents reproved him for this) helping 'escapism' to acquire a clear social conscience. In its most rigorous form, which predominated around 1900, the autonomy concept said nothing less than that art and science, which were both accorded the same hypothetical status, are principles which do not, for example, serve people, but which on the contrary are there to be served by people inasmuch as they lay claim to being members of civilised society [Kulturmenschen]. In contrast to this there is the simplistic objection that what human beings make must, in order not to seem superfluous, be for human beings; and this has become the ruling paradigm. People are no longer prepared to revere what Schelling lauded as 'the sublime indifference of beauty'.

Thus 'communication' is the slogan of the day. The relationship to the category of the self-contained work, which claims to exist for its own sake, is, however, as we have seen, not at all as straightforward as it seems in the dichotomy which opposes an alienated concept of work with an abstract concept of communication, in other words, which places entrenched extremes in confrontation with one another instead of pursuing the mediation which is distinctly possible. Countless informal groups have become painfully aware that communication – the idea to which they cling obsessively – always fails and remains abstract if it exhausts itself in the attempt to exchange 'empty inwardness', as Hegel would have put it. Obviously it requires an object in order to be meaningful, an object which brings about the interaction between subjects who are in pursuit of communication. And by concentrating on a common object, and indeed on an object which is worth the effort, we are far more likely to attain an intersubjectivity which will do justice to the subject as a person and not merely as the incumbent of a function than by attempting to establish it in objectless immediacy. But music performs the function of acting as a mediating authority, and it does so all the more precisely the less it allows itself to loosen or even suspend its internal claims on account of the envisaged aim. Adaptation for teaching purposes always does pedagogical as well as material harm.

Yet although communication has to avoid the danger of getting lost in the cul-de-sac of an abstract immediacy and objectlessness, the idea (which is subject to continual attack) that a musical work as a rounded whole is divorced from the productive subject to the same extent that in the 'sublime indifference of the beautiful' it does not really require a receptive subject is an extreme position of art metaphysics which even Arnold Schoenberg, who did not fight shy of extreme consequences in certain pronouncements, did not seriously wish to insist upon. He did, it is true, feel himself to be the instrument of a power which worked through him, and he despised the public, which repaid the low opinion he had of it with animosity; but he spoke in music and through music as a person – though expression in works such as *Erwartung* is less expressive communication than the eruption of deeper layers. He wished to be understood and sought sympathy. And if we put the rigorous formulations of art metaphysics aside, we can probably come closest to the present function of the concept of the work – a function which is mediated through the concept of communication – if we remember how Friedrich Schleiermacher, in formulating a theory of textual exegesis which he called hermeneutics, based his approach on the model of a conversation which requires a certain amount of help and support in order to be a truly understanding dialogue. According to New Criticism, which, without the knowledge of the protagonists, represented the real aesthetics or poetics of serial music, it was – contrary to Schleiermacher – one of the fundamental rules of textual exegesis to belittle the intentions of the author, or to suspect their being taken into account, as 'intentional fallacy', and to declare the work itself, abstracted from the composer and his intentions, to be the sole authority for an adequate reception. The danger that in this way the text, which in the first instance is nothing but the dead letter of the work, provided the occasion for subjective projections which misconstrued themselves as the objectified spirit of the work was, however, not small in view of the fact that aesthetic perception, however much it may consider itself to be unprejudiced, is always prestructured in a manner which can hardly be determined. Some composers even declared that they were supplying nothing except a bundle of acoustical stimuli, the structuring of which was solely a matter for the listener.

In contrast to this, Schleiermacher's seemingly outmoded dialogue model at least keeps alive the possibility that the factors which the recipient himself contributes can be caused to interact with those which emanate from the work, so that the effect is one of mutual modification. It is not unthinkable, at all events, that it might be possible to mediate between the illusion that a text speaks of its own accord – the illusion that, by excluding one's self, one simply has to absorb what it has to say – and the arbitrary view that in point of fact reception is solely resident in the subject, the listener.

But if we assume that a non-alienated concept of the work, which leaves open the possibility that the reception process might follow the dialogue model, and a concrete concept of communication which manages to resist the temptation to indulge in abstractions and, in theory, recognises the need to secure an element of interaction by means of something common to both, actually complement each other instead of remaining mutually exclusive, then this would appear to be a way of describing the central insight at the very core of the present uninhibited relationship between the idea of the restored work concept and the notion of communication that has nonetheless been retained.

Notes

Progress and the avant garde

1 Paul Valéry, 'Bemerkungen über den Fortschritt', in *Über Kunst* (Frankfurt, 1959), p. 119. It cannot be ruled out that Valéry was thinking of Baudelaire's *Fusées* when referring to the 'idolisation of the rejection of progress'.

2 Ernst Bloch, 'Philosophie der Musik', in *Geist der Utopie* (Frankfurt, 1964); translated as 'The Philosophy of Music', in *Essays on the Philosophy of Music*, trans. Peter Palmer (Cambridge, 1985). Cf. also T. Kneif, 'Ernst Bloch und der musikalische Expressionismus', in *Ernst Bloch zu ehren* (Frankfurt, 1965).

3 W. R. Inge, *The Idea of Progress* (Oxford, 1920); J. B. Bury, *The Idea of Progress* (New York, 1932).

4 G. W. F. Hegel, *Die Vernunft in der Geschichte* (Leipzig, 1917), p. 25.

5 Ibid. p. 24. See also J. G. Droysen, *Grundriss der Historik* (Halle, 1925), paragraph 48.

6 K. Löwith, *Weltgeschichte und Heilsgeschehen* (Stuttgart, 1953); L. Kolakowski, 'Der Priester und der Narr', in *Der Mensch ohne Alternative* (Munich, 1960).

7 Hegel, *Die Vernunft in der Geschichte*, p. 53.

8 Stravinsky writes in the introductory chapter of the *Poetics of Music*: 'Our vanguard elite, sworn perpetually to outdo itself, expects and requires that music should satisfy the taste for absurd cacophony.'

9 Pierre Boulez, 'Eventuellement . . . ', *Revue musicale* (1952), p. 119.

10 Hans Magnus Enzensberger, 'Die Aporien der Avantgarde', in *Einzelheiten* (Frankfurt, 1962), pp. 299ff. According to H. E. Holthusen avant garde and revolutionary politics are related in a complementary manner, even though there is a gap between them and though it seems that the West has the avant garde and the East the revolution. The hardening of the revolution and its petrification in the shape of a dictatorship corresponds to the ossification of the avant garde in 'imitating itself'. 'Kunst und Revolution', in *Avantgarde: Geschichte und Krise einer Idee* (Munich, 1966).

11 Karlheinz Stockhausen, 'Musik und Graphik', in *Texte zur elektronischen und instrumentalen Musik* (Cologne, 1963), p. 188.

12 Eduard Hanslick, *The Beautiful in Music*, trans. Gustav Cohen (London, 1891), p. 81.
13 H. H. Eggebrecht, 'Der Begriff des "Neuen" in der Musik von der Ars nova bis zur Gegenwart', in *Kongress-Bericht New York 1961*, pp. 195ff.
14 Zofia Lissa, *Über das Spezifische der Musik* (Berlin, 1957), p. 70.
15 Walter Benjamin, 'Der Autor als Produzent', in *Versuche über Brecht* (Frankfurt, 1966), p. 108.
16 B. Eichenbaum, 'Die Theorie der formalen Methode', in *Aufsätze zur Theorie und Geschichte der Literatur* (Frankfurt, 1965).
17 Northrop Frye, *Anatomy of Criticism* (New Jersey, 1957), p. 73.
18 W. H. Wackenroder, *Werke und Briefe* (Jena, 1910), vol. 1, p. 294.
19 Henri Pousseur, 'Zur Methodik', in *Musikalisches Handwerk, Die Reihe*, vol. 3 (Vienna, 1957); K. Stockhausen, 'Momentform', in *Texte zur elektronischen und instrumentalen Musik*, pp. 189ff.
20 In paragraph 2 of the *Vorschule der Ästhetik* (Munich, 1963), p. 31, under the heading 'Poetic Nihilists', Jean Paul speaks of the 'lawless capriciousness of the present spirit of the age – which would rather destroy the world and the universe in its love of self, only in order to empty free space for itself in the void . . . '
21 A. Andersch, *Die Blindheit des Kunstwerks und andere Aufsätze* (Frankfurt, 1965), pp. 26f. Similar views, though more guardedly formulated, have been expressed by the English art critic Herbert Read.
22 Arnold Gehlen, 'Über kulturelle Evolutionen', in *Die Philosophie und die Frage nach dem Fortschritt* (Munich, 1964).
23 J. Ortega y Gasset, *The Dehumanization of Art* (New Jersey, 1968).
24 W. Benjamin, 'Ursprung des deutsches Trauerspiels', in *Schriften*, vol. 1 (Frankfurt, 1955), p. 172.
25 H. Kuhn, *Die Kulturfunktion der Kunst*, vol. 1 (Berlin, 1931).
26 Immanuel Kant, *Kritik der Urteilskraft*, paragraph 53.
27 Karl Popper, *The Poverty of Historicism* (London, 1960).
28 B. Croce, *Ästhetik als Wissenschaft vom Ausdruck* (Tübingen, 1930), p. 145.
29 Kant, *Kritik der Urteilskraft*, paragraph 47.
30 Theodor W. Adorno, *Philosophy of Modern Music*, trans. Anne G. Mitchell and Wesley V. Bloomster (London, 1973).
31 Stockhausen, 'Erfindung und Entdeckung', in *Texte zur elektronischen und instrumentalen Musik*, pp. 222ff.
32 C. S. Benedict, 'Gibt es in der Musik einen "Fortschritt"?', *Neue Musikzeitschrift*, vol. 1 (1947), pp. 187ff. On the other hand, writers of music history in the early part and the middle of the eighteenth century emphasised the 'progress of harmony', of regulated style (F. W. Marpurg, *Kritische Einleitung in die Geschichte und Lehrsätze der alten und neuen Musik* [Berlin, 1759], pp. 227f.).
33 H.-K. Metzger ('Das Altern der Philosophie der Neuen Musik', in *Junge Komponisten, Die Reihe*, vol. 4 (Vienna, 1958), p. 76) speaks of the 'pseudo-function of a technological progress à la branlette'.
34 Adorno, *Philosophy of Modern Music*.
35 G. Ligeti, 'Wandlungen der musikalischen Form', in *Form-Raum, Die Reihe*, vol. 7 (Vienna, 1960).
36 Stockhausen, 'Erfindung und Entdeckung'.
37 J. N. Forkel, *Allgemeine Geschichte der Musik*, vol. 1 (Leipzig, 1788), p. 1. Cf.

also vol. 2, p. 484: the description of the 'gradual expansion and improvement' of polyphony.

38 Adorno, 'Reaktion und Fortschritt', in *Moments musicaux* (Frankfurt, 1964), pp. 153f. Cf. also *Klangfiguren* (Frankfurt, 1959), pp. 27f.; *Quasi una fantasia* (Frankfurt, 1963), p. 375: in poetry one meets, as Walter Benjamin noted, in the case of Valéry, 'once more the idea of progress . . . and here it is the valid and authentic one – that of what can be transferred in the methods, which in Valéry corresponds as clearly to the concept of construction as it runs against the compulsive idea of inspiration'.

39 'A third culture, the synthesis of the two which we have attempted to describe in this book, may be expected. It will be the whole culture of music and not only one culture. . . . ' August Halm, *Von zwei Kulturen der Musik*, 3rd edn (Stuttgart, 1947), p. 253.

40 Schoenberg, 'New Music, Outmoded Music, Style and Idea', in *Style and Idea*, ed. Leonard Stein (London, 1975), pp. 39f. Cf. also Boulez, 'Ästhetik und Götzendienst', *Melos*, vol. 34 (1967), p. 233.

41 Schoenberg, 'New Music, Outmoded Music, Style and Idea', pp. 40f.

42 Kurt von Fischer, 'Der Begriff des "Neuen" in der Musik von der Ars nova bis zur Gegenwart', in *Kongress-Bericht New York 1961*, pp. 184ff.

43 *Summa musicae*, GS III, 238b.

Avant garde and popularity

1 *The Pleasure of the Text*, trans. Richard Miller (London, 1976), p. 40.
2 *Materialen zu einer Dialektik der Musik* (1973), p. 109.

Schoenberg's aesthetic theology

1 *Style and Idea*, ed. Leonard Stein (London, 1975), p. 85.
2 Ibid. pp. 214–15.
3 Ibid. p. 442. [Translation slightly amended.]

Schoenberg and programme music

1 Translation from Willi Reich, *Schoenberg: a Critical Biography*, trans. Leo Black (London, 1971), p. 51. [Translation amended.]
2 Translation from *Arnold Schoenberg Letters*, ed. Erwin Stein, trans. Eithne Wilkins and Ernst Kaiser (London, 1964), p. 148.
3 Thomas Mann, *The Genesis of a Novel*, trans. Richard and Clara Winston (London, 1961), p. 172.

Musical prose

1 'Singstil und Instrumentalstil in der europäischen Musik', in *Kongressbericht Bamberg 1953*, p. 224.
2 *Style and Idea*, ed. Leonard Stein (London, 1975), p. 415.
3 Ibid. p. 399.
4 Ibid. p. 426.

5 'Der Begriff der Kunstkritik in der deutschen Romantik', in *Schriften* (Frankfurt, 1955), vol. 2, p. 505.

6 *Style and Idea*, p. 431. Ernest Ansermet objected that Schoenberg's interpretation of the second phrase was a 'véritable abstraction' (*Les fondements de la musique dans la conscience humaine* [Neuchâtel, 1961], vol. 1, p. 532). Ansermet's argument implies a denial of the variation principle, for to recognise the model in a variant is impossible without 'abstraction' from the non-identical.

7 *Style and Idea*, p. 435. The inclusion of 2 + 2 + 2 crotchets (beats) in one bar, to which Schoenberg is referring, cannot be expressed unambiguously, for the beat in 6/4 time refers to the 3 + 3 grouping, and in 3/2 time to the minim.

8 *Gesammelte Schriften über Musik und Musiker*, ed. Heinrich Simon, vol. 1, p. 95.

9 *Werke*, ed. Stefan Hock, vol. 12, pp. 104, 90.

10 *Style and Idea*, p. 411.

11 'Aus der Musiksprache des Mozart-Theaters', *Mozart-Jahrbuch 1950*, p. 85.

12 Ibid. p. 86.

13 Cf. I. Bengtsson, 'On Relationships between Tonal and Rhythmic Structures in Western Multipart Music', *Svensk tidskrift för musikforskning 1961*.

14 *Mozart-Jahrbuch 1950*, p. 93.

15 *Gesammelte Schriften und Dichtungen*, ed. Wolfgang Golther, vol. 4, p. 114.

16 Ibid. pp. 113f.

17 The fact that not all the stresses in a line are assigned to logical accents (only two of the five stresses in George's line 'Ich bin im Boot, die Laubgewölbe wahren' are accented) led Wagner to the polemical conclusion that regular lines were poetic 'monstrosities' which 'mutilated' the accentual patterns of language (p. 106).

18 Ibid. p. 131.

19 Ibid. p. 327.

20 *Style and Idea*, p. 411.

Emancipation of the dissonance

1 Schoenberg, 'Gesinnung oder Erkenntnis', in *25 Jahre Neue Musik: Jahrbuch 1926 der Universal Edition* (Vienna, 1926), p. 25; *Style and Idea*, ed. Leonard Stein (London, 1975), pp. 216f.; *Structural Functions of Harmony*, ed. Leonard Stein (London, 1954), p. 193.

2 Schoenberg, *Theory of Harmony*, trans. Roy E. Carter (London, 1978), p. 21.

3 Gottfried Weber, *Versuch einer geordneten Theorie der Tonsetzkunst*, 2nd edn. (Mainz, 1824), vol. 1, p. 252; cf. also A. B. Marx, *Die alte Musiklehre im Streit mit unserer Zeit* (Leipzig, 1841), pp. 79f.

4 Pierre Boulez, *Boulez on Music Today*, trans. Susan Bradshaw and Richard Rodney Bennett (London, 1971), p. 36.

5 *Style and Idea*, pp. 216–17. [Translation slightly amended.]

6 Johann Mattheson, *Der vollkommene Capellmeister* (Hamburg, 1739); facsimile reprint (Kassel, 1954), p. 253.

7 Riemann's attempt to deduce compositional rules from the definitions of tonal meanings led to unfounded consequences which were refuted by Ernst Kurth. *Die Voraussetzungen der theoretischen Harmonik und der tonalen Darstellungssysteme* (Berne, 1913), pp. 110f.

8 Hugo Leichtentritt, *Musikalische Formenlehre*, 5th edn. (Leipzig, 1952), pp. 436ff.; cf. also E. von der Nüll, *Moderne Harmonik* (Leipzig, 1932), pp. 102ff.

9 Theodor W. Adorno, *Philosophy of Modern Music*, trans. Anne G. Mitchell and Wesley V. Bloomster (London, 1973), pp. 53f., 82–3.

10 In his third edition of *Grundlagen des linearen Kontrapunkts* Kurth defended himself against the misunderstanding that he had been in favour of 'counterpoint which took no notice of harmony' (Berlin, 1922, p. xiii).

11 This is true not only of the Piano Pieces, Op. 11, the relatively simple structure of which, compared to Opp. 9 and 10 may have been prompted by the instrument, but also of the Five Orchestral Pieces, Op. 16.

12 *Theory of Harmony*, pp. 309ff. Cf. E. Toch, *Melodielehre* (Berlin, 1923), pp. 108ff.

13 Weber, *Versuch einer geordneten Theorie der Tonsetzkunst*, p. 217.

14 D'Alembert, *Eléments de musique théoretique et pratique* (Paris, 1752); F. W. Marpurg, *Systematische Einleitung in die Musicalische Setzkunst* (Leipzig, 1757).

15 *Theory of Harmony*, p. 343.

16 Ibid. p. 329.

17 Ibid. p. 328: '[Bach] followed his urge to accommodate more complicated harmonies, wherever he thought he could do it without danger to the intelligibility of the whole. But the essential thing, the urge to write harsh harmonies . . . this urge was there.'

18 Ibid. p. 317.

19 Adorno, *Philosophy of Modern Music*, p. 72.

20 Schoenberg, *Style and Idea*, pp. 225, 232f.; Milton Babbitt, *The Function of Set Structure in the Twelve-Tone System* (Princeton, 1946); George Perle, *Serial Composition and Atonality* (Berkeley and Los Angeles, 1962), pp. 99ff.

21 Rudolf Stefan, *Neue Musik* (Göttingen, 1958), pp. 32ff.

22 Schoenberg, *Structural Functions of Harmony*, p. 194.

23 Ernst Kurth, *Romantische Harmonik und ihre Krise in Wagners 'Tristan'* (Berne, 1920), p. 61.

24 Alfred Lorenz, *Der musikalische Aufbau von Richard Wagners 'Parsifal'* (Berlin, 1933), pp. 29ff.

25 Adorno, *Philosophy of Modern Music*, pp. 51f. Later Adorno emphasised the importance of counterpoint for the creation of twelve-note technique: see 'Die Funktion des Kontrapunkts in der Neuen Musik' in *Klangfiguren* (Frankfurt am Main, 1959), pp. 210ff.

26 *Structural Functions of Harmony*, pp. 194–5.

27 Ibid. p. 194.

28 *Style and Idea*, p. 407: 'No matter what the purpose or meaning of an idea in the aggregate may be, no matter whether its function be introductory, establishing, varying, preparing, elaborating, deviating, developing, concluding, subdividing, subordinate, or basic, it must be an idea which had to take this place even if it were not to serve for this purpose or meaning or function; and this idea must look in construction and in thematic content as if it were not there to fulfill a structural task.'

29 *Theory of Harmony*, pp. 27ff., 128f.; 'Gesinnung und Erkenntnis', p. 26.

30 *Arnold Schoenberg Letters*, ed. Erwin Stein, trans. Eithne Wilkins and Ernst Kaiser (London, 1964), p. 164.

What is 'developing variation'?

1 Manuscript held in the Arnold Schoenberg Institute, Los Angeles [the so-called 'Gedanke Manuscript'].
2 *Style and Idea*, ed. Leonard Stein (London, 1975), p. 290.
3 Ibid. p. 397.
4 Ibid. pp. 122–3.
5 *Fundamentals of Musical Composition*, ed. Gerald Strang and Leonard Stein (London, 1967), p. 16.
6 *Style and Idea*, p. 91. [Translation amended.]

Schoenberg and Schenker

1 Vienna, 1911. Translated by Roy E. Carter as *Theory of Harmony* (London, 1978), pp. 318f.
2 Munich, 1926 [reprinted Hildesheim, 1974], pp. 30ff. Partially translated by Sylvan Kalib as *Thirteen Essays from the Three Yearbooks 'Das Meisterwerk in der Musikz' by Heinrich Schenker: An Annotated Translation* (Ph.D. Diss., Northwestern University, 1973; Ann Arbor: University Microfilms, 1973): see vol. 2, pp. 199ff.
3 Schenker, pp. 34f.; Kalib, pp. 206f.
4 Schenker, p. 25; Kalib, p. 189.
5 Schoenberg, *Theory of Harmony*, p. 318.
6 Ibid. pp. 311f., pp. 342ff.
7 Ibid. pp. 309ff.
8 Ibid. pp. 321ff.
9 Schenker, p. 31; Kalib, pp. 200f.
10 Schoenberg, *Theory of Harmony*, pp. 318–19.
11 Schenker, p. 35; Kalib, p. 208.
12 Schenker, p. 32; Kalib, p. 202.
13 Schoenberg, *Theory of Harmony*, pp. 316–17.

Schoenberg's Orchestral Piece Op. 16, No. 3 and the concept of *Klangfarbenmelodie*

1 Schoenberg, *Harmonielehre* (Vienna, 1911), p. 471. Translated by Roy E. Carter as *Theory of Harmony* (London, 1978), pp. 421–2. [Translation slightly amended.]
2 H. H. Stuckenschmidt, *Arnold Schoenberg*, trans. Edith Temple Roberts and Humphrey Searle (London, 1959), p. 52.
3 E. Doflein, 'Schönbergs Opus 16 Nr. 3. Der Mythos der Klangfarbenmelodie', *Melos*, vol. 36 (1969), pp. 203f.
4 Schoenberg, *Theory of Harmony*, p. 422. [Translation amended.]
5 H. von Helmholtz, *Die Lehre von den Tonempfindungen als physiologische Grundlage für die Theorie der Musik* (Brunswick, 1863), pp. 343f.; Schoenberg, *Theory of Harmony*, p. 21.
6 Helmholtz, *Die Lehre von den Tonempfindungen*, p. 358; Schoenberg, *Theory of Harmony*, pp. 9, 27.

7 Helmholtz, *Die Lehre von den Tonempfindungen*, p. 556.
8 Ibid. p. 107.

'The Obbligato Recitative'

1 Schoenberg, *Berliner Tagebuch*, ed. Josef Rufer (Frankfurt, 1974), p. 11.
2 Schoenberg, 'The Relationship to the Text', in *Style and Idea*, ed. Leonard Stein (London, 1975), pp. 141ff.
3 *Berliner Tagebuch*, p. 14.
4 Quoted in H. H. Stuckenschmidt, *Arnold Schoenberg: His Life, World and Work*, trans. Humphrey Searle (London, 1977), p. 70. [Translation amended.]
5 Wagner, 'Zukunftsmusik', in *Gesammelte Schriften und Dichtungen*, vol. 7, p. 130.
6 Schoenberg, *Style and Idea*, p. 407.
7 Jan Maegaard, *Studien zur Entwicklung des dodekaphonen Satzes bei Arnold Schoenberg* (Copenhagen, 1972), vol. 2, pp. 285ff. Maegaard's interpretation of the term 'obbligato' as 'worked-out motivically' is probably wrong. The recurring 'motifs' that Maegaard has discovered in Op. 16, No. 5 (pp. 281ff.) are two- or three-note figures with no fixed, repeated rhythms, figures which are too indistinct to be perceived as motifs whose return would provoke the idea of an obbligato style.
8 *Style and Idea*, p. 415. Maegaard is of the opinion (vol. 2, pp. 291f.) that there is no mention of contradiction between idea (*Gedanke*) and formula (*Formel*) in Schoenberg's text. The postulate of a 'direct and straightforward presentation of ideas, without patchwork, without mere padding and empty repetitions' is aimed not at 'ideas' ('Gedanken') but at 'concepts' ('Ideen'). In the context of Schoenberg's aesthetics an idea is always a formulational idea, and a concept is that which stands behind it; only a concept and not an idea can be expressed directly or indirectly. An idea differently formulated is a different idea. Yet Maegaard's argument has certain loopholes. First, there is no change in the difference between what is musically 'eloquent' and what 'has nothing to say'. Secondly, in the passages quoted by Maegaard, Schoenberg was thinking of 'concept' as referring to the idea of a whole work, whereas in the definition of musical prose he was concerned with individual ideas. Thirdly, the fact that Schoenberg did not always distinguish between a musical idea and its formulation is not a sufficient reason to avoid making the distinction and to deny that there is a difference.
9 *Style and Idea*, pp. 415–16.
10 Cf. *Style and Idea*, pp. 417–18 with 411.

Expressive principle and orchestral polyphony in Schoenberg's *Erwartung*

1 Cf. Erwin Stein, *Orpheus in New Guises* (London, 1952), p. 53: 'It is a tour de force of musical form without formative devices'; Luigi Rognoni, *Espressionismo e dodecafonia* (Turin, 1954), p. 75: 'Il più assoluto atematismo caratterizza questa partitura schönbergiana'.
2 Theodor W. Adorno, *Philosophy of Modern Music*, trans. Anne G. Mitchell and Wesley V. Bloomster (London, 1973), p. 50.
3 Ibid. p. 42. [Translation amended.]

4 Adorno, *Ästhetische Theorie* (Frankfurt am Main, 1970), p. 174.
5 See Carl Dahlhaus, *Wagners Konzeption des musikalischen Dramas* (Regensburg, 1971), pp. 71ff.
6 Jan Maegaard (*Studien zur Entwicklung des dodekaphonen Satzes bei Arnold Schoenberg*, [Copenhagen, 1972], vol. 2, p. 322) combines the recurring three-note groups in Schoenberg's *Erwartung* in structures independent of the sequence of the notes. However, the similarity between D–C sharp–F and F–D–C sharp, which belong to the same Maegaardian structure, is less important than the connection, which Schoenberg achieved in compositional terms, between the basic shape and the inversion, which Maegaard assigns to different groups.
7 Schoenberg, *Style and Idea*, ed. Leonard Stein (London, 1975), p. 143.

Schoenberg's late works

1 *Philosophy of Modern Music*, trans. Anne G. Mitchell and Wesley V. Bloomster (London, 1973), p. 122.
2 Ibid. p. 123.
3 Ibid. p. 113.
4 Ibid. p. 117.
5 Ibid. p. 115.
6 Ibid. pp. 122–3.
7 Ibid. p. 127.
8 Ibid. p. 128.
9 Ibid. p. 115.
10 *Denkbare Musik* (Cologne, 1972), pp. 195–7.
11 'Arnold Schoenberg von hinten', in *Arnold Schoenberg: Musik-Konzepte* (Munich, 1980), pp. 29–34.
12 *Schoenberg and His School*, trans. Dika Newlin, 2nd edn. (New York, 1970), p. 116.
13 Ibid. pp. 119, 126.
14 Adorno, *Philosophy of Modern Music*, p. 118.

The fugue as prelude: Schoenberg's *Genesis* composition, Op. 44

1 See Arnold Schoenberg, *Stil und Gedanke. Gesammelte Schriften*, ed. Ivan Vojtech (Frankfurt am Main, 1976), vol. 1, p. 501. Cf. *Style and Idea*, ed. Leonard Stein (London, 1975), p. 523. [Translation amended.]
2 *Style and Idea*, pp. 248–9.
3 Willi Reich, *Schoenberg: A Critical Biography*, trans. Leo Black (London, 1971), p. 215.
4 *Style and Idea*, p. 393.
5 Rudolf Smend, 'Goethes Verhältnis zu Bach', in *Bach-Studien* (Kassel, 1969), p. 214.
6 Ibid. p. 228.
7 Walter Wiora, 'Goethes Wort über Bach', in *Historische und systematische Musikwissenschaft* (Tutzing, 1972), pp. 251ff.
8 Smend, 'Goethes Verhältnis zu Bach', pp. 216f. and 222.
9 Wiora, 'Goethes Wort über Bach', pp. 253f. and 256.

Analytical instrumentation: Bach's six-part ricercar as orchestrated by Anton Webern

1 Quoted in Josef Rufer, *The Works of Arnold Schoenberg*, trans. Dika Newlin (London, 1962), p. 94. [Translation slightly amended.]
2 Letter to Hermann Scherchen of 1 January 1938, quoted in *Die Reihe*, vol. 2, 2nd [Eng.] edn. (Bryn Mawr, 1959), p. 19.

Schreker and modernism: on the dramaturgy of *Der ferne Klang*

1 H. Schreker-Bures, 'Franz Schreker und seine Zeit', in *Franz Schreker*, Österreichische Komponisten des XX. Jahrhunderts, vol. 17 (Vienna, 1970), p. 31.
2 Theodor W. Adorno, 'Schreker', in *Quasi una fantasia* (Frankfurt am Main, 1963), pp. 182–3: 'Schoenberg himself always treated him with great respect, quoting a passage from *Der ferne Klang* (as one of several) among the first examples of unresolved chords with six or more notes. But the younger generation, not least Schreker's pupils, reacted vehemently against him, even while he was still the head of the Berlin Hochschule, on the lines of avant-garde painters who reject the successful figures of their own age and of their own circles as being purveyors of kitsch.'
3 In making a sharp distinction between Schoenberg and Schreker, Paul Bekker allows himself to be led astray by the prejudiced view of Schoenberg as a musical engineer. 'It would be very wrong to put Schreker in the same category as Schoenberg. Schoenberg is a talent with a penchant for the abstract and the speculative; he feels with his brain . . . ' ('Franz Schreker', in *Klang und Eros* [Stuttgart, 1922], p. 21).
4 Paul Bekker, *Franz Schreker* (Berlin, 1919), pp. 21–2; R. Louis also linked Wagner's idea that drama constituted 'musical deeds made visible' with the postulate that the emphasis had to shift from 'music drama' to 'opera' if musical drama after Wagner were still to be possible (*Die deutsche Musik der Neuzeit*, 3rd edn. [Munich, 1912], pp. 121–2, 129–30).
5 Bekker, *Franz Schreker* (1919), p. 28.
6 Richard Wagner, 'Über die Benennung "Musikdrama" ', in *Gesammelte Schriften und Dichtungen*, vol. 9, p. 306.
7 Adorno, 'Schreker', pp. 183–4.
8 Schreker-Bures, 'Franz Schreker und seine Zeit', p. 14.
9 Bekker, *Klang und Eros*, p. 26.
10 Bekker, *Franz Schreker* (1919), p. 44.
11 In an analysis of the 'Nachtstück' Gösta Neuwirth comes to the conclusion that the music identifies Fritz 'as a petit bourgeois' (*Die Harmonik in der Oper 'Der ferne Klang' von Franz Schreker* [Regensburg, 1972], p. 165).
12 P. von Matt, 'Das literarische Gespenst "klassisches Drama" ', *Merkur*, vol. 30 (1976), pp. 735, 739.
13 Bekker, *Klang und Eros*, pp. 23–4.
14 Louis, *Die deutsche Musik der Neuzeit*, pp. 88–9.
15 For Bekker the idea of 'drama' in the shape of 'musical deeds made visible', which he applied to Schreker, was the key to the whole of Wagner's work.

The musical work of art as a subject of sociology

1 T. W. Adorno, 'Ideen zur Musiksoziologie', in *Klangfiguren* (Frankfurt am Main, 1959), p. 11.

2 A. Silbermann, *Wovon lebt die Musik?* (Regensburg, 1957).

3 M. K. Cerny, 'Das musikalische Kunstwerk unter dem Gesichtspunkt der Musik-geschichte', in *De musica disputationes Pragenses* (Prague and Kassel, 1972), p. 98.

4 Adorno, 'Thesen zur Kunstsoziologie', in *Ohne Leitbild: Parva Aesthetica* (Frankfurt am Main, 1967), pp. 95f.

5 T. Kneif, 'Der Gegenstand musiksoziologischer Erkenntnis', *Archiv für Musik-wissenschaft*, vol. 23 (1966), p. 216.

6 C. Dahlhaus, 'Gefühlsästhetik und musikalische Formenlehre', *Deutsche Viertel-jahresschrift für Literaturwissenschaft und Geistesgeschichte*, vol. 41 (1967), pp. 510ff.

7 W. Hilbert, *Die Musikästhetik der Frühromantik* (Remscheid, 1911), p. 120.

8 P. Spitta, 'Kunstwissenschaft und Kunst', in *Zur Musik* (Berlin, 1892), pp. 4f.

9 R. Ingarden, 'Das Musikwerk', in *Untersuchungen zur Ontologie der Kunst* (Tübingen, 1962), pp. 3ff.

10 F. Engels, letter to H. Starkenburg of 25 January 1894, in *K. Marx und F. Engels: Werke* (MEW), vol. 39, p. 206.

11 K. Kosík, *Dialektik des Konkreten* (Frankfurt am Main, 1967), pp. 104ff.

12 Ibid. p. 116.

13 Adorno, *Klangfiguren*, p. 11.

14 Ibid. p. 11.

15 Adorno, *Mahler: Eine musikalische Physiognomik* (Frankfurt am Main, 1960), pp. 10ff.

16 Adorno, *Klangfiguren*, p. 21.

17 Ibid. p. 24.

18 Ibid. p. 16.

19 Adorno, 'Zur Vorgeschichte der Reihenkomponisten', in *Klangfiguren*, p. 113.

20 *Kongressbericht Kassel 1962*, pp. 3ff.; 'Generalthema I: Die musikalischen Gattungen und ihr sozialer Hintergrund'.

List of sources

' "New Music" as historical category': ' "Neue Musik" als historische Kategorie', in *Das musikalisch Neue und die Neue Musik*, ed. H.-P. Reinecke (Mainz, 1969)*

'Progress and the avant garde': 'Fortschritt und Avantgarde', in *Bericht über den internationalen musikwissenschaftlichen Kongress Leipzig 1966* (Kassel, 1970)*

'*Avant garde and popularity*': 'Avantgarde und Popularität', in *Avantgarde und Volkstümlichkeit* (Veröffentlichungen des Instituts für Neue Musik und Musikerziehung, vol. 15) (Mainz, 1975)*

'New Music and the problem of musical genre': 'Die Neue Musik und das problem der musikalischen Gattungen', in *Gestaltungsgeschichte und Gesellschaftsgeschichte: Festschrift für Fritz Martini*, ed. Helmut Kreuzer (Stuttgart, 1969)*

'Problems of rhythm in the New Music': 'Probleme des Rhythmus in der Neuen Musik', in *Terminologie der Neuen Musik* (Veröffentlichungen des Instituts für Neue Musik und Musikerziehung Darmstadt, vol. 5) (Berlin, 1965)*

'Tonality: structure or process?': 'Tonalität – Struktur oder prozess', *Darmstädter Beiträge zur Neuen Musik* (forthcoming)

'Schoenberg's poetics of music': 'Schönbergs musikalische Poetik', *Archiv für Musikwissenschaft*, vol. 33 (1976)*

'Schoenberg's aesthetic theology': 'Schönbergs ästhetische Theologie', in *Bericht über den 2. Kongress der internationalen Schönberg-Gesellschaft 1984* (Vienna, 1984)

'Schoenberg and programme music': 'Schönberg und die Programmmusik', *Arnold Schoenberg* (Katalog der Akademie der Künste) (Berlin, 1974)*

'Musical prose': 'Musikalische Prosa', *Neue Zeitschrift für Musik*, vol. 125 (1964)*

'Emancipation of the dissonance': 'Emanzipation der Dissonanz', in *Aspekte der Neuen Musik*, ed. W. Burde (Kassel, 1968)*

'What is "developing variation"?': 'Was heisst "entwickelnde Variation"?', *Bericht über den 2. Kongress der internationalen Schönberg-Gesellschaft 1984* (Vienna, 1984)

'Schoenberg and Schenker': 'Schoenberg and Schenker', *Proceedings of the Royal Musical Association*, vol. 100 (1973–4)*

'Schoenberg's Orchestral Piece Op. 16, No. 3 and the concept of "Klangfarben-melodie"': 'Schönbergs Orchesterstück op. 16, 3 und der Begriff der "Klang-farbenmelodie"', in *Bericht über den internationalen musikwissenschaftlichen Kongress Bonn 1970* (Kassel, n.d.)*

' "The Obbligato Recitative" ': ' "Das obligate Rezitativ" ', *Melos/NZ*, vol. 3 (1975)*

'Expressive principle and orchestral polyphony in Schoenberg's *Erwartung*': 'Ausdrucksprinzip und Orchesterpolyphonie in Schönbergs "Erwartung"', *Wiener Schönberg-Kongress 1974* (Vienna, n.d.)*

'Schoenberg's late works': 'Zum Spätwerk Arnold Schönbergs', in *Die Wiener Schule heute* (Veröffentlichungen des Instituts für Neue Musik und Musikerziehung Darmstadt, vol. 24) (Mainz, 1983)

'The fugue as prelude: Schoenberg's *Genesis* composition, Op. 44': 'Die Fuge als Präludium: Zur Interpretation von Schönbergs Genesis-Komposition Opus 44', *Musica*, vol. 37 (1983)

'Rhythmic structures in Webern's Orchestral Pieces Op. 6': 'Rhythmische Strukturen in Weberns Orchesterstücken opus 6', in *Webern-Kongress* (Beiträge 1972/3 der Österreichischen Gesellschaft für Musik (Kassel, 1973)*

'Analytical instrumentation: Bach's six-part ricercar as orchestrated by Anton Webern': 'Analytische Instrumentation – Bachs sechsstimmiges Ricercar in der Orchestrierung Anton Weberns', in *Bach-Interpretationen*, ed. Martin Geck (Göttingen, 1969)*

'Schreker and modernism: on the dramaturgy of *Der ferne Klang*': 'Schreker und die Moderne – Zur Dramaturgie des "Fernen Klang"', in *Franz Schreker. Am Beginn der Neuen Musik* (Studien zur Wertungsforschung, vol. 5) (Vienna, 1978)*

'Structure and expression in the music of Scriabin': 'Struktur und Expression bei Alexander Skrjabin', in *Musik des Ostens*, vol. 6 (Kassel, 1972)*

'Plea for a Romantic category: the concept of the work of art in the newest music': 'Plädoyer für eine romantische Kategorie – Der Begriff des Kunstwerks in der neuesten Musik', *Neue Zeitschrift für Musik*, vol. 130 (1969)*

'On the decline of the concept of the musical work': 'Über den Zerfall des musikalischen Werkbegriffs', in *Beiträge 1970/1 der Österreichischen Gesellschaft für Musik* (Kassel, 1971)*

'The musical work of art as a subject of sociology': 'Das musikalische Kunstwerk als Gegenstand der Soziologie', *International Review of the Aesthetics and Sociology of Music*, vol. 5 (1974)*

'Form': 'Form', in *Darmstädter Beiträge zur Neuen Musik*, vol. 10 (Mainz, 1966)*

'Composition and improvisation': 'Komposition und Improvisation', *Neue Zeitschrift für Musik*, vol. 133 (1972)*

'A rejection of material thinking?': 'Abkehr von Materialdenken?', *Darmstädter Beiträge zur Neuen Musik (Die 31. Internationalen Ferienkurse für Neue Musik: Algorithmus, Klang, Natur: Abkehr von Materialdenken?)*, ed. Friedrich Hommel (Mainz, 1984)

---

* Reprinted in *Schönberg und andere: Gesammelte Aufsätze zur Neuen Musik* (Mainz, 1978)

Index